100 THINGS WARRIORS FANS SHOULD KNOW & DO BEFORE THEY DIE

Danny Leroux

D0064520

TRIUMPH
BOOKS

No part of this publication may be reproduced, stored in a retrieval system, or transmitted in any form by any means, electronic, mechanical, photocopying, or otherwise, without the prior written permission of the publisher, Triumph Books LLC, 814 North Franklin Street, Chicago, Illinois 60610.

Library of Congress Cataloging-in-Publication Data available upon request.

This book is available in quantity at special discounts for your group or organization. For further information, contact:

Triumph Books LLC
814 North Franklin Street
Chicago, Illinois 60610
(312) 337-0747
www.triumphbooks.com

Printed in U.S.A.
ISBN: 978-1-62937-479-6
Design by Patricia Frey
Photos courtesy of AP Images unless otherwise indicated

To Grammy and Grandpa,
the bearings in my moral compass

Contents

Foreword

I'm one of those guys who gets a twitch whenever I see a basketball court. I could be driving down a street and see a roll-out court in a driveway and, somewhere inside of me—pressed under the other 50 million things I have to think about—is an inkling to go play on that court. That's how much I love the game. The itch to play is always there, waiting for me to scratch it. I can watch the game, at any level, and find some measure of enjoyment.

So this current existence I have, to be part of this amazing run, is surreal. It can be overwhelming if I allow myself to get lost in the experience. This is sensory overload. I may be the president of basketball operations and general manager, but I am also a fan of the game and sometimes I want to go find a seat in the crowd and yell like a 10-year-old.

When I sit back and think of what we've accomplished, I feel so privileged. I've always been fortunate to be around the game and this organization gave me a chance to help build something special in our community.

When I was coming up in Alamo, the Bay Area was in a glory era of high school hoops. Players were cropping up all over the East Bay, and Jason Kidd was royalty.

Then I got lucky enough to play at UCLA, winning a national championship. After college as an agent, I worked for an elite mentor in the profession, Arn Tellem, and found myself in the same room as Kobe Bryant, Reggie Miller, and Tracy McGrady.

Next thing I know, I have the opportunity to build a storied franchise. My childhood franchise.

Most probably think the Warriors just became worth something. But there has always been an aura about this franchise. Even when the teams weren't good, the fans were the stuff of legend.

Part of what has made the Warriors special is that even though success came intermittently over the decades, they have consistently produced fascinating players, teams, and personalities, along with the best fans in the league.

Wilt Chamberlain, Rick Barry, Nate Thurmond, Chris Mullin, and 10 other Hall of Famers have played for the franchise since their move to the Bay Area in 1962. Al Attles, who has been with the organization for over 50 years as a player, coach, and executive, is possibly the franchise's most beloved figure. But those luminaries are only part of the team's legacy, because fan favorites such as Larry Smith, Baron Davis, Tom Meschery, Phil Smith, Antawn Jamison, Jason Richardson, and Monta Ellis are essential elements of the story as well. The Warriors also featured key figures off the court, including Don Nelson and Alex Hannum on the sideline and Bill King on the microphone. This franchise delivered definitive moments like Wilt Chamberlain's 100-point game, Sleepy Floyd becoming Superman, Davis' dunk over Andrei Kirilenko, and Klay Thompson's 37-point quarter.

Over the past 55 years, Golden State has also produced some of the NBA's most memorable teams. In 2007, the We Believe Warriors shocked the basketball world 16 years after Run TMC electrified the league. Nellie Ball helped key stunning playoff upsets on three occasions and those came decades after the 1975 team pulled off one of the biggest shockers in league history when they swept the heavily favored Bullets in the NBA Finals.

And now here we are, fortunate enough to have Hall of Famers on our roster. To win 73 games and two championships. To watch crazy records fall before our eyes. To play for the highest stakes in the game and compete against all-time greats, waging the kind of battles that will outlive us all.

This is a culmination for a franchise and a region that has always found a way to be special in the world of hoops. The passion for basketball in these parts is rich enough to consume and properly appreciate this historic era.

Perhaps, the Warriors were meant to experience this. Maybe this area was meant to be home to this. Maybe I was meant to see it up close.

—Bob Myers

1 Stephen Curry

Stephen Curry became a game breaker, lightning rod, and singular figure all before his 30th birthday.

Curry's defining characteristic on the court is his ability to shoot off the dribble and pull up effectively from places that were previously inconceivable. The NBA's present and past are full of talented catch-and-shoot marksmen but Curry breaks defenses because his shot requires substantially more planning, talent, and execution to slow down, much less stop.

It took nine seasons for the first NBA player to make 100 three-pointers in a season and another seven years plus moving the three-point line in for anyone to crack 200. Stephen Curry ousted Ray Allen's record of 269 in his fourth season and has already broken his own record two more times in four seasons, only falling short of Allen's 269 in 2013–14.

However, Curry's status as the best shooter of all time only tells part of the story. Over the years, he has combined the ability to draw immense amounts of defensive attention and much improved passing to orchestrate some of the most effective offenses in league history. While Klay Thompson, Draymond Green, Andre Iguodala, and more recently Kevin Durant have integral parts to play, Curry is the focal point and mandatory centerpiece of the system.

His other defining characteristic is also the reason fans all over the league come when doors open for Warriors games: his preparation. While spectators ooh and ahh at dribbling exhibitions and shots from the center court logo or Oracle tunnel, those demonstrations come on top of a foundation built through immense amounts of time and remarkable diligence. In the off-season, Curry challenges himself through complicated drills like one where people stand on the edge of his vision holding numbers and he has to dribble while responding to lights and reading the numbers or another where he dribbles a basketball in one hand and throws around a tennis ball in the other while wearing vision-limiting goggles.

While many focus on Curry's unusual stature and build for a superstar, his uncommon path to this point may be even more remarkable. After all, the giants of league history, like Wilt Chamberlain, Michael Jordan, Magic Johnson, Kareem Abdul-Jabbar, and LeBron James, were all undeniable combinations of physical ability and prodigious talent, while Curry faced doubters and skeptics even while building an impressive résumé.

Curry lays it up just out of reach of LeBron James during the second half of Game 1 of the 2017 Finals on June 1, 2017. (AP Photo/Marcio Jose Sanchez)

It is somewhat rare for the child of an NBA player to fly under the radar but being Dell Curry's son did not compel any NCAA powerhouses to offer a scholarship. Leading college basketball in scoring as a junior the year after propelling Davidson College to the Elite Eight in the 2008 NCAA Tournament also did not inspire any NBA general manager to select him with a top-five pick.

Even then, after impressing early in his time on the Warriors and finishing second in Rookie of the Year voting, Curry ended up sitting behind Acie Law IV in coach Keith Smart's rotation during his sophomore campaign, often in fourth quarters. The next season, Curry only appeared in 26 games as the team shut him down in March after numerous ankle and foot issues and that fall he agreed to a four-year, $44 million contract extension, a lower salary than his performance and potential justified, due to those persistent health concerns.

All of the doubt that could have defined Curry's basketball life ended up being the prologue for a story even his most optimistic supporters did not see coming.

Golden State began the 2012–13 season with Curry as the centerpiece of their offense after trading Monta Ellis during the prior season. Curry responded with his best performance as a pro to that point, as his 22.9 points and 6.9 assists per game helped drive the Warriors to their first playoff appearance since the We Believe team six years before. On top of that, Curry only missed four games, assuaging the injury concerns that dogged his early career and contributed to his less-lucrative extension the prior November.

He built on that success with another strong campaign in 2013–14, increasing his scoring to 24 points per game and assists to 8.5 per game, both new career highs. Again, he missed only four games as the Warriors improved to 51–31, their first season with 50 or more wins in 20 years. While Golden State fell to the Los Angeles Clippers in the first round of the playoffs that season, Curry battled established star Chris Paul for all seven games, including 33 points and nine assists in their 126–121 Game 7 loss. His improvement and the hard-fought series set the table for a truly remarkable stretch.

While the 2014–15 season started with considerable turnover due to the firing of Mark Jackson and hiring of Steve Kerr, Curry quickly turned the focus his direction with the best season of his career to that point. Despite playing four fewer minutes per game, he averaged 23.8 points, 7.7 assists, 4.3 rebounds, and two steals per game as the Warriors jumped from the 12th best offense all the way to second, and Curry's emergence played a major part in that meteoric rise.

While increasing his role in the offense under the new coaching staff and system, Curry also improved his efficiency as a shooter while reducing his turnovers. That transformation turned him from a captivating novelty to genuine force and the league's best offensive player. While Coach Jackson protected Curry on defense by frequently giving his fellow Splash Brother Klay Thompson the more challenging assignment, Kerr entrusted Curry with added responsibilities on that end. Curry responded with a solid performance that was more than enough, considering Golden State's other talent on that end, and they finished the season with the league's best defense.

After beating fellow 2009 draftee James Harden for his first Most Valuable Player Award, Curry averaged 28.3 points per game in the playoffs, including 25 or more points in the clinching game of every round on the Warriors' way to their first championship in 40 years. While Andre Iguodala won Finals MVP due to his defense on LeBron James, Curry's 37 points and four assists in Game 5 helped give the Warriors the 3–2 series lead they never relinquished.

Winning the league MVP and championship in the same season made Curry a household name. With an elevated platform and expectations, the sports world eagerly anticipated Curry's encore. He responded with one of the best offensive seasons in

NBA history by leading the league in scoring, annihilating his own record for most made three-pointers in a season and powering the Warriors to a remarkable 73–9 regular season record that bested the 1995–96 Chicago Bulls' all-time mark. Yet again, Curry managed to accomplish the extraordinary double of increasing his role in the Warriors offense (which led the league) while also improving his efficiency, which pushed him toward the best seasons by Wilt Chamberlain and Michael Jordan. His outrageous regular season received appropriate acclaim when Curry became the first unanimous MVP in league history.

The sky-high expectations and a potential coronation for the league's newest dynasty came to a halt when Curry slipped on a wet spot in Game 4 of the Warriors' first-round series against Houston. A sprained medial collateral ligament in his right knee forced him to miss the closeout game against the Rockets and the first three games against the Trail Blazers. While he had a few truly electrifying moments in the playoffs, including an NBA-record 17 overtime points in his first game back, Curry did not have the possession-by-possession impact of his prior two seasons and the Warriors ended up falling to the Cavaliers in the NBA Finals.

After a history-making regular season that ended in injury and disappointment, Curry cultivated a new kind of interest in his follow-up. That fascination only grew when 2013–14 MVP Kevin Durant decided to join the Warriors, making them the first set of Most Valuable Players to be teammates while still in their twenties. With those massive expectations, Curry ended up closer to his 2013–14 and 2014–15 campaigns with 25.3 points and 6.6 assists per game as the team finished with the league's best record despite Durant missing 19 games with his own MCL sprain. The disappointment of 2016 put extra pressure on Curry to deliver in the playoffs. He became the key stabilizing force, averaging 28.1 points and 6.7 assists while shooting 42 percent from three as the Warriors dominated their opponents, finishing with a 16–1 record.

Echoing the 2015 playoff run, Curry scored 30 or more points in every closeout game, including 34 in the title-clincher at Oracle.

After the parade, Curry had the chance to be an unrestricted free agent for the first time but chose to return to the Warriors on the league's very first Designated Veteran contract: a five-year, $201 million agreement that was the largest in NBA history. At just 29 years old, he should be able to expand his already massive imprint on the franchise for years to come.

2 Rick Barry

Perhaps the best encapsulation of Rick Barry came from his first NBA coach, Alex Hannum, in a piece he wrote for *Sports Illustrated* in 1969:

"Of all the rookies I ever saw break in, Rick Barry was the most special. It was something to remember, that first day as a Warrior, when he scrimmaged against Tom Meschery, whom we called 'the Mad Manchurian.' After a while they were just going one-on-one, at and over each other and ignoring everyone else. I was refereeing and I let a Barry basket go on a dubious play, but then I whistled a charging foul on Meschery when he came through Barry like the Normandy invasion. Meschery went into a rage. It was so bad I had to rearrange things so they were no longer guarding each other. But as soon as Tom got the ball again, Barry left his new man, picked Meschery up, and stole the ball as he blocked the shot. Meschery was so enraged I had to call off the whole practice.

"Half an hour later, calmed down and getting dressed, Tom couldn't contain his enthusiasm. 'Hey, Alex,' he said, 'that Barry's going to be a great one.'"

Along with his signature underhanded free throw form, Barry's incredible talent, intensity, and divisive personality became trademarks of a truly remarkable career. Teammate Clifford Ray said it well when he told *Sports Illustrated*, "Rick may not be the kind of guy to say please, but he's in it to win."

Barry grew up in Roselle Park, New Jersey, before starring at the University of Miami, where he averaged more than 30 points per game each of his final two seasons and led the NCAA in scoring as a first team All-American as a senior.

The Warriors had the first two non-territorial picks in the 1965 Draft and took Barry second. The team had traded Wilt Chamberlain to Philadelphia in the middle of the prior season, though they still had star-caliber players in Guy Rodgers and Nate Thurmond. Barry fit in right away, leading the Warriors in scoring with 25.7 points per game while also making both the All-Star team and first team All-NBA as San Francisco improved from 17–63 to 35–45. After a historic rookie season, Barry upped the ante by leading the league in scoring at 35.6 points per game and finishing fifth in MVP voting behind Chamberlain, Thurmond, Bill Russell, and Oscar Robertson. That season, the Warriors won 44 games and the Western Division, then made the NBA Finals after defeating both the Lakers and Hawks. Chamberlain's 76ers won the series 4–2, but Barry averaged 40.8 points and 8.8 rebounds in a losing effort, proving his mettle on the largest stage. Shortly after his 23rd birthday, Barry was a star and key contributor on a contending team. Future Hall of Famer Billy Cunningham called Barry "by far the toughest forward in the NBA to guard because he is in constant movement."

That optimism changed quickly as Barry's disappointment over his second year salary (just a $10,000 raise in base pay from his rookie year despite his success) created a fissure at exactly the wrong time for the Warriors. The newly formed American Basketball Association was going to have a team in Oakland and owner Pat Boone offered him an intriguing contract to play for the Oakland Oaks that included an ownership stake and the opportunity to play for his father-in-law and University of Miami head coach Bruce Hale.

Barry accepted but Mieuli sued with the argument that it violated the terms of his contract. The court forced Barry to sit out for one year, which he partially spent broadcasting Oaks games, but he did play for them in 1968–69 for former coach Alex Hannum because Hale left while Barry sat out. He was sharp after the layoff, averaging 34 points per game before tearing ligaments in his knee which eventually forced him to sit out the rest of the year as his teammates won the 1969 ABA championship. Even though they went 60–18 and won the league title, the Oaks only drew 2,800 fans per game and Boone sold the team to Earl Foreman, who moved the team to Washington, D.C., where they became the Washington Capitols.

Barry's ABA gamble had not paid off but his ordeal was not over. Frustrated with the move, he told the *Los Angeles Times*, "If I wanted to go to Washington, I'd run for president" and tried to re-join the Warriors but lost in court again, forcing him to fulfill his contract. A disappointed Barry still averaged 27.7 points per game but missed 30 games due to another knee injury. After that season, the team announced they were moving again, this time to Virginia, and their star told sportswriters, "I don't want my son coming home saying 'Howdy, y'all'" before forcing a trade to the New York Nets.

Even with all the change, Barry still produced and helped the Nets reach the 1972 ABA Finals after scoring 27 points on the road against his former team in Game 7. One month after the Nets lost to the Pacers in the ABA Finals, the U.S. District Court issued a preliminary injunction that Barry would have to re-join the Warriors after his contract with the Nets ended, which he did four months later.

Barry was a meaningfully different player after five years away from the Warriors. While still a gifted scorer, knee injuries had sapped some of the athleticism that earned him the "Miami Greyhound" nickname from Warriors broadcaster Bill King. In its place, Barry became more of a distributor and eventually the forerunner to the "point forward," though the term did not exist yet. Astonishingly, he led Golden State in scoring and assists for five straight seasons after his return.

The highlight of Barry's second stint with the Warriors came in 1974–75, when the team retooled and he reached 30 points per game for the first time since his final season in New York, finishing fourth in MVP voting. Barry again led the team in points and assists as they won the Pacific Division with a 48–34 record. After defeating the Sonics in six games, Golden State had to face a formidable Chicago Bulls team that had beaten them three times in the regular season. Facing a must-win Game 6 in Chicago, Barry scored 36 points in a huge comeback victory before a team effort carried them to the 1975 NBA Finals, eight years after the team lost to Chamberlain's 76ers in Barry's second season.

Despite being massive underdogs to the Washington Bullets, Golden State won Game 1 before having to play two games in the Cow Palace, their home arena in the 1967 Finals. Barry loved the shooter-friendly dead rims he called "sewer pipes" there and scored 36 and 38 points in two Warriors wins as they took a commanding 3–0 series lead. Two nights later, Barry and the Warriors had their first NBA championship and completed the biggest upset in league history and the star earned Finals MVP honors after averaging 29.5 points per game in the sweep.

While Barry and the Warriors never reached those heights again despite coming brutally close the next year, he stayed a central figure on the team for another three seasons before signing with the Houston Rockets in 1978. The presence of other scorers moved Barry into an even more pronounced "point forward" role. Assistant Del Harris described it by saying, "He would sort it out. He would make the plays. He was really the first guy to be utilized in that role very heavily. But there was no name attached to it." That fairly describes his later years in Oakland as well. After two seasons in Houston, Barry retired shortly after his 36th birthday.

Despite spending five years of his prime outside the organization, Barry is the second-leading scorer in Warriors history (No. 1 since the move to California), fourth in assists, and seventh in rebounds. The Warriors retired his No. 24 jersey on March 18, 1988, and he was enshrined in the Naismith Memorial Basketball Hall of Fame in 1987.

3 2015 Championship

The Warriors knew the 2014–15 season would involve massive changes after firing head coach Mark Jackson two days after losing to the Clippers in the first round of the 2014 playoffs. A little over a week later, they replaced Jackson with former player, general manager, and broadcaster Steve Kerr, who, like Jackson, had never coached at any level. While Kerr compiled a staff that included Alvin Gentry and Ron Adams, general manager Bob Myers added pieces to the two-time playoff squad, including signing guards Shaun Livingston and Leandro Barbosa to back up Stephen Curry and Klay Thompson.

Returning talent faced adjustments as well. Before the season, Kerr asked lifelong starter and 2013 signee Andre Iguodala to come off the bench in favor of third-year forward Harrison Barnes. The veteran appreciated Kerr's candor and directness when making the tough ask and changed roles, which again strengthened the bench. Shortly thereafter, necessity became the mother of invention as David Lee suffered a strained hamstring in the team's final preseason game and Kerr decided to start Draymond Green in his place. The new starting five of Curry, Thompson, Barnes, Green, and Bogut had played 51 minutes together the season before.

During training camp, Kerr told his new team, "We have the pieces here for a championship. Now I'm not going to talk about that again."

Even with the significant turnover, the Warriors started out the season strong by winning their first five games and 21 of their first 23. Curry transformed from fascination to star in the new coaching staff's more sophisticated offensive scheme and fueled Golden State's jump from 12th to second in offense on his way to earning the league's Most Valuable Player Award. The Warriors were also able to maintain the successful defense from Jackson's tenure and that potent combination produced a 67–15 record that led the league by seven games.

Even with that success, there were plenty of reasons to question whether Golden State would be able to win the title. After all, those Warriors had never made it past the second round while San Antonio was a reigning champion who retained their key contributors and LeBron James had taken his talents back to his hometown Cleveland Cavaliers, who finished second in the East despite adding new pieces throughout the season. On top of those two, the Clippers and Rockets had put together strong seasons and looked dangerous at full strength.

On the last day of the regular season, the New Orleans Pelicans jumped into the No. 8 seed by shockingly beating the Spurs, who fell all the way from second to sixth. While the Pelicans staged a late comeback in Game 1, the Warriors won both contests at Oracle without too much incident. New Orleans took a huge 20-point lead into the fourth quarter in their first home playoff game since 2011, but the Warriors battled all the way back and Curry made a three-pointer deep in the corner to complete the comeback, sending the game to overtime, where Golden State closed it out before finishing off the sweep two days later.

From there, they had to face Memphis, a battle-tested opponent with quality size in Marc Gasol and Zach Randolph. The Warriors won Game 1 behind a strong defensive effort, but the Grizzlies took Game 2 in Oracle after receiving an emotional lift from returning point guard Mike Conley and then won Game 3 at home, putting Golden State in a 2–1 hole with another game in Memphis. That night, Green, Curry, Lee, and Festus Ezeli went to dinner at the Blues City Café to collect themselves and the coaching staff adjusted by putting center Andrew Bogut on noted non-shooter Tony Allen, allowing the big man to help all over the floor. The Warriors won each of the remaining three games by double digits.

On the other side of the bracket, the Clippers knocked out the Spurs in a seven-game classic before falling to the second-seeded Rockets. In Game 1 of the Western Conference Finals, the Rockets took a 16-point lead in the first half but the Warriors again came all the way back and won behind 34 points from Curry and a complete game from Green, who came two assists short of a triple-double. Golden State took that momentum and won Game 2 despite MVP runner-up James Harden fueling a Houston comeback with a near triple-double of his own. Unlike their prior two series, the Warriors started strong in their first road game, controlling the whole way as Curry scored 40 points in a 115–80 win. The drama in the series came when Curry had a bad fall in Game 4 and needed to pass the concussion protocol before rejoining the game. Harden's 17 points in the fourth quarter helped secure a Rockets victory but Golden State closed out the series in Game 5 with a stressful 104–90 win.

Returning to their first NBA Finals in 40 years, the Warriors had to defeat LeBron James' Cleveland Cavaliers. Game 1 was an absolute battle and Iman Shumpert missed a potential game-winning shot at the end of regulation. Cleveland point guard Kyrie

Irving had played one of the best defensive games of his career but fractured his kneecap in overtime and missed the remainder of the Finals. Even without him, Cleveland won Game 2 in overtime as James dominated with a triple-double that was just enough to overcome a late Warriors rally. As was the case against Memphis, the Warriors also fell in Game 3, putting them in a familiar 2–1 hole.

This time, the coaching staff's adjustment was even more significant: moving Andre Iguodala into the starting lineup in place of Andrew Bogut and shifting Green to starting center. Alignments with Green at center had fared well at moments in the first three rounds of the playoffs but that five-man lineup had only played a total of 62 playoff minutes together to that point. Coach Kerr credited the change to special assistant Nick U'Ren, who pointed to a similar adjustment the Spurs had made against James' Heat team in the middle of their NBA Finals the previous season. Beyond playing their best defense of the series—including Iguodala spending more time guarding James—the man who gave up his starting spot played a major offensive role as well, chipping in 22 points and actually outscoring James by two. With newfound confidence, the Warriors returned home and Curry produced his best performance of the Finals, with 37 points and a definitive highlight when he crossed over Matthew Dellavedova and nailed a three-pointer.

One win away from an NBA championship, the Warriors had to return to Cleveland for Game 6. The Cavaliers fought their way back from a first-quarter deficit to only trail by two at halftime but Golden State closed it out with a strong third quarter that provided the margin they carried through the fourth and to their first championship in 40 years. Both Curry and Iguodala scored 25 points and the sixth-man-turned-starter won Finals MVP due to his defense on James and scoring punch those final three games. The championship cemented Curry's place as a superstar and also made history as the first time a team won a title with a first-year coach since Pat Riley and the Lakers in 1982. Guard Leandro

Barbosa, who ended a March 21 postgame interview with sideline reporter Rosalyn Gold-Onwude with, "We gonna be championship," reveled in the moment and changed the tense of his famous proclamation to "We are championship."

Two days later, the Warriors held their championship parade and approximately 1 million people filled the streets of Oakland to celebrate a remarkable season in a moment of true catharsis for a long-tortured fan base. In three years, the franchise had finally and improbably completed the journey from black sheep to gold standard.

4 1975 Championship

After making three consecutive playoff appearances from 1971–73, the Warriors missed out on the final spot by three games in 1973–74, but that helped set the table for a remarkable season.

It ended up being an off-season featuring some meaningful turnover, with guard Cazzie Russell leaving for the Lakers as a free agent, the New Orleans Jazz selecting guard Jim Barnett in the expansion draft, and a September blockbuster when they traded star center Nate Thurmond to the Chicago Bulls for Clifford Ray and a future first-round pick. In total, four of the Warriors' top seven players in minutes played on the 1973–74 team did not return. On top of those changes, the Warriors drafted UCLA standout forward Jamaal (then Keith) Wilkes in the first round and local product Phil Smith of USF in the second.

Even with all that change and guard Jeff Mullins missing the first 13 games of the season due to injury, the Warriors started the season strong, including a six-game win streak that pushed their record to 7–2. Charles Johnson took Mullins' place in the starting lineup and held onto it even after the three-time All-Star returned. Part of what made Mullins' acceptance of the demotion easier was the presence of Bill Bridges, another former All-Star who came off the bench for the Warriors that season.

At the All-Star break, they were a surprising 27–13, as rookies Wilkes and Smith had already become established parts of the rotation while Rick Barry continued to excel, making yet another All-Star team with full-season averages of 30.6 points, 6.2 assists, 5.7 rebounds, and a league-leading 2.9 steals per game. In a comparatively down year for elite teams (the powerhouse Bucks lost Oscar Robertson and Kareem Abdul-Jabbar missed 16 games with a broken hand), Golden State's 48–34 record led the Western Conference. For their efforts, Wilkes won Rookie of the Year while Barry made first team All-NBA for the second consecutive season and finished fourth in MVP voting.

The Warriors stood out in their era because coach Al Attles relied on a deep bench. Beyond Johnson replacing Mullins in the starting lineup, 10 different players averaged more than 10 minutes per game on a team that stayed largely healthy throughout the season. While the team was very close-knit, the second unit was strong as well, including advocating sticking together in scrimmages when Attles wanted to shift some starters around to make it more balanced. Even more remarkably, Attles maintained his deep bench in the playoffs, when most coaches pare down their rotation to give their stars more playing time. In their 17 playoff games, only Barry averaged more than 30 minutes per game.

In their first playoff series, the Warriors faced off against the Seattle SuperSonics, who were coached by 1960s nemesis Bill Russell and making their playoff debut. After a comfortable Golden State win in Game 1, the Sonics rebounded with a nice Game 2 comeback victory behind 28 points from star Spencer Haywood and 26 from future All-Star guard Fred Brown. In Seattle's first home playoff game, Barry scored 33 in a significant 105–96 Warriors win that ensured at least a split before the series returned to the Bay Area. After Seattle squared the series, the Warriors dominated Game 5 then closed out the series behind 31 points from Barry and 20 from Wilkes in a 105–96 win.

From there, the Warriors had to face the Chicago Bulls and former teammate Nate Thurmond, though he was not their best player in either that regular season or their first-round win over the Kings. Despite Golden State having the better regular-season record by one game, Chicago had beaten Golden State three of four times in convincing fashion. Like in the first round, the Warriors started strong with a double-digit Game 1 win behind a fourth-quarter push, despite Bulls forward Bob Love scoring 37 points.

Since the Oakland Coliseum Arena was booked for the day of Game 2, the Bulls hosted both Games 2 and 3. In Game 2, the Warriors led by one and Barry got a steal from Chet Walker with 22 seconds left but Barry misheard the bench yelling "move the ball" as "shoot the ball," so he forced a shot and missed when the league's best free-throw shooter could have held the ball for shots and a prohibitively likely win. Instead, Chicago got one more chance and center Tom Boerwinkle made a layup to give the Bulls an unlikely win. After the crushing loss, Attles actually let his players out a side door in the locker room before the media came in so they would not have to answer questions. That disappointment grew as Chicago won Game 3 behind 35 points from Norm Van Lier, then the Bulls started Game 4 with a big first-quarter lead but the deep Warriors pushed and made it a single-possession game by halftime before winning 111–106 behind Barry's 26 second-half points.

After the home team had won the first four games of the series, Chicago took control and a 3–2 series lead with an 89–79 win in Oakland. *San Francisco Chronicle* beat writer Art Spander wrote, "Despite the usual words to the contrary, it looks very much like

Jeff Mullins (23) of the Warriors goes by Doug Collins of the 76ers for a first-quarter layup in a 1975 game. (AP Photo/RBK)

the Warriors will lose." He also noted that the Warriors had not won in Chicago all season.

Despite falling behind in the first quarter, Golden State rallied with a 28–13 second quarter and took an eight-point lead to the locker room, eventually holding ground and surviving a Bulls comeback attempt as Barry scored 36 points to fuel the team's offense. Chicago guard Jerry Sloan credited former teammate Clifford Ray's effort for Golden State, saying, "Ray really stepped up when it counted," when recounting the game he called, "the most memorable game of my career," despite it ending in a brutally disappointing loss.

After six grueling contests, the Warriors and Bulls had a Game 7 for a spot in the Finals. Chicago again controlled early, leading by 14 before the Warriors narrowed the margin to 11 at halftime. With 12 minutes to go in the series, the Bulls still led 65–59. Barry struggled immensely in the first three quarters, making just two of 15 shots, so Attles kept him on the bench to start the fourth.

A lineup of Charles "Grasshopper" Dudley, Jeff Mullins, Wilkes, Derrick Dickey, and journeyman center George Johnson held the Bulls to a draw with each team scoring just two points in the first five minutes of the quarter. Barry then came in and immediately hit three shots, tying the game, and he eventually converted six of his eight fourth-quarter attempts as the Warriors took the game and the series.

Years later, Barry still credits his teammates' defensive effort for the win, saying, "If it weren't for my teammates playing at that level, I would have never had a chance to come back in and play reasonably well the last five minutes of the game for us to be able to win that conference title."

The Warriors' depth and defense had fueled one upset but they still needed one more to come away with a championship. The Washington Bullets won 60 games in the regular season and dispatched the Buffalo Braves and Boston Celtics in their first two series, both of whom had better records than the Warriors. Even before the series, there was another issue to deal with because the Oakland Coliseum Arena was booked for the Ice Follies and the arena refused to move or reschedule it for the NBA Finals, leading to the Warriors hosting games at the Cow Palace, their home for much of the 1960s. Even then, the Cow Palace had a karate tournament on the scheduled date for Game 4, so the league gave the Wizards the choice of hosting Game 1 at home before two in California or Game 1 on the road and then Games 2 through 4 at home with Washington preferring the first option and a home Game 1.

Due to the seven-game Western Conference Finals, the Warriors flew to Washington overnight after their Thursday win and then played Game 1 Sunday afternoon. While the Bullets took a 16-point lead early in the second half, the Warriors finished the third quarter on a 31–16 run. Phil Smith played more minutes due to starting guard Butch Beard's trouble defending Bullets guard Kevin Porter and the second round pick scored 20 points, including 8-for-12 from the free throw line. In total, Golden State's bench outscored their counterparts 44–15 in the surprising 101–95 victory.

With one big win under their belts, the series headed to the Cow Palace due to the Ice Follies and scheduling snafu. While playing in a different arena was an adjustment, Barry had experience and loved shooting at the Cow Palace, noting, "The place was horrible and the locker room was horrible, but you don't play in the locker room, and those baskets were very forgiving." He ended up scoring 36 points in Game 2 and 38 in Game 3 on those "shooter-friendly" rims.

In Game 2, the Bullets again started out strong and faded down the stretch before making a comeback of their own in the final seven minutes of the game and taking the lead with less than a minute to go. After a missed Bullets free throw, Barry was fouled hard by Mike Riordan and made both shots to give the Warriors the lead. Bullets star Elvin Hayes was having a rough series due to heavy minutes and strong defense from Wilkes and Dickey but had a shot to win the game. His turnaround missed and the Warriors moved into a stunning 2–0 series lead. Game 3 was less dramatic, as Barry's 38 points and another strong bench performance put the Warriors one win away from history.

Desperate and down 3–0, Riordan committed a hard foul on Barry minutes into Game 4, ostensibly in an effort to get Golden State's star ejected, though Barry says he "wasn't stupid enough to fall into that trap." Coach Al Attles burst onto the court to keep Barry from Riordan and was thrown out but Riordan stayed in the game. Beyond that, the game followed the now-standard format: Bullets early lead followed by Warriors comeback followed by Bullets comeback. Washington held a 92–84 lead with less than five minutes remaining. The visiting Warriors then went on a 10–1 run and took the lead. After a few miscues by the Bullets, Beard went to the line on two separate occasions and made two free throws to put the Warriors up by three and shortly thereafter they were NBA champions.

After what can still be argued to be the biggest upset in NBA history, the Warriors won their first title in the Bay Area and Barry was named the Finals MVP, averaging 29 points per game in the series. Even with his individual brilliance, the championship was a team accomplishment. Barry described the team as "such a close-knit group, such a family."

Attles said, "Every coach should have one team like that."

The Finals MVP summarized the season and remarkable playoff run best, saying, "We made reality out of fantasy. This is the type of season you only dream about. It just doesn't happen."

5 2017 Championship

The Warriors put a massive target on their backs just 17 days after their brutal Game 7 loss in the 2016 NBA Finals when Kevin Durant announced he was joining the team. The basketball world reacted strongly to a superstar who came so close to the summit joining the team that stopped him, but the greater concern was competitive balance, as the Warriors became the first team in NBA history to start a season with two MVPs still in their twenties. Durant's decision also necessitated a massive turnover of a roster that had just won 73 regular season games, with six new Golden State players on Opening Night, including veteran big men Zaza Pachulia and David West, who both took significant pay cuts to join the team. Bob Myers also worked to rebuild the team's depth by buying the 38th pick in the draft to select UNLV guard Patrick McCaw while also taking a flier on enigmatic center JaVale McGee, both of whom became vital contributors to the team's remarkable season.

Unsurprisingly, adding a new star and replacing almost the entire center rotation required an adjustment period. While Golden State still dominated most opponents due to their superior talent, they had high-profile fourth-quarter collapses in Cleveland on Christmas Day and at home against Memphis less than two weeks later. Stagnant offense was a key factor both times and those disappointments helped push Stephen Curry to take more control instead of ceding too much to Durant. The early portion of the season had two major highlights: Curry responding to his first game without a made three-pointer in 196 contests by setting an NBA record with 13 threes against the Pelicans and Klay Thompson's remarkable scoring barrage with 60 points in the first three quarters against the Pacers. In 29:03, the combustible scorer shot 21-of-33 from the field (8-for-14 from three) while only touching the ball for 90 seconds and taking just 11 dribbles.

After a loss to Memphis in early January, the Warriors won 12 of their next 13 games as extended playing time for Curry and Durant together helped foster more cohesion between the two MVPs. Even though their nine losses at the All-Star break equaled their total for the entire 2015–16 regular season, Golden State was in good shape.

The season changed abruptly on February 28 when Wizards center Marcin Gortat threw Zaza Pachulia down and the big man careened into Durant's left leg. Initially, the injury was diagnosed as a fractured tibia, which would have put him out for months, potentially the entire remainder of the season. Later that same day, doctors checked the CT scan and determined Durant's leg was not broken. Instead he had suffered a grade II sprain of his medial collateral ligament and a bone bruise. Durant returned to the court late in the regular season after missing 19 games.

While challenging, that absence allowed some of the Warriors' role players to step up. Second-round pick McCaw started 15 of those 19 games and impressed playing with the starters, while Andre Iguodala increased his workload and Myers signed former We Believe contributor Matt Barnes to step in as well. The team rallied to some of their most impressive wins of the regular season, including back-to-back victories in Houston and San Antonio, the latter of which required coming back from a 16-point first-quarter deficit.

Golden State finished with the league's best record for the third consecutive season and was close to full strength to start the playoffs, but that would not last. Durant strained his calf in the third quarter of their first game, forcing him to miss Games 2 and 3 against Portland. During that time, Coach Kerr suffered new complications from the back surgery that caused him to miss half of the 2015–16 regular season and had to hand over the reins to assistant coach Mike Brown in his first season with the team. Even with that much turmoil, the Warriors swept the Trail Blazers as Curry averaged just under 30 points per game.

While the top of the Western Conference had looked strong all season, returning to the NBA Finals ended up being a less challenging road than expected. The Utah Jazz won a seven-game series against the Clippers but point guard George Hill only played 28 minutes in a second Warriors sweep that included a 38-point barrage by Durant in Game 3 and another 20-plus point lead in the first quarter of a closeout Game 4. In the next round, the San Antonio Spurs stunned Oracle Arena by storming out to a 46–21 lead in Game 1, but star Kawhi Leonard re-sprained his ankle twice in the third quarter as Golden State came back for a shocking win. Leonard never returned to the series and the Warriors finished off their third consecutive sweep with another dominating Game 4.

That 12–0 start put the Warriors on a collision course with the Cleveland Cavaliers, who made it through the Eastern Conference playoffs with only one loss. The much-anticipated rubber match between the two rivals inspired even more excitement because it was the first time in their three Finals matchups that both teams came in at close to full strength, particularly in terms of their star players.

Durant made his presence felt immediately, pouring in 38 points in his first NBA Finals game since falling to LeBron James and the Heat five years earlier as the Warriors won comfortably to the thrill of the home crowd. Three nights later, the Cavs cleaned up many of their defensive flaws but Golden State took control in the second half, winning Coach Kerr's return to the sideline behind strong performances from Curry and Durant.

The series moving to Cleveland for Game 3 brought a fascinating dynamic. Golden State looked clearly superior in the first two contests, but had done the same a year before and still lost the series. The ghosts of 2016 looked to make a return in Game 3 as the Cavs built a five-point lead by the end of the third quarter, fueled by James and Kyrie Irving, who had 32 and 33 points, respectively, with 12 minutes still to play.

Cleveland led by four with the ball and 1:50 remaining but the Warriors went on a 9–0 run in just 66 seconds, turning that four-point deficit into a five-point lead and a signature win. The definitive moment again came from Durant, who rebounded Kyle Korver's missed three and pulled up from 26 feet, making the three that gave the Warriors a lead they never relinquished. Iguodala also had the chance to redeem himself in a huge Finals moment, stripping James as he attempted a potential game-tying three with 12 seconds to go.

While the Warriors were on the doorstep of history with a potential 16–0 playoff run, they had already made some of their own because their 15–0 start represented the longest postseason win streak ever in the NBA, NFL, MLB, or NHL. Still, the prospect of an undefeated playoffs had a special ring to it. However, perfection eluded them as Cleveland staved off elimination with a forceful Game 4 win, creating an all-too-familiar 3–1 margin as the series shifted back to Oakland.

That set the stage for Game 5, the Warriors' first chance to clinch a series at home since Game 7 of the 2016 Finals and an opportunity to be the first Bay Area team since the 1974 Oakland A's to win a championship in their home arena. After stubbornly relying on traditional big men for the first four games, Coach Kerr reacted to an early Cleveland lead by turning to small lineups. While Iguodala and McCaw both thrived with more playing time than they had become accustomed to in the playoffs, the key run came with West on the floor alongside Curry, Iguodala, Durant, and Green. That quintet outscored the Cavs 22–7 in five minutes, fueling Golden State's 11-point halftime lead.

After a burst from Irving, James and J.R. Smith made it a one-possession game in the fourth quarter. Another Warriors run pushed the margin back to double digits with nine minutes remaining. To the delight of a raucous Oracle crowd, Golden State held on and secured their second championship in three years. Nine Warriors players celebrated their first title, including Kevin Durant, the unanimous selection for Finals MVP due to his 35.2 points, 8.2 rebounds, 5.4 assists, and 1.6 blocks per game, coupled with active defense on James. Durant also became only the sixth player to score 30 or more points in every game of a Finals series.

While there were adjustments, surprises, and speed bumps along the way, the Warriors' first season with Durant went as well as could be expected. The franchise faced a new level of attention from opponents, media, and the sports world more broadly without getting sidetracked by what Pat Riley characterized as the "Disease of More."

Significantly, the 2016-17 season also marked what could be a fundamental change in the way Coach Kerr and the team approach the regular season. After battling each and every night the year before made 73–9 possible, the players and coaching staff were successfully able to throttle back for most of those first 82 games and reaped the rewards. That shift also opened the door for more experimentation with lineups and players while also reducing the strain on stars and veteran role players alike. While much can change over the next few years, that could end up being one of the larger legacies of the 2016–17 campaign as the Warriors adjust to being a force in the league dominant enough to have success solely defined by whether or not their season ends with a championship.

Of course, the other major story was the formation of a truly formidable, durable juggernaut. Curry and Durant found a potent offensive equilibrium and the Warriors were able to accomplish that without sacrificing the Strength in Numbers approach that already helped fuel two NBA Finals appearances and a championship before Durant's arrival. It also answered the question of whether Golden State's four All-Stars would be able to play together, as the quartet of Curry, Durant, Green, and Thompson outscored opponents by 22.6 points per 100 possessions in the regular season and 20 points per 100 possessions in the playoffs. It may not have been as resonant as either the 1975 or 2015 championships since the Warriors spent the entire season as prohibitive favorites, but Golden State's third title in the Bay Area definitively marked the transition from laughingstock to success story to superpower.

Al Attles

Al Attles did not think he was going to stick in the NBA and later said that "the first thing on [his] mind was to teach school in Newark and play in the Eastern League on the weekend," and that he "planned to go to training camp for a week." That week has turned into 57 years and counting, giving him a unique place both in Warriors history and in the NBA today.

After four years at North Carolina A&T, Attles' tenure with the Warriors began as a player in Philadelphia when they drafted him in the fifth round of the 1960 Draft, which Attles found out from a fellow student who heard it on the radio. A month after the training camp where Attles realized he was talented enough to make the team, owner Eddie Gottlieb told the young guard, "You're not very good. But we're going to keep you."

He fit in the guard rotation behind Hall of Famers Guy Rodgers and Tom Gola in an important role on the final two Philadelphia Warriors teams before the move to San Francisco. In that final season in Philadelphia, Attles was the team's second-leading scorer in Wilt Chamberlain's 100-point game, leading to the classic line, "I'll never forget the night me and Wilt combined for 117 points."

In San Francisco, Attles fully embraced his role of key reserve guard and earned the nickname "the Destroyer" due to his intensity on the court, particularly on the defensive end. He averaged 13.3 points per game in their 1964 Western Division Finals win over the St. Louis Hawks and 10.6 per game in their subsequent NBA Finals loss to the Celtics. Shortly thereafter, Attles helped the team transition after trading Chamberlain and played an almost identical 25.6 minutes per game when the Warriors returned to the NBA Finals in 1967 behind Nate Thurmond and Rick Barry.

Attles' role shifted for the 1968–69 season when he took on the responsibilities of being an assistant coach behind former teammate and longtime player–assistant coach George Lee. For two and a half seasons, he ably filled both roles before owner Franklin Mieuli came to him in January 1970 and said, "Al, we want you to coach the team." Attles turned Mieuli down three times that day, infuriating the rarely angry owner. The next day, Mieuli returned with Lee and Attles eventually accepted the position. For the remainder of that season and the full '70–71 campaign, Attles served as a player/coach, sometimes checking himself in to take a foul because he did not want to have one of his teammates do it.

In 1971, Attles made the transition to full-time coach in the team's first season as the Golden State Warriors. They went 51–31 and made it back to the playoffs before falling to the Kareem Abdul-Jabbar/Oscar Robertson Bucks. The next season, Attles' Warriors overcame the Bucks in six games but lost to the 60–22 Lakers and former teammate Chamberlain in his final season.

After finishing one spot out of the playoffs in 1973–74, the Warriors finished first in the Western Conference but with the fourth-best record in the league, 12 games behind the Celtics and Bullets. Golden State dispatched Seattle in six games but had to win a Game 6 in Chicago to force a climactic Game 7 in Oakland to end the Western Conference Finals. A huge defensive effort earned the team a spot in the NBA Finals against the Bullets, who had already defeated two opponents with better season records than the Warriors.

Golden State understood that they were underdogs, with Attles saying, "Nobody expected much of us and felt that we were just lucky to even reach the Finals." They stunned the favorites by winning Game 1 in Washington and kept on rolling, eventually sweeping the heavily favored Bullets in one of the greatest upsets in NBA history. Even now, Attles thinks fondly of that season and noted 40 years after their title win that, "Every coach should have one team like that."

Attles coached the Warriors for another eight seasons and they made the playoffs two more times, including a crushing 1976 Western Conference Finals loss to the Phoenix Suns in seven games that ended their attempt to repeat as champions. Attles eventually passed his first coach, Eddie Gottleib, for the longest-tenured coach in franchise history, a distinction he holds to this day. He transitioned into a front office position in 1983 and ran basketball operations for another three seasons.

For the last 30-plus years, Attles has served as a community ambassador for the Warriors and in 2014 he received the Naismith Memorial Basketball Hall of Fame's John R. Bunn Lifetime Achievement Award, the most prestigious honor outside of Enshrinement. He is also one of only six Warriors players to have their jersey numbers retired and remarkably he played with, coached, and/or drafted all of the other five. Now in his eighties, Attles still attends almost every Warriors home game.

7 Chris Mullin

Few players in Warriors history were more enjoyable to watch than Chris Mullin. He captured the hearts of the Bay Area with his beautiful shooting long before Stephen Curry and Klay Thompson did.

At 6'7", he had a sweet lefty stroke that seemed to never fail and it worked in transition, spotting up and off the dribble.

That was Mullin's distinctive trait, the truest of Warriors fans know Mullin was more than his shooting. While that jumper captivated the basketball world and earned him a spot on the greatest basketball team ever assembled, the Dream Team, Mullin's all-around game was essential for the Warriors.

He was a talented, underrated passer and a decent rebounder despite his wanting athleticism. Critically, Mullin played the game with an instinct and feel that had to be witnessed to be appreciated. The anticipation and vision that allowed him to see two steps ahead enabled Mullin to overcome his deficiencies in quickness and jumping ability.

"He was exciting, had all sorts of style and charisma," said Tim Hardaway in a 2011 interview with the *San Francisco Chronicle* that previewed Mullin's induction to the Naismith Memorial Basketball Hall of Fame.

"He surprised people with his hands, footwork, just beating people to the shot," Hardaway told the *Chronicle*. "He'd drive to the hoop, get hammered in mid-air, and still come up with some crazy bank shot. He played in slow motion, yet he dictated; you just don't see that. Plus, on an NBA court—hey, anywhere—I have never seen a better lefty shooter."

Mullin came to the Warriors having succeeded at every level of basketball he had faced. As a Brooklyn teen, he would find his way to Harlem and the Bronx to play pickup games against New York City's best.

He became legendary for his play in CYO, dominating for St. Thomas Aquinas Parish. He played for Lou Carnesecca's camp, where he was branded by the heralded coach. Mullin went to Power Memorial Academy, where he played with future teammate Mario Elie, before transferring to Xaverian High in Brooklyn.

In 1981, Mullin led Xaverian to the state championship, made the McDonald's All-America team, and earned the title of New York state's Mr. Basketball.

In 1982, he set St. John's record for points by a freshman and the following season Mullin was named Big East Player of the Year and selected to the All-American team. As a junior, he repeated as Big East Player of the Year and All-American, then also made the US Olympic team that won gold in 1984 in Los Angeles.

In 1985, Mullin led the Red Storm to a No. 1 ranking and the Final Four. He became the first player to ever win Big East Player of the Year three times, was chosen as All-American for the third time, and received the John Wooden Award for best collegiate player in the country.

After four remarkable years at St. John's, the Warriors selected the lefty seventh overall in the 1985 Draft, shipping the New York kid all the way across the country.

Despite all his success to that point, Mullin's Warriors career did not start well.

After winning consistently as a high schooler and collegian, he joined a team that had not made the playoffs since 1977 and was coming off its sixth losing season in eight years. The move also kept Mullin far from his family and friends, making him a loner in the Bay Area.

Chris Mullin drives against Glen Rice and the Heat. (AP Photo/Al Messerschmidt)

As a rookie, Mullin struggled in coach Johnny Bach's system, which used him primarily as a spot-up shooter. He made just 46.3 percent of his shots and 18.5 percent of his three-pointers that season and averaged 14 points per game. While his scoring average only went up to 15.1 points per game the next season under new coach George Karl, Mullin's problems were bigger than the system.

He started gaining weight, ballooning up to 250 pounds, well above his eventually stable playing weight of 200 pounds. While Karl questioned Mullin's work ethic and his commitment to defense, the issues went far deeper than that.

Don Nelson was hired as executive vice president of the Warriors for Mullin's third season and Nelson confronted Mullin about his drinking after he missed several practices. While the 24-year-old had been a beer drinker since college, he was not getting arrested or embarrassing himself, so classifying that behavior as a drinking problem had not crossed his mind.

However, Nelson knew. People were whispering about Mullin appearing at bars all over and the team's young shooter was frequently late. While Nelson got Mullin to commit that he would stop drinking for six months, it lasted only four days.

Nelson suspended Mullin on December 10, 1987, and Mullin checked into Centinela Hospital in Inglewood, California, not far from The Forum where the Lakers played, for a month-long rehabilitation program.

A new man emerged from that program. One with a maniacal work ethic, incredible focus, and an unshakable commitment.

Mullin sweated through his cravings, willed away his urges with intense and consistent exercise. He lived in the gym instead of bars and his game took off. Mullin returned to the court January 29 and came off the bench. While it took him a few games to regain his groove, in the first game after the All-Star break, the Warriors hosted the Kings and Mullin exploded for 27 points on 11-for-18 shooting off the bench.

The Warriors finished with just 20 wins, but Mullin was back. He regained his starting role for the remainder of the season and averaged 22.0 points on 52.2 percent shooting and 5.0 assists in 34.2 minutes.

Nelson took over as coach the next season and the revitalized Mullin became a key figure in the team's overhaul. He moved Mullin to small forward, drafted Mitch Richmond out of Kansas State to play shooting guard, and implemented the uptempo style of play known as Nellie Ball. The changes worked wonders for Mullin. The Warriors returned to the playoffs and Mullin became a star: 26.5 points, 5.9 rebounds, 5.1 assists, and 2.1 steals per game. That season, Mullin played in his first All-Star Game and made the All-NBA second team.

1988–89 was the first of five straight seasons where Mullin averaged at least 25 points and shot at least 50 percent from the field. His fame grew as an integral part of Run TMC, particularly during their memorable 1990–91 season, but that prominence arose out of his success on the court. After his breakout in 1988–89, Mullin made another three consecutive All-NBA teams and was even voted an All-Star starter by the fans.

After winning gold with the Dream Team in the 1992 Olympics, Mullin's 1992–93 season was cut short by surgery to repair a ligament in his right thumb. He tried to play through it but was held to four points in a game against Washington, snapping his streak of 301 games scoring in double figures.

Unfortunately, that would be the last time Mullin dominated as an elite NBA player. At that point, his body began to break down. The longtime star missed 87 games over the next three seasons and never averaged more than 19 points per game, eventually declining into little more than a shooter and veteran presence.

After four years filled mostly with decline, Golden State traded Mullin to the Indiana Pacers in 1997, giving him a chance to win while the Warriors rebuilt. By that point in his career, Mullin was limited to spot-up shooting and eventually lost his starting job to Jalen Rose. After three years with the Pacers, he re-signed with the Warriors for the 2000–01 season, his last as a pro.

Ten years later, Mullin was enshrined in the Naismith Memorial Basketball Hall of Fame. On March 19, 2012, the Warriors retired his No. 17 and Mullin is currently the franchise's all-time leader in both games played and steals with a place in their top five for points and assists.

8 Don Nelson

Don Nelson is a singular figure in Warriors history and his imprint on the team shines through in two of their brightest moments in the last 30 years, but he also played an underappreciated part in setting the table for their current success.

After a 13-season playing career that included five championships as a member of the Boston Celtics, Nelson rapidly transitioned to general manager and assistant coach of the Milwaukee Bucks in 1976 before taking over as head coach two months into the season. He helped Milwaukee rebuild about a year after they traded Kareem Abdul-Jabbar by challenging basketball conventions and maximizing players' potential contribution with what became known as "Nellie Ball," including using point forwards like Paul Pressey to run the offense. The Bucks made the playoffs in eight of Nelson's 10 full seasons at the helm and he finished there with an 540–344 record and two Coach of the Year Awards.

After a year away from the league, Nelson reconnected with longtime Bucks owner Jim Fitzgerald, who purchased the Warriors in 1986. Fitzgerald hired Nelson as the general manager in December

1987 but he returned to the bench for the 1988–89 season, following George Karl's resignation late in the prior season. Fueled by Chris Mullin, rookie Mitch Richmond, and Nellie Ball, the Warriors improved by 23 games, made the playoffs, and swept the second-seeded Utah Jazz in the first round that first season. That summer, Nelson drafted Tim Hardaway and signed Šarūnas Marčiulionis, the final pieces in what became known as Run TMC.

In 1989–90, Nelson's fingerprints were firmly on the roster but he still needed to identify the right fits with their newly assembled core, which became even more challenging after losing center Alton Lister to a ruptured Achilles tendon three months after trading a first-round pick for him. During that season of exploration, the Warriors led the league in scoring due to their breakneck pace but struggled immensely on defense, finishing second to last. They showed significant potential and improvement but finished 37–45, a few games outside the playoffs.

The next season, everything started coming together. Hardaway looked more comfortable running the offense, Mullin continued to score efficiently overall despite dropping from 37 percent to 30 percent from three, Richmond had his best all-around season to that point, and Nelson's rotation stabilized a little because big man Alton Lister was healthy enough to play in 77 games. The Warriors improved by seven games and made the playoffs as the No. 7 seed. In the first round, after falling in Game 1, a starting five of Mullin, Richmond, Hardaway, Jim Petersen, and Mario Elie ran through David Robinson's Spurs for three straight wins, two of them by double digits. Nelson's willingness to play and stay small created problems for Larry Brown's team as the Warriors' offense dominated. While the Warriors fell to Magic Johnson, James Worthy, and a strong Lakers team, Run TMC was a phenomenon and Nelson was again the talk of the league.

That off-season, Nelson shocked the basketball world by trading Richmond to Sacramento for rookie Billy Owens in an attempt to add size while maintaining the Nellie Ball identity. While Owens produced when he was able to stay on the court, Run TMC was over and Richmond had a Hall of Fame career for the Kings. Even so, the 1991–92 Warriors improved offensively as they continued to run and Nelson continued to tinker with various combinations built around his key players. They ended the season with a 55–27 record, their best since 1975–76, Nelson won his third Coach of the Year Award, and the perennial underdogs actually had home-court advantage in their first-round series.

They matched up against the Seattle SuperSonics, who had become reinvigorated behind George Karl, the Warriors' coach when Nelson took over as general manager, and Gary Payton, an Oakland product who Seattle selected with a first-round pick Nelson traded them for Lister. After losing Game 1, the Warriors won Game 2 despite athletic forward Shawn Kemp tallying 17 points and 19 rebounds. Nelson responded to Kemp's dominant performance by fouling him incessantly in Game 3, but he made 12-of-15 free throws and Seattle won 129–128 after two Kemp free throws with 6.1 seconds left and a missed shot by Marčiulionis. Kemp then unloaded two definitive highlights in Game 4 by viciously dunking on Lister and Chris Gatling and the Sonics upset Nelson's Warriors 3–1 despite Golden State outscoring Seattle in the series.

While the 1992–93 season was lost due to injuries, it gave Nelson the chance to add and cultivate talent. Second-round pick Latrell Sprewell played well in larger-than-expected playing time and falling out of the playoffs gave them a spot in the draft lottery, which ended up moving them from seventh to third. Nelson then traded three future first-round picks to move up and draft Chris Webber No. 1 overall, with a vision of him as the perfect multifaceted big man for Nellie Ball. Webber bristled at the idea of playing center and that created one of the early points of conflict. Nelson and Webber battled all season on and off the court and reports of the first overall pick and eventual Rookie of the Year using an unusual opt-out after his rookie year hung over the team. Despite all the drama and Hardaway missing the entire season, the Warriors won 50 games before being swept by the Phoenix Suns due to an authoritative performance from Charles Barkley.

After that season, Webber opted out then held out, effectively forcing ownership to choose between their young star and coach. In one of the all-time "what ifs" for the NBA, Nelson offered to leave and actually had a tantalizing offer on the table during that drama because former assistant Gregg Popovich, who had left Golden State to become the general manager of the San Antonio Spurs, was "holding the job open for" Nelson but the team sided with their coach and traded Webber to Washington. The Warriors struggled to a 14–31 record as Nelson dealt with physical and mental fatigue before resigning, with the *Los Angeles Times* saying it was a mutual parting of the ways with owner Chris Cohan "ready to be rid of him" less than three months after choosing Nelson over Webber.

Nelson recharged for the remainder of that season in Maui, then returned to the NBA the next season to coach the Knicks. There, his system did not mesh with their existing talent and the Knicks fired him in March of his first season. Even in that one season, John Starks said the issues between him and Nelson "would never heal," further diminishing Nelson's reputation as a player's coach.

After some time off, Ross Perot Jr. hired Nelson in Dallas in February 1997 and he followed a similar path to his time with the Warriors: starting as general manager before eventually taking over as head coach as well. It took Nelson longer to turn around the Mavericks than the Bucks or Warriors but he built a young core on draft night in 1998 by drafting Dirk Nowitzki and trading for Steve Nash. Nelson established "Hack-A-Shaq" in 1999–2000 by intentionally fouling Shaquille O'Neal, though he had used the strategy two years before on Dennis Rodman. Nelson intended to fluster the star and succeeded, noting that "Shaq was so upset, he grabbed the TV in the visiting locker room and threw it in the shower, which I thought was pretty funny."

In 2000–01, Dallas had the first of four consecutive 50-plus win playoff seasons under Nelson. Nowitzki, Nash, and Michael Finley had become All-Stars but owner Mark Cuban's refusal to match Nash's contract offer from the Phoenix Suns in 2004, Nash's immediate success there, and assistant coach Avery Johnson's success when Nelson missed 13 games helped inspire him to resign before the end of the 2004–05 season.

That same year, former Nelson player Chris Mullin traded for Baron Davis as the Warriors' general manager. After a disappointing season with Mike Montgomery, Mullin approached his former coach about taking over as head coach. It made sense, as Nelson's creativity and understanding of the game could cover the Warriors' flaws and accentuate their strengths. It was going to take a mastermind of sorts to work magic for a franchise that had a hard time luring top talent via free agency and tended to strike out during the draft. Despite his issues with Cohan since the owner had sued Nelson for $1.6 million when he became the coach of the Knicks, Nelson agreed on August 29, 2006. That season, Mullin and Nelson acquired Stephen Jackson and Al Harrington from the troubled Indiana Pacers for Mike Dunleavy and Troy Murphy in a massive eight-player trade and the We Believe Warriors won 14 of their final 21 games to make the playoffs.

Finishing as the No. 8 seed pitted the Warriors against Nelson's prior team and former protégées Nowitzki and Johnson. Nelson got Nowitzki off his game by putting the smaller, stronger Jackson on him and fear of Nellie Ball inspired Johnson to start Game 1 without a traditional center despite their 67–15 regular season record. Eventually the Warriors pulled the biggest first-round upset in league history, stunning the Mavericks in six games in a massive triumph for Nelson.

After falling to the Jazz in the second round, Golden State actually improved by six games the next season despite trading Jason Richardson for a first-round pick, but that team shares the distinction for the best record in NBA history (48–34) for a team that failed to make the playoffs. Davis left for the Clippers after that season and the team fell off, though their struggles in 2008–09 opened the door for Nelson's last major contribution to the franchise.

The Warriors had the seventh pick in the 2009 Draft with plenty of uncertainty ahead of them. While general manager Larry Riley was also in love with guard Stephen Curry's potential after seeing him play against Purdue, Nelson's vision for Curry as a star and point guard helped firm up the team's commitment to keep him instead of trading the pick to the Suns for Amaré Stoudemire. "That was our guy–that was *my* guy anyway," Nelson said of Curry years later.

Nelson had the opportunity to coach the player he felt was the second-best talent in that class for his rookie year. The Warriors struggled to a 26–56 record but Nelson passed Lenny Wilkens for the most coaching wins in NBA history a week before the end of the season in Minnesota. The longtime coach savored the moment, calling it "such a neat feeling," particularly since Wilkens was an "idol of [mine] for a long time." With the change in ownership, Nelson resigned and returned home to Maui.

While Nelson's unquenchable thirst for innovation changed the entire NBA for decades, he had a much larger impact on the Warriors as a franchise. For a 25-year period, Nelson was the only coach to take Golden State to the playoffs, despite only spending all or part of 11 of those seasons on their bench.

9 Nate Thurmond

On January 15, 1965, the San Francisco Warriors made a move that would get around-the-clock analysis in the modern sports world when they traded Wilt Chamberlain.

They sent the centerpiece of the franchise and arguably the best player in the world to Philadelphia for three hardly known players and cash. Far from a dimming star, Chamberlain was 28 years old at the time and the Warriors had made the NBA Finals the previous year behind his 36.9 points and 22.3 rebounds per game.

While deciding to trade a megastar is and will always be a major decision, it was more palatable for the Warriors because they had Nate Thurmond.

At 6'11", 225 pounds, Thurmond did not cast as long a shadow as Chamberlain, but what he lacked in size he made up for in strength. Similarly, he did not have Chamberlain's incredible skill but used toughness to make up much of that margin.

Before LeBron James, Thurmond was the original son of Akron, Ohio, where he played with Hall of Famer Gus Johnson at Central High School. Thurmond passed up a chance to play at Ohio State to attend Bowling Green State University, where he became a *Sporting News* first team All-American in 1963.

Thurmond was the Warriors' first draft pick after moving to the West Coast when they selected him third overall. He learned the game behind Chamberlain and became a premier force in the NBA after the trade, eventually rivaling both Chamberlain and Bill Russell, the other dominant big man of their day.

Just over a month after the trade, Thurmond set a record with 18 rebounds in a quarter at Baltimore and later that same year had a 42-board performance against Detroit. While building a reputation around the league, he averaged more than 16 points and 18 rebounds in about 40 minutes per game over the first two seasons after Chamberlain's departure and made the next four All-Star teams (1965–68).

While already a valued contributor and All-Star, Thurmond's game, especially his offense, continued to develop. He finished second in MVP voting behind Chamberlain for the 1966–67 season, then built on that by averaging 20.5 points and 22.0 rebounds the next year.

Plus, when the team added Rick Barry in 1965, they began to win. After finishing 35–45 in 1965–66, they won the Western Division the next season with a 44–37 record and the Thurmond/Barry duo propelled San Francisco to the NBA Finals, where they faced off against Chamberlain's 76ers.

Thurmond had 31 rebounds in Game 1 as the Warriors pushed it to overtime before losing in Philadelphia. He averaged 14.2 points and 26.7 rebounds in the series as he and Chamberlain became the only two players to record 20 or more rebounds in every game of the same playoff series.

While the Warriors fell to that loaded 76ers team, they had two players in Thurmond and Barry who finished in the top five of MVP voting that season and were both 25 or younger.

Shockingly, that was as close as the Warriors would come to a title with Thurmond, who had grown into a Bay Area sports icon. Barry ended up leaving the team after that season due to a financial dispute with owner Franklin Mieuli and Thurmond took the reins. He scored 20 or more points per game for the next five seasons and averaged 21 points and 17.4 rebounds during Barry's half-decade odyssey. That time also allowed Thurmond to bolster his defensive reputation and he made five of six All-Defensive teams from 1968–69 to 1973–74.

Barry returned in 1972–73 and Thurmond was still going strong, having carried the Warriors through the transition to

Oakland. That season was a high point for Thurmond and the franchise's recent history, as he stayed healthy and dominated to the tune of 17.1 points and 17.1 rebounds and Golden State ended up beating Kareem Abdul-Jabbar, Oscar Robertson, and the Bucks in the first round of the playoffs. That allowed Thurmond to face off against Chamberlain again in the 1973 Western Conference Finals and again the Stilt's team came out on top, though neither pivot man was at the peak of their respective powers by that point.

After a disappointing follow-up in 1973–74, the Warriors decided to trade Thurmond to the Chicago Bulls shortly before the 1974–75 season for the startling return of fellow center Clifford Ray, a first-round pick, and cash. Bay Area fans, who saw Major League Baseball's San Francisco Giants trade Willie Mays and Willie McCovey, experienced the familiar discomfort of watching a longtime star in an unfamiliar uniform.

Richard Vertlieb, general manager of the Warriors at the time, said age was a key factor in trading the 33-year-old Thurmond.

"We are acquiring an outstanding young performer who has been an integral part of Chicago's success the past three seasons and who has his best seasons before him," Vertlieb said. "In return we gave up one of the game's great players who is nearing the end of his career."

While it was hard to trade Thurmond after 11 transformative seasons for the franchise, Ray helped anchor the defense for the 1975 championship team that very season before playing seven total seasons for the Warriors. Thurmond would play that 1974–75 season with the Bulls and become the first player to ever record a quadruple-double with 22 points, 14 rebounds, 13 assists, and 12 blocks against the Atlanta Hawks on October 8, 1974. After that stint in Chicago, Thurmond finished his career playing for the team he grew up rooting for, the Cleveland Cavaliers.

Thurmond's 14-season NBA career ended after the 1976–77 season and he stands with Chamberlain, Russell, Bob Pettit, and

Jerry Lucas as the only players to average at least 15 points and 15 rebounds for their career. He remains the Warriors' all-time leader in rebounds (12,771) and minutes played (30,735) and trails only Chris Mullin in games played.

Thurmond was inducted into the Naismith Memorial Basketball Hall of Fame in 1985 and named one of the 50 Greatest Players in NBA History 11 years later. He is still the only NBA player to have his number retired by two teams, as the Warriors and Cleveland Cavaliers gave him the honor.

Despite ending his career elsewhere, Thurmond's presence in the Bay Area extended far beyond his No. 42 hanging in the rafters at Oracle Arena. He maintained his ties with San Francisco, even living in the city while playing in Chicago. Big Nate's Barbeque became a staple on Folsom Street for almost 20 years and he served as a community advisor who was a consistent presence with the Warriors and in the community until his passing on July 16, 2016.

10 Run TMC

The Run TMC era for the Warriors stands out due both to its brilliance and brevity.

Tim Hardaway, Mitch Richmond, and Chris Mullin were all homegrown products, drafted by the Warriors in 1989, 1988, and 1985, respectively. Don Nelson's move from the front office to head coach in 1988 set the table for the group as his high-energy Nellie Ball ensured a dynamic and eminently watchable team.

The three worked as a cohesive unit. While Hardaway ran the offense in half-court sets, each of the three could handle well enough to bring the ball up and keep opponents off balance as the other two and their teammates streaked down for an easy basket. When they were not able to run, Hardaway handled the ball while Mullin and Richmond worked off-ball and maximized their ability to score in different ways. Importantly, all three were capable shooters who could make their free throws. As Mullin described it years later, "Our talents really meshed. Timmy was the ball-handler, the dominant personality, the leader. I was more of an outside shooter, a finesse guy. And then we mixed with that power guard in Mitch, who could go in the post. We really complemented each other."

The trio's first season, 1989–90, was a little rocky, but the Warriors led the NBA in scoring at 116.3 points per game despite starting Hardaway at point guard as a rookie, which typically

Mitch Richmond, Chris Mullin, and Tim Hardaway pose for photographs before Mullin's jersey retirement. (AP Photo/Jeff Chiu)

means a rough, slow adjustment. Nelson used Mullin, Richmond, and Hardaway as his foundation but continued to tinker with the other players around them, including Terry Teagle, Šarūnas Marčiulionis, Winston Garland, and Rod Higgins, while running through a wide array of big men trying to find the right fit, including Manute Bol, Tom Tolbert, Uwe Blab, and Jim Petersen. Even with that much turnover and experimentation, there were signs of what was to come, including two different six-game win streaks and home wins over the Lakers, Pistons, and Trail Blazers. Mullin made the All-NBA third team as the Warriors won 37 games, good enough for 10th in the conference.

One of the most important elements of the trio's first season together was developing a connection on and off the court. Mullin said, "Once we got on the court, we clicked for sure."

They also appreciated the personal relationships, with Richmond noting that the team "had a whole roster of guys…that did really like being with each other."

That potential metamorphosed into a force in 1990. Nelson named Mullin, Richmond, and Hardaway co-captains and all three scored at least 22.9 points per game as Golden State actually outscored their blistering 1989–90 campaign with 116.6 points per game.

Both Mullin and Hardaway made the 1991 All-Star team as the run-and-gun Warriors became a genuine phenomenon. During the season, the *San Francisco Examiner* ran a "Name the Warriors Trio Contest" with the best submissions going to the players themselves for the final decision. The three agreed on "Run TMC," inspired by the hip hop group Run-DMC, and the name stuck instantly.

What made Warriors fans fall in love and enthralled the rest of the league was the team's combination of youth, excitement, and talent. While playing fast had become more commonplace (after all, the 1990–91 team did not even lead the NBA in pace), no one did it quite like Golden State. On opening night, they played against the Nuggets and the two teams combined for 320 points in a 162–158 Warriors win, still the most total points in league history for a regulation game. Each night, they had the potential for unforgettable moments, sometimes for either team.

While deploying a series of different lineups due to injuries, most notably Marčiulionis missing almost half the regular season, and Nelson simply wanting to try out new combinations, the team finished the season 44–38 and never dropped below .500 at any point.

In the first round of the playoffs, the No. 7-seeded Warriors faced the second-seeded San Antonio Spurs. After falling 130–121 in Game 1, Nelson changed the starting lineup to Mullin, Richmond, Hardaway, Petersen, and swingman Mario Elie, going even smaller against an opponent that relied heavily on center David Robinson. Golden State's 111–98 road victory stole control of the series. All three members of Run TMC scored 22 or more in their first home playoff game together as they eked out a 109–106 victory and a 2–1 lead in the best-of-five series. Hardaway said, "I was pumped up all night. I didn't sleep last night. I woke up, my stomach was turning, and I was ready to play the game." It showed as he took the lead, scoring 32 points and dishing out nine assists. While the Spurs cut the lead to five in the fourth quarter, it never got closer than that and the young team won their first playoff series.

Yet again, the Warriors' unconventional nature and Nelson's ability to get opponents out of their comfort zone played a major factor in the upset. Describing that team, Nelson said, "We had a small team, so we had to create mismatches however we could."

Hardaway described the challenge for opponents facing them. "They didn't know how to even play against us. They didn't know how to discuss it. They didn't know how to plan for it. It was mind-boggling to the other team."

With momentum and confidence, Golden State had to face the Lakers, who went 58–24 on the season behind Magic Johnson,

James Worthy, and a deep supporting cast that included former teammate Teagle. While the Lakers won Game 1 as Johnson logged an impressive triple-double, the Warriors stunned them with a 125–124 upset in Game 2 as Mullin scored 41 and Run TMC combined for 91 points.

The series moved to Oakland and Run-DMC introduced the team before Game 3. Lakers coach Mike Dunleavy shifted Worthy on to Mullin after his scoring outburst and the sharpshooter's scoring total dropped from 41 to 13. Los Angeles built an 11-point lead with 3:25 remaining, but the Warriors roared all the way back to a one-point deficit after a Marčiulionis shot with 37 seconds remaining. After Byron Scott made a two-pointer, Hardaway missed two game-tying threes and the Lakers took back home court.

Two nights later, the Lakers held a lead and then made it insurmountable with a 16–3 run early in the fourth quarter. Mullin struggled again with Worthy on him, scoring nine points on 4-for-13 from the field. Facing elimination, the Warriors led for most of Game 5 but another fourth-quarter surge from the Lakers closed the gap and eventually a Sam Perkins layup forced overtime. The game stayed close during the entire extra period but the Lakers scored just enough to win 124–119.

Even though their season ended in disappointment, Richmond, Mullin, and Hardaway were just 25, 27, and 24, respectively, when the series ended. Pulling an upset and pushing the eventual Western Conference champions established Run TMC as one of the league's most intriguing young trios in a long time.

However, that May 14 loss would be the last game they ever played together because Nelson traded Richmond for the 1991 Draft's No. 3 overall pick, Billy Owens, on November 1. While Nelson called the decision to trade Richmond "the toughest I ever made" at the time, it was even harder for the team and fans to take since it was consummated just before the Warriors' first regular season game of the 1991–92 season.

In devastating fashion, Run TMC was over.

Nelson justified the move with the rationale that the team needed more size and ideally skilled taller players like Owens to reach greater success. But that never materialized. While Hardaway remained on the team for another four seasons and Mullin six, the Warriors never reached the second round of the playoffs again, despite surpassing their 1990–91 win total twice during that time, including that first season immediately following the trade.

Richmond summarized the era and its legacy well almost 25 years later when he remarked, "It's funny. I played three years there and people think that I played 10." Despite its brevity, Run TMC had a lasting impact on the Warriors, basketball fans, and the sport as a whole.

11 We Believe

The 2006–07 season started out in surprisingly nondescript fashion. Despite having an offensive linchpin in Baron Davis and Don Nelson back on the sidelines, on January 16 the Warriors were 19–20 and on the fringes of the Western Conference playoff chase. Plus, talented swingman Jason Richardson had recently broken his hand and would not return after the All-Star break in late February.

That January day, general manager Chris Mullin made a move Golden State had been on the opposite side of many times in the preceding years. The Indiana Pacers were still reeling from the nasty on-court melee with the Detroit Pistons, now known as the "Malice at the Palace," which happened 14 months earlier. Mullin made an offer for troubled swingman Ron Artest (now known as Metta World Peace) before he was traded to Sacramento, but

Stephen Jackson was still on the team and had been charged with a felony count of criminal recklessness in October of that season.

Eventually, the two franchises agreed to a massive deal: Mike Dunleavy, Troy Murphy, Ike Diogu, and Keith McLeod for Jackson, Al Harrington, Šarūnas Jasikevičius, and Josh Powell.

While Jackson and Harrington immediately became massive pieces of the team's rotation, an adjustment period and Davis needing surgery to relieve knee soreness in early February pushed the team closer to the brink. The Warriors were 27–35 and seemed to be heading toward another disappointing end to the season as a six-game losing streak had their playoff hopes on life support. However, they were coming off a big road win over Eastern Conference powerhouse Detroit and showing a sign of life that had been missing for a while.

So Paul Wong, an Alameda resident and owner of a Korean BBQ joint, printed up 150 signs and passed them out at the Warriors' next game, a home tilt vs. Denver on March 7, 2007. Each one had two words that would become the mantra for the rest of the season and eventually Warriors lore:

We Believe

The Warriors beat Denver and Wong printed out more placards before the Warriors defeated the Clippers two nights later. After a loss in Portland, Golden State ran off another three-game win streak and Wong handed out signs at each home game. On March 29, the "We Believe" signs were seen during the nationally televised game on TNT as Jason Richardson scored 36 in a 124–119 win over the Phoenix Suns, who finished with the second-best record in the West. Behind a starting five of Davis, Richardson, Jackson, Harrington, and second-year guard Monta Ellis, the Warriors won their next three games as well, including road victories over the Rockets and Grizzlies.

We Believe had life. The fan base was engaged. The team was maxing out. Something special was brewing.

Wong took it to another level in the last week of the season. On April 13, he printed up some signs and took them to Sacramento. It was a critical game for the Warriors and We Believe traveled to see the Warriors rout the Kings, including 51 points combined from Davis and Jackson. Two nights later, the Warriors were back at home and so was Wong with his signs.

Suddenly, the Warriors were unbeatable. With three straight wins under their belt, they hosted the Dallas Mavericks, who had already clinched the best record in the Western Conference. With their seed assured and two games left in the regular season, former Nelson assistant Avery Johnson rested many of his key players, which infuriated the Clippers, who were in a fight with the Warriors for the final spot in the playoffs. The Warriors cruised and set up a win-and-in scenario in Portland for the season finale.

Wong made that trip too, bringing signs to the game. Golden State won 120–98 and the We Believe mantra was about to receive a much bigger platform.

Due to losing a tiebreaker with the Lakers, the Warriors were the No. 8 seed and faced off against the Mavericks. That provided a massive tactical advantage for Golden State because Nelson had coached Dallas from 1997 to 2005 but also played an instrumental role in finding, drafting, and developing league MVP Dirk Nowitzki. That knowledge proved invaluable from the start as the Warriors won Game 1 with a strong team performance and a massive game from Baron Davis: 33 points, 14 rebounds, and eight assists. They also gained an advantage when Mavericks coach Avery Johnson changed his starting lineup in the first game of the series despite Dallas winning a league-best 67 games with Nowitzki typically playing power forward next to starting center and former Warrior Erick Dampier. Johnson pre-adjusting to the Warriors' smaller, quicker lineup at the outset gave Nelson and his team confidence they were in the Mavericks' heads.

After a competitive Game 2, which Dallas won 112–99, the Warriors were ready for the series to head to Oracle. "I can't wait to get home to see our fans," Richardson said from Dallas. "It's going to be crazy."

Was it ever.

The Warriors returned home to a surreal setting as the team printed up gold T-shirts with bold navy blue letters saying "We Believe" on the front. Each seat had one and Oracle Arena became an intimidating sea of gold.

The stadium was practically full as soon as it opened for Game 3, as fans were eager to experience the first playoff game in Oakland in nearly a generation. The energy in the building was epic. When the players came out for warm-ups, it sounded like a championship had been clinched.

In his first home playoff game, Richardson—the long-suffering soldier for the Warriors who survived long enough to see good times—exploded for 30 points and released 13 years of suppressed cheering among the Oracle fan base in a resounding 109–91 victory. In Game 4, Golden State erased a four-point deficit with four minutes remaining to take a 3–1 series lead on the heavily favored Mavericks.

The Warriors should have ended the series in Game 5 but blew a nine-point advantage in the final 3:20 as the Mavericks forced a return to Oracle. There, the home team left no doubt with a massive 36–15 third quarter that unleashed a raucous, defiant Oracle crowd. The Warriors had just produced the biggest first-round upset in league history. Nowitzki was so angry postgame that he threw a 60-pound trash can at the wall opposite the visitors' locker room, putting a dent about 13 feet up that still exists, covered by Plexiglas with a We Believe shirt above it.

Their second-round series with the Jazz produced fewer bright spots but did include the single most definitive highlight of the season: Baron Davis' dunk on Andrei Kirilenko in Game 3. While the Warriors came close in Game 1 and forced overtime in Game 2, Davis' dunk punctuated their only win of the series.

Rather than seek another 15 minutes, Wong instead savored his discreet rewards: witnessing Oracle Arena turn into a den of basketball passion, having fans from around the country visit his restaurant to meet him and shake his hand, and, most important, getting his wife back.

That was all he needed.

"It was crazy," Wong says. "I really paid a price…. I'm happy with being a regular fan. The whole celebrity thing was too much for me."

While the We Believe campaign started in earnest on March 7, when the Warriors hosted the Denver Nuggets, the motivation for it came earlier. At the time, Wong told everyone that the reason he started We Believe was to motivate Warriors fans to be zealous about the team again and said the idea came from *The Secret*, a self-help book made popular by Oprah Winfrey that focuses on positive reinforcement, which is true.

What Wong did not tell everyone was that his wife of 10 years, Mai, gave him the book. Their marriage was in trouble because, as Wong admitted, he was a workaholic and they grew apart. She suggested the book because she did not think he believed in their relationship anymore. "We were going to get a divorce," Wong acknowledged, his reluctance negated by the glee from his now-stronger marriage. "We had been trying to make it work, but we were headed for divorce."

Paul and Mai Wong are still married and watched the Warriors win the 2015 championship together at Oracle Arena.

12 Experience Roaracle

There are some truly special arenas in the NBA. In some of these basketball palaces, you can just feel the vibe as soon as you walk in. You know you are in a unique place.

That feeling is probably most present in Madison Square Garden, considered the Mecca of basketball. It has been the home to so many historic basketball moments, including both amateur and professional hoops, and its legend creeps under the skin to create goose bumps.

Another example is Staples Center, Hollywood's version of basketball. Even though the Lakers moved there from The Forum in 1999, no basketball arena feels as extravagant. It is a foray into an exclusive party filled with wealth and fame, a paradise for celebrity watching, fashion gawking, and, until recently, watching future Hall of Famers.

Oracle Arena has forged its way into the sanctified realm of NBA venues. It hits you when the entire arena bellows in unison from the diaphragm, "Warriors! Warriors! Warriors!"

There is nothing special about the design of Oracle Arena. Built in 1966 and renovated in 1996, it is far from state-of-the-art. Unlike many more modern arenas, Oracle is not in an especially attractive location, nestled in the corner of an expansive complex sandwiched by a freeway and East Oakland.

Instead, the fans transform it into a marvel of a setting. It has become known as "Roaracle" and it should be on the bucket list of Warriors fans, even those who do not live in the Bay Area.

It is one of the true home-court advantages in the NBA, with the crowd being frenetic and engaged enough to fuel the Warriors players. It also makes for a daunting obstacle for the visitors.

Kobe Bryant, before his final game in Oakland, held a press conference with the media. The future Hall of Famer, who earlier in the season announced he was retiring, was asked if he regrets not playing a playoff game in Oakland.

"I'd rather not," Bryant said. "If I had to and the challenge presented itself, of course I'd rise to the challenge. But if I had a choice, I don't want to deal with this crowd."

Even visiting players revere the setting the Warriors enjoy. After losing to the Warriors on Christmas Day in 2015, Cleveland star LeBron James tweeted out his admiration, saying, "Nothing like playing in atmospheres like Oracle Arena." And, during the 2015 NBA Finals, James said the environment moved him to want to be remembered there, something that happened definitively almost exactly a year later.

There have been moments in Oracle where you could not hear yourself think.

Like the introductions before Game 3 of the 2007 first-round series against Dallas, the first playoff game in the building since 1994, or when Baron Davis dunked over Andrei Kirilenko in Game 3 of the second-round series against Utah in 2007.

Another special moment came back in November 2012, when Harrison Barnes posterized Minnesota center Nikoka Pekovic. The crowd became increasingly raucous as the dunk was repeatedly played on the video screen.

Five months later, the Oracle crowd exploded when the Warriors closed out the Denver Nuggets for their first playoff series win since We Believe. That series also had Stephen Curry's explosion in Game 4 of the 2013 first-round series against Denver. He scored 22 points in the third quarter, none louder than his pull-up three-pointer on a fast break that sent Oracle to new levels of crazy.

There was also the magical night when Klay Thompson scored 37 points in a quarter, turning an NBA arena into Rucker Park as he made nine straight three-pointers.

Game 5 of the 2015 Western Conference Finals, when Barnes took over down the stretch to send the Warriors to their first NBA Finals in 40 years, rivaled just about any moment as the confetti fell from the rafters.

One of the most special moments happened with the Warriors out of town. Fans packed Oracle Arena for Game 6 of the NBA Finals in Cleveland. And after the Warriors clinched the title, thousands converged for an impromptu party outside the arena.

After a disappointing end to the Finals a year later, Oracle crowds had two special moments during the 2016–17 season. First, Thompson exploded for 60 points in three quarters in the same game where Draymond Green threw a full-court outlet pass to Curry, who alley-ooped it to Kevin Durant in one of the highlights of the year. Five months later, the Oracle crowd finally had the chance to experience a trophy presentation in person as Warriors won their first championship on their home floor since moving to the Bay Area.

The Warriors will move to San Francisco and the Chase Center for the 2019–20 season, so time is running short to make a pilgrimage to the home of the most raucous atmosphere in the NBA and so many Warriors memories.

13 The Making of a Monolith

Building a powerhouse takes time, effective management, and plenty of good fortune. While many steps of the Warriors' long process from frequent lottery team to multiple-time champion were incredibly important, three factors stand out as being central to the success that followed:

1. Stephen Curry's extension: Back in October 2012, giving Curry four years and $44 million guaranteed carried risk since the point guard had missed time in each of the prior two seasons due to ankle issues, playing only 26 games in the lockout-shortened 2011–12 campaign. By the end of the season between that agreement and when the extension actually kicked in, it had already become apparent that it would be a huge bargain and that only intensified over time. The Warriors used cap space to sign Andre Iguodala in 2013 and Kevin Durant in 2016 with flexibility that largely stemmed from having a superstar making around $11 million per season. If Golden State had let Curry hit restricted free agency in 2013 instead of agreeing to that extension a year early, at least one but likely both of those key signings never happens and the franchise is in a very different place as a result.

2. Hiring Steve Kerr: While Mark Jackson's contributions to the Warriors must be properly appreciated, Kerr and his staff actualized and maximized the team's talent. His system emphasizing active ball and player movement unlocked Curry's truly special offensive potential while also unearthing Green's value with the ball in his hands. Thanks to an already-solid defensive foundation, overhauling the offense amplified those improvements because greater efficiency led to even more possessions defending in the half-court, producing a system of positive feedback loops that fueled Golden State's trademark devastating runs. Beyond helping Curry, Green, Thompson, and their teammates reach new heights, Kerr's system and Strength in Numbers approach made playing on the Warriors more appealing for talent around the league. The successful incorporation of Kevin Durant, David West, Zaza Pachulia, and David West in 2016–17 confirmed Kerr's value, even as he spent a significant portion of their 16–1 playoff run away from the sideline.

3. Timing: Many focus on the Warriors taking advantage of a huge salary cap spike to sign Durant, but they benefitted from timing for years, with the whole sequence culminating in that opportunity. While Iguodala, Thompson, and Green all took less

Durant and Curry during the first half of Game 4 of the 2017 Finals.
(AP Photo/Tony Dejak)

than their maximum when they hit free agency, each of those negotiations occurred before the league had incorporated the new national television contract, which helped keep all contracts signed and low, relative to recent off-seasons. Additionally, those factors combined with a comparatively small mid-level exception in 2014 allowed Golden State to hold on to Shaun Livingston while fitting Durant in two summers later, helping them retain depth that proved vital during their championship run.

While those were the key factors, many other decisions and events are pivotal parts of how the Warriors became a force.

June 25, 2009: Drafted Stephen Curry seventh overall despite him refusing to work out for the team, then refused to trade him despite extended pre-draft negotiations with Phoenix about using that selection in a deal for Amar'e Stoudemire. Three days before, they traded Corey Maggette to Milwaukee with three years and $31 million remaining on his contract.

April 14, 2011: Hired former player agent Bob Myers to be assistant general manager. One month later, ownership brought in Jerry West as an executive board member. They become two of the key figures in the personnel moves that followed.

June 6, 2011: Hired Mark Jackson as head coach. Less than two years later, he became the first coach other than Don Nelson to lead the franchise to the playoffs since 1987.

June 23, 2011: Drafted Klay Thompson with the 11th pick. He is one of only five players taken in that first round to be an All-Star in any of their first six seasons.

December 2011: Waived Charlie Bell using the amnesty provision and cut guard Jeremy Lin to clear additional salary cap space for restricted free agent center DeAndre Jordan. After the Clippers matched that offer sheet, the front office used the space on contracts for Kwame Brown, Dominic McGuire, and Brandon Rush (via trade) that all expired the following summer, maintaining financial flexibility.

March 13, 2012: Traded Monta Ellis, 2010 lottery pick Ekpe Udoh, and Kwame Brown for center Andrew Bogut and Stephen Jackson, who was then moved to San Antonio for Richard Jefferson and a 2012 first-round pick. While attributable to more factors than just the Australian center, Golden State had a top-five defense each of Bogut's three years after finishing outside the top 10 for the previous 14 seasons.

June 28, 2012: Drafted Harrison Barnes (No. 7), Festus Ezeli (No. 30—the choice from the Jefferson/Jackson trade), Draymond Green (No. 35), and Ognjen Kuzmic (No. 52). All four won at least one championship with the Warriors.

October 31, 2012: Agreed to a contract extension with Curry for four years and $44 million, running through the 2016–17 season. Curry made an All-NBA team each of the four seasons under that contract and won two league MVP Awards.

July 2013: Secured a commitment from free agent swingman Andre Iguodala, then traded two first-round picks to Utah with Andris Biedrins, Richard Jefferson, and Brandon Rush to clear the necessary salary cap space. Also signed center Marreese Speights to a three-year contract.

October 25, 2013: Agreed to an extension with Bogut for three years and $43 million that descended in salary each season. The decision to front-load his contract became more significant in July 2016 when the team needed to shed salary in order to sign Durant using cap space.

May 2014: After a tumultuous season, management decided to fire Mark Jackson despite a 121–109 record in three seasons. Two weeks later, they hired Steve Kerr. The Warriors have made the NBA Finals in each of Kerr's three seasons, including two championships. Kerr received the 2015–16 NBA Coach of the Year Award.

July 2014: Signed guard Shaun Livingston for the mid-level exception and refused to include Klay Thompson in trade negotiations for power forward Kevin Love, partially due to Jerry West threatening to resign if the Warriors went through with the deal over his objection. Later that off-season, they also brought in veteran guard Leandro Barbosa and undrafted big man James Michael McAdoo.

October 31, 2014: Agreed to four-year, $69 million contract extension with Klay Thompson, which ended up being less than his maximum as the salary cap rose above the expected level, saving the Warriors an eventually significant million dollars in the summer of 2016.

July 2, 2015: After winning their first championship since 1975, the Warriors re-signed restricted free agent Draymond Green for five years, $82 million. Like Thompson, the $2.3 million Green signed for below his maximum became important later on. Later that off-season, they traded David Lee to Boston for Gerald Wallace before moving Wallace to Philadelphia for Jason Thompson. Myers also re-signed Barbosa and brought in guard Ian Clark, who eventually replaced Barbosa on the second unit.

July 4, 2016: Secured the commitment of Kevin Durant, then cleared salary cap space for him by trading Bogut to Dallas and rescinding the qualifying offers on both Barnes and Ezeli. Later that summer, they signed big men Zaza Pachulia, David West, and JaVale McGee; retained McAdoo and Clark; and drafted center Damian Jones and guard Patrick McCaw.

July 2017: Re-signed Curry using the new Designated Veteran contract for five years and $201 million. Durant also agreed to take less money to return, making it easier for the team to retain Iguodala and Livingston. The Warriors also re-signed Pachulia, West, and McGee, signed veterans Nick Young and Omri Casspi, and purchased a second-round draft pick, which they used to select Jordan Bell.

14 The 1975–76 Season

After shocking the basketball world by winning the 1975 championship, the Warriors faced a new challenge.

The prior off-season was full of changes but the front office largely kept the successful group together, with the notable exception of trading guard Butch Beard for forward Dwight Davis and the addition of second-round pick Gus Williams, who earned a role quickly and made the All-Rookie second team. That continuity paid off with a blistering 22–6 start that included a 10-game winning streak and a 35–13 record at the All-Star break. While Rick Barry maintained his place as a star and leading scorer, 1974–75 rookies Jamaal Wilkes and Phil Smith took on larger roles and both made the 1976 All-Star team, which was again coached by Al Attles.

Amazingly, Golden State kept up that torrid pace and finished with a 59–23 record that led the league by five games and was the high-water mark in franchise history, including their time in Philadelphia. Barry again finished fourth in MVP voting but had ceded some of his shots to Smith, who increased his scoring from 7.7 to 20 points per game in his first season as a starter. The University of San Francisco product went from second-round pick to second team All-NBA in his second season, a truly remarkable accomplishment. Wilkes was honored as well, making the All-Defensive second team. The league's most surprising champion had become a powerhouse remarkably quickly.

One year later, the Warriors saw a very different Western Conference playoff picture. The Chicago Bulls missed the playoffs entirely after a mass exodus following their devastating loss in the 1975 Conference Finals and the only holdover teams besides them were the final two to make it in the season before: Detroit and Seattle.

Golden State faced Hall of Famer Bob Lanier and the Detroit Pistons in the first round. Following a pattern from the year before, Golden State won Game 1 at home before falling in Game 2 when both Lanier and forward Curtis Rowe went 31 and 33 points, respectively. Smith took the lead with 34 points in Game 3 as the Warriors took back control, but another 30-point showing for Lanier allowed the Pistons to hold on and bring the series back to Oakland tied at two.

Smith and Barry combined for 53 points in Golden State's Game 5 win. With their backs against the wall, the Pistons erased Warrior leads six times in the fourth quarter alone and forced overtime, but Golden State ended up winning with Phil Smith scoring 37 points, inspiring Detroit writer Curt Sylvester to say Smith "doesn't even know the word pressure exists." Sylvester summarized the series beautifully: "The Pistons simply could not have come any closer, or force the Warriors to work any harder and make things any less comfortable for the Warriors than they did." After overcoming that challenge, Golden State moved on to the Western Conference Finals.

The Phoenix Suns had finished the season 42–40 but had new addition Paul Westphal thriving with increased playing time after three seasons on the Celtics, as well as Rookie of the Year Alvan Adams at center. Following their typical pattern, the Warriors won Game 1 comfortably but then lost Game 2 despite Barry's 44 points. Phil Smith picked up three early fouls in Game 3 but his 15 second-half points helped Golden State regain control of the series after a 53–48 halftime deficit in a 99–91 victory. Game 4 still haunts Attles and the Warriors. They had the lead and the ball in the final 10 seconds of both regulation and the first overtime but Phoenix gained possession and made shots to keep the game going both times. In the second overtime, they again built a lead, this time four points, before allowing a 14–0 Suns run, including eight points by former Warrior Keith Erickson, that tied the series at two.

With the series tied and home-court advantage, the Warriors still had the upper hand in the series even though the Suns were giving them quite a fight. They returned home and took control early with a 40–24 first quarter, including 10 early points from Charles Johnson, and largely held that margin for a 111–95 win. Center Clifford Ray's 17 points and 16 rebounds complemented scoring from Smith (25) and Barry (23), who Attles had shifted to guard during that game to help the team's defense.

Holding a 3–2 series lead meant Golden State needed to win one of the final two games in order to return to the NBA Finals and defend their championship. Like Game 4, they led inside the final minute but Adams made a layup with 12 seconds remaining and Gar Heard blocked Wilkes' shot to end the game. Barry showed frustration at his change in role, noting that the team had "won 59 with me at forward. I just do what I'm told."

After the disappointing loss in Game 6, the Warriors faced their second straight Game 7 in the Western Conference Finals but with largely flipped circumstances, since this time they were the stunned favorites being pushed to the brink. Like the year before, Game 7 became a defensive struggle but the Warriors' stars were not producing as the offense stagnated in what Barry characterized to *Sports Illustrated* as a "total breakdown."

Barry and Smith had carried the scoring load all season, but each went 20 or more minutes between made baskets and the Suns outrebounded the Warriors 57–49, including a career-high 20 from Adams. Even with all that, the teams were tied at 70 with nine minutes to go. The Suns maintained their defensive pressure and used a 10–2 run to build a lead they never relinquished. Minutes later, the team's dream for a repeat and enhanced place in history were over. Barry said the team "had enough chances to win, but we didn't take advantage of them," while Attles said he "did not see 100 percent effort," without singling any Warrior out for criticism.

While inevitably both the Suns' effort and the Warriors' failure to execute played a role in their demise, the defending champions finished the most successful regular season in franchise history with a shockingly stagnant offense and a crushing Game 7 loss on their home floor.

73–9

The Warriors started out the 2015–16 season with a potent combination of continuity and talent as young reigning NBA champions returning almost all of their key pieces from the team that won 67 games the year before.

One big challenge presented itself before the start of the season, as head coach Steve Kerr faced complications from two off-season back surgeries that ended up keeping him out for the first 43 games of the regular season. Despite assistant coach Ron Adams' more extensive experience, Kerr elected to give the interim head coaching responsibilities to Luke Walton, who had only retired from playing two years earlier. Walton's easygoing demeanor helped keep the squad balanced during their intense drive to surpass their recent success and they began the season by setting an NBA record with 24 consecutive wins.

While wins defined Walton's tenure as interim coach, the stretch also provided drama through close calls against the Nets and Celtics, a dramatic win over Cleveland on Christmas Day, and Draymond Green testing Walton's resolve by checking himself in against the Suns to secure a triple-double. When Coach Kerr returned to the team full time, they were already 39–4.

Stephen Curry ratcheted up his game yet again after his MVP campaign and fueled the league's best offense by leading the league in scoring while adding 6.7 assists per game and obliterating his own record for most made three-pointers in a season with 402. The Warriors ended up finishing the season first in offense, one of the few achievements that eluded them the season before.

Beyond being motivated by their own desire to dominate, Golden State also received additional stimulus from the San Antonio Spurs, the 2013–14 champions who finished with the best regular season in their illustrious history. Coach Kerr openly spoke about the importance of going through the playoffs with home-court advantage for the second year in a row and the Spurs' eventual 67–15 record pushed the Warriors until the final two weeks of the regular season. On top of that, both the Warriors and Spurs spent a vast majority of the season chasing another piece of history as no NBA team has ever gone undefeated at home. After finally clinching the No. 1 seed in the West on March 28, the Warriors were looking down the barrel of history at the 1995–96 Chicago Bulls' record of 72–10.

With just over two weeks remaining in the regular season, the Warriors had secured home court for the playoffs but needed a 7–2 finish to surpass the Bulls. After beating the Wizards, they needed a Klay Thompson three to force overtime the next night against the Jazz but emerged victorious. Two nights later, the Warriors lost their other chance at history when the Celtics became the first visiting team to win at Oracle Arena, and that also meant they had to finish the season 5–1 in order to stand alone in the record books. A stunning home loss to the young Minnesota Timberwolves made the challenge even more stark: win four straight, including road games in Memphis and San Antonio, plus a second battle with the Spurs.

While Memphis had to deal with injuries to stars Mike Conley and Marc Gasol, they held an eight-point lead with six minutes to go thanks to a big night from former Warrior Matt Barnes. A 12–3 run cut the lead to one point and after a Green layup and a crazy final possession, the Warriors were two wins away but had to face the still-undefeated-at-home Spurs in San Antonio the next night. An early fourth-quarter scoring binge by Harrison Barnes created a small lead that the Warriors eventually expanded to double digits as Golden State made history with their 72nd win while preventing San Antonio from making their own.

On the final night of the regular season, the Warriors hosted the same Grizzlies that had given them such a scare four days earlier. Stephen Curry scored 20 points as the home crowd erupted during a 37–23 first quarter. Curry put the finishing touches on his eventually unanimous MVP season with 46 points in three quarters and the celebration was on.

After the game, Coach Kerr, a member of those 1995–96 Bulls, said, "I thought [72 wins] was like [Joe] DiMaggio's hit streak, and I was wrong."

Green added, "[Seventy-three wins means] I'm a part of the best team ever…. Not many people can say that. Fifteen guys can say that, and that's amazing."

While the 2015–16 season ended in disappointment three months later, 73–9 stands as a significant accomplishment and a piece of NBA history.

16 The 2016 Playoffs

The Warriors began the 2016 playoffs as both the defending champions and the team that just topped the Bulls' incredible NBA record for regular season wins with Stephen Curry weeks away from being named the league's first unanimous Most Valuable Player.

Interestingly, their first-round foe was the Houston Rockets, their first repeat opponent since their 2013 return to the postseason. Their animosity helped add another layer of intrigue to the series and the Warriors received what turned out to be a little piece of foreshadowing when Curry rolled his left ankle in Game 1 of the series. He sat out the next two games, which the teams split.

Curry returned for Game 4 and the moment that changed their playoffs and arguably league history. On the last play of the first half, Curry was defending Trevor Ariza as he angled for a buzzer-beating shot in the tie game. Unbeknownst to Curry, Rockets center Donatas Motiejunas fell while making his way down the court and slid toward the free throw line. Turned and focused on Ariza, Curry fell on a wet spot on the floor and suffered a grade one sprain of his medial collateral ligament (MCL). While Curry rarely looked like his MVP self even after returning, he provided an indelible performance by coming off the bench in his first game back before scoring 10 points in the fourth quarter and an NBA-record 17 in overtime to push the Warriors past Portland, giving them a 3–1 series lead.

Klay Thompson starred in Curry's absence, averaging 31.5 points per game while defending Houston and Portland's talented guards for long stretches. Those four games served as a statement for Thompson and Draymond Green, All-Stars who do not get the chance to flex their individual capabilities with the team's surrounding talent.

With Curry back, the Warriors squared off with the Oklahoma City Thunder in the Western Conference Finals. Due to injuries and misfortune, the two teams had never faced off in a playoff series after playing a slew of memorable regular season games over the years. The Thunder shocked the Warriors with a 14-point comeback in Game 1 at Oracle, then dominated Games 3 and 4 at home by a combined 52 points.

Draymond Green caused a firestorm in Game 3 when a kick on Oklahoma City's Steven Adams inspired calls for suspension from Game 4. The league did not suspend Green but gave him two flagrant foul points, which loomed large later in the playoffs.

Down 3–1, the Warriors rallied behind 36 points from Curry to stay alive. Returning to Oklahoma City, Golden State needed both a heroic 41 points from Thompson, which included a playoff-record 11 three-pointers, and a massive fourth quarter offensive collapse from the Thunder, who committed six turnovers in the final three minutes, to force Game 7 in Oakland. There, behind a strong defensive performance and 36 points from Curry, the Warriors became the 10th team to come back from a 3–1 deficit to win a playoff series.

After all of the drama in the first three rounds, the Warriors needed to overcome the Cleveland Cavaliers to complete a picture-perfect season. They dominated the first two games, winning by 15 and 33 points behind big performances from Draymond Green and superior bench play. Following the pattern of their first two series, Golden State fell in their first road game, setting up a huge Game 4. Curry scored 38 points, almost matching his total from the first three contests, while Thompson chipped in 25 and the Warriors took control late, winning by 11 and securing a significant 3–1 series lead.

Ahead by 10 with three minutes left in Game 4, Green fell to the floor while setting a screen and LeBron James stepped over him. Green took offense, swiped at James, and the two exchanged both words and elbows for the remainder of the possession. The league reviewed the incident and assessed Green a flagrant 1 foul. That held massive significance because Green was at the limit with three previous flagrant foul "points" from incidents in the Houston and Oklahoma City series, meaning he was suspended for Game 5 of the Finals.

Cleveland won Game 5 as Green watched from the next-door Oakland Coliseum and center Andrew Bogut suffered a sprained knee that kept him out for the remainder of the Finals. A returning Green and 30 points from Stephen Curry were not enough for Golden State to pick up their second road win of the series, so they faced a Game 7 at Oracle.

After missing the previous game in Oakland due to his suspension, Green had one of the best performances of his career with 32 points, 15 rebounds, and nine assists. A close, hard-fought game throughout, Thompson made a layup to tie the score at 89 with 4:39 remaining. After both teams failed to score until the game's final minute, including James' chase-down block on Iguodala, Kyrie Irving made a three-pointer over Curry and the MVP failed to create separation on Kevin Love after a switch twice on the Warriors' final full possession of the game. Thompson's layup with 4:39 left ended up being the Warriors' final points of the NBA Finals and their historic season ended with a 93–89 loss in their own building.

While Curry's injury, Green's suspension, James' dominance, Irving's shot-making, and Coach Kerr's overreliance on Festus Ezeli and Anderson Varejão after Bogut's injury were all significant factors in Golden State's season ending in disappointment, falling in the 2016 Finals arguably set the table for adding Kevin Durant just two weeks later and helped shape their 2016–17 season.

17 Draymond Green

In the back of a black SUV, riding to a Foot Locker in Toronto, Draymond Green pondered his improbable rise. He was headed to an appearance and autograph signing the night before his first All-Star game.

"I'd be lying if I told you I expected this," Green said.

When the SUV arrived, Green could barely get out of the car because a crowd of fans hovered at the store's entrance. When he emerged from the vehicle, they cheered like a rock star had shown up. Indeed, Green had arrived.

It has been a long, crazy ride for Green, who took a nontraditional path to NBA stardom. He played four years in college, which is scarcely the case for players who end up in the NBA, much less starring. He was projected to be a late first-round pick but dipped to the second round because teams were worried about his conditioning and size. At 6'7", Green was a classic 'tweener, as he was considered too small for his style of play and not skilled enough to play the position that matched his size.

The Warriors, who had already drafted two players in the first round, snatched Green up when he was on the board at No. 35 overall. It might have been the best thing to happen to Green because he wound up on a team with an established player at his position (David Lee) and with a coach (Mark Jackson) who was emphasizing Green's skill set.

In the course of his rookie season, Green went from little-used reserve in November to pivotal bench player in the playoffs. The next season, he was a staple in the rotation at the outset and had established himself as a defensive anchor by his second playoff appearance. Green's third season began with him filling in as a starter due to a Lee injury and ended with him becoming the second best player on the NBA champions, the first Warrior to ever make the All-Defensive first team and runner-up for Defensive Player of the Year.

His fourth season? All-Star, second team All-NBA, first team All-Defense, and runner-up for Defensive Player of the Year for the second time as a star on the team that broke the NBA record for most wins in a regular season. He capped the year with the performance of his life in Game 7 of the NBA Finals and a spot on the 2016 Olympic team.

Without many accolades left to attain, Green excelled again in 2016–17 by finally winning Defensive Player of the Year and leading the league in steals per game for the first time. He again made the All-Star team and the All-Defensive first team.

Draymond Green poses for photos with his Defensive Player of the Year Award.
(*USA TODAY* Sports Images/Brad Penner)

That is an awe-inspiring progression for any player, but for a second-round pick who started toward the back end of the bench, it was especially incredible. It becomes a little less of a surprise considering Green's impressive history and incredible skill set.

Green has been a winner throughout his basketball career. As a junior at Saginaw High School in Michigan, he helped lead his team to a state championship in 2006–07. The team won the state title again the following season and was ranked fourth in the nation by *USA Today*.

A successful high school basketball career earned Green a scholarship to play for legendary coach Tom Izzo at Michigan State. Green mostly came off the bench in a freshman season that saw the Spartans make a run to the national title game. During the NCAA Tournament, Green more than doubled his regular season averages with 8.5 points and 5.3 rebounds per game. The next year, he won Big 10 Sixth Man of the Year honors and was named Michigan State's Most Improved Player. As a junior, Green became the third player in school history to notch a triple-double—the first was Magic Johnson. His senior season, Green was team captain, led the Spartans to their third Big 10 title in four years, and was named Big 10 Player of the Year.

The same way Green made his mark in college translated to the professional ranks, despite his many doubters. He was able to play power forward full time in the NBA though his height led to many pegging him as a small forward. Green's defensive abilities made him impossible to keep off the court as his wingspan, basketball IQ, and toughness compensate for his lack of height. He grabs tough rebounds and protects the rim better than many seven-footers.

During the 2015 playoffs, the Warriors even used him at center in what became known as the Death Lineup. Head coach Steve Kerr started that group in the final three games of the NBA Finals to secure the championship. As a big man, Green has a quickness and skill advantage. Already a good passer who can handle the ball and read what's happening on the floor, his limited athleticism became less of an issue when defended by plodding big men. Since he was able to hold his own and even thrive defensively, playing center made him a significant contributor on both ends of the floor.

Green worked on his three-point shooting, improving from a rough rookie season. That development, along with his other skills, made him an ideal partner for Stephen Curry in the pick-and-roll. Green is physical enough to set great screens and skilled enough to turn into a playmaker or shooter when defenses give him an opening.

Just as pivotal to Green's success is his fire. Despite racking up the accomplishments—including a five-year, $82 million contract in the summer of 2015—Green still plays with a hunger. The same drive that got him to this level in the NBA is still present.

He is the Warriors' heartbeat: their emotional leader, enforcer, defensive stopper, and fiery motivator. The only question about Green now is if he can control that fire.

Over the years, he became a magnet for technical fouls and has a penchant for arguing with referees, since Green is an elite, relentless trash talker. In the 2016 playoffs, his accumulation of flagrant fouls, including an infamous kick on Steven Adams in the Western Conference Finals and his confrontation with LeBron James in the NBA Finals, which earned him a suspension in Game 5, proved to be pivotal in preventing the Warriors from winning back-to-back championships. While the Warriors fell without Green in Game 5, he responded with a spectacular Game 7 at Oracle, finishing just short of a triple-double with 32 points, 15 rebounds, nine assists, and two steals.

Green bounced back from the high-profile disappointment by putting together one of his best all-around seasons, especially since he had to shoulder a larger defensive burden since Golden State lost both of their rim-protecting centers to clear space for Kevin Durant. The Warriors still finished second in defense and Green won his first Defensive Player of the Year Award. That February,

Green demonstrated his unique ability to affect games by recording the NBA's first triple-double without scoring 10 points: four points, 11 rebounds, 10 assists, 10 steals (a franchise record), and five blocks. In the 2017 playoffs, he was able to stay under control and never risked suspension as Golden State won their second championship in three years.

The Warriors' third selection of the 2012 Draft has made two All-Star teams, two All-NBA teams and three All-Defensive first teams all while establishing himself as the heartbeat of some of the greatest teams of all-time and he still has more time to build an even stronger legacy.

18 Klay Thompson

It was a home game against Denver, on national television. The Warriors led by two and coach Mark Jackson implored his players to pressure up on defense.

The Nuggets had several offensive weapons, so the Warriors could not key on any one player and they had not been able to stop Denver all game. To get one more stop and secure the home victory, they needed one possession of focus and crisp execution.

Klay Thompson drew the assignment of Danilo Gallinari, the long forward who shot like a guard. Instead of staying between Gallinari and the basket, Thompson overplayed to take away the three-pointer. Gallinari cut backdoor, took the inbounds pass, and tied the game with a dunk.

The Warriors lost in overtime.

After the game, there was no trace of Thompson. His clothes remained in his locker but he was long gone. Thompson was so frustrated, he went in, grabbed his keys, and took off, driving home in his uniform.

That was young Klay. Talented but prone to mental breakdowns, whether it was losing focus on defense or taking a bad shot on offense.

In many ways, Thompson's immense improvement from that low point mirrors the growth of his team. He steadily improved and worked on his game, eventually turning some of his weaknesses into strengths.

Thompson will always be known for his shooting ability. Beyond his current standing as the league's most prolific shooter other than his fellow Splash Brother, Thompson also stands out because of his astonishing ability to score in bunches. Those skills were never more evident than on January 23, 2015. That night he broke the NBA record for points in a quarter with 37 in the third, including nine three-pointers and a perfect 13-for-13 shooting in an unforgettable 9:40.

He produced another historic performance on December 5, 2016. Thompson again drove the Oracle crowd into a frenzy, this time scoring 60 points in the first three quarters of action. Incomprehensibly, he only held the ball for 90 seconds and took just 11 dribbles on his way to those 60 points, shooting 21-for-33 from the field and 8-for-14 from three.

While that level of proficiency would be enough to sustain a career, Thompson became more than a shooter. Under head coach Mark Jackson, Thompson developed one of the weaknesses that stuck to him coming out of the 2011 Draft: defense. After working hard on his skill and stamina, the 6'7" shooting guard often received the assignment of hounding opposing point guards and became an expert at using his superior size and strength to apply pressure to the ball-handler.

In the 2013 playoffs, Thompson made life rough for Ty Lawson, the speedy point guard who ran the Denver Nuggets. In the next round against San Antonio, the tide of Game 1 changed when Thompson fouled out and Spurs point guard Tony Parker finally saw daylight.

Over time, Thompson grew into the protoypical "3 and D" player, someone capable of playing tough defense and hitting shots from long range. Still, he kept working and becoming a more complete player. He developed a post game and worked hard at dribbling, which improved his drives to the basket. Through effort and experience, the mental lapses that far too often characterized his early career lessened and he became a more reliable producer.

Playing next to Stephen Curry also afforded Thompson the luxury of having attention drawn away from him. Opposing defenses focusing so hard on Curry put the ball in Thompson's hands, often in big moments. Over the years, he frequently hit big shots in the fourth quarter when Curry was swarmed.

While he has not had many chances to prove his mettle as a lead performer, one of those opportunities came when Curry sprained his MCL during the team's first-round series in the 2016 playoffs. Thompson stepped up without the unanimous MVP, scoring 31.5 points and playing strong defense on Portland's electric guard duo of Damian Lillard and C.J. McCollum. He also produced one of the most indelible moments of the season with 41 points in Game 6 of that season's Western Conference Finals, almost single-handedly keeping the Warriors alive as they came back to win the game and eventually the series to make their second straight NBA Finals.

It looked like adding Kevin Durant that off-season would dramatically affect Thompson's role on the team and he reacted with enthusiasm and a team-centric approach by saying, "I'd sacrifice everything for championships. When you win, you don't really sacrifice anything because everybody gets love when you win." However, he also famously said, "But I'm not sacrificing shit, because my game isn't changing. I'm still going to try to get buckets, hit shots, come off screens." Thompson was proven right, as his production stayed almost perfectly in line with prior seasons as the Warriors again pushed to the league's best record and another championship.

The talented but inconsistent kid who left locker rooms before the media entered after bad games became a complete player and leader, making three consecutive All-Star games from 2015 to '17 and third team All-NBA in both 2014–15 and 2015–16.

19 Bad Trades

While almost every franchise with a long history has trades that haunt them, the Warriors stand out for the volume and degree of pain caused in this way. There are more that could be included but these were the most important of the bunch.

Mitch Richmond for Billy Owens (1991)

After two seasons of Run TMC, Don Nelson felt he "was under pressure to get bigger" and traded Richmond to the Sacramento Kings with Les Jepson and a second-round pick for rookie forward Billy Owens. While Nelson called the decision to trade Richmond "the toughest I have ever made" at the time, the final results made it even harder to take. While Owens played three seasons for the Warriors, where he was reasonably productive when healthy, Richmond made six straight All-Star teams and five All-NBA teams in Sacramento and was enshrined in the Naismith Memorial Basketball Hall of Fame in 2014. Richmond later said Nelson "broke up something special that could have went on for a long time," and that is putting it kindly.

Wilt Chamberlain to the 76ers (1965)

Owner Franklin Mieuli was frustrated with Chamberlain and the team's trouble drawing fans and told head coach Alex Hannum that Wilt would "be traded before I go home" from the 1965 All-Star Game. Mieuli kept his word and traded the star back to Philadelphia for Connie Dierking, Paul Neumann, Lee Shaffer, and cash. Shaffer was an All-America at North Carolina who scored 18.6 points per game for Syracuse the year before, but broke his leg earlier that season in Philadelphia and never reported to San Francisco, walking away from the NBA entirely at 24 to work for a transportation company in North Carolina. Dierking played 565 total minutes as a Warrior before being traded again and Neumann ended up being a key piece on San Francisco's next NBA Finals team in 1967 but retired after that season at 29 years old.

Parish and McHale for Carroll and Brown (1980)

While likely the most devastating trade in franchise history in terms of value, this deal is a little different from the first two because the mistakes became more obvious in hindsight than they were at the time. Boston had the No. 1 overall pick in the 1980 Draft and the Warriors coveted big man Joe Barry Carroll from Purdue. They had the third pick and eventually agreed to give up starting center Robert Parish to move up from No. 3 to No. 1, while also receiving the 13th pick. The Celtics would then use the third pick on power forward Kevin McHale from Minnesota.

Parish had already come into his own for the Warriors and eventually he and McHale became foundational pieces in the Celtics' dominant '80s, winning three championships and making a combined 16 All-Star appearances as Celtics. Thirteenth pick Rickey Brown played in 340 NBA games (177 with the Warriors) before a long career in Europe.

Chris Webber to Washington (1994)

Just three years after trading Richmond, the Warriors caught lightning in a bottle again with the combination of Latrell Sprewell and No. 1 overall pick Chris Webber added to the remaining

Chris Mullin, Tim Hardaway, and Šarūnas Marčiulionis. Despite Hardaway and Marčiulionis missing the 1993–94 season, Golden State still won 50 games and looked to be a team on the rise. Due to a conflict with Nelson and an ill-advised opt-out in his contract, Rookie of the Year Webber was able to force his way off the team and the Warriors ended up trading him to the Washington Bullets. Their return for him was Tom Gugliotta (who would be traded three months later for Donyell Marshall) and three first-round picks. In an amazing twist, two of the three picks Washington sent Golden State were originally their own, having been sent to Orlando in the Webber/Penny Hardaway draft-night deal, the Bullets later acquired them from the Magic for Scott Skiles over that summer. Webber made five All-Star teams and five All-NBA teams after the trade.

Tim Hardaway to Miami (1996)

Don Nelson resigned in 1995 and the Warriors were 25–27 heading into the 1996 trade deadline. They reacted by trading Hardaway and former first-round pick Chris Gatling to the Miami Heat for Bimbo Coles and Kevin Willis. Willis would finish out the season and Coles would disappoint for another three seasons before being traded in another disastrous deal for Mookie Blalock. Meanwhile, Hardaway starred in Miami, finishing fourth in MVP voting his first full season there and making three more All-NBA teams in six seasons.

Jason Richardson for No. 8 (2008)

Less than two months after the We Believe Warriors shocked the Dallas Mavericks in the 2007 playoffs, Jason Richardson was already gone, traded to the Charlotte Bobcats for eighth overall pick Brandan Wright. While future All-Star Joakim Noah was chosen next, the most haunting part of the trade did not come out until later: Richardson was originally supposed to be part of a much larger deal for superstar Kevin Garnett, which owner Chris Cohan vetoed when an extension with Garnett was already "basically done."

Latrell Sprewell to the Knicks (1999)

After choking P.J. Carlesimo, Sprewell was an unusual case as an unquestionably talented player with an infamous red flag. The Warriors wanted to move Sprewell before the start of training camp and traded him to the New York Knicks for John Starks, Chris Mills, and Terry Cummings, older players with significant contracts. Starks was a Warrior for a season and a half before being involved in another strange trade for Larry Hughes and Billy Owens, while Mills battled injuries for five seasons and Cummings retired after two years. Meanwhile, Sprewell revitalized his career in New York, including starting all five NBA Finals games that season and making the 2001 All-Star team. To make matters worse, Golden State could have reportedly received Brent Barry, Dan Majerle, and future Warrior Bobby Sura for Sprewell instead, but that deal fell through.

A First-Round Pick for Marcus Williams (2008)

After Baron Davis left for the Clippers in early July 2008, GM Chris Mullin needed a point guard. He decided on Marcus Williams of the New Jersey Nets, who had averaged 16 minutes per game in two seasons for the team after a tumultuous time at the University of Connecticut. Desperate for a lifeline at the position, Mullin gave up a 2011 lottery-protected first-round pick for him. Williams came to camp out of shape and was out of the rotation before Thanksgiving, appearing in just nine games and making just four shots before being cut in March of that season. After giving up a 2011 second-round pick to loosen that protection, the pick eventually became Gorgui Dieng in 2013.

20 Tim Hardaway

Before Allen Iverson made the crossover famous, before YouTube was replete with highlights of fancy dribble moves, the Warriors had the UTEP Two-Step.

Tim Hardaway's famous crossover was one of the signature moves during one of the Warriors' most memorable eras of basketball and he ran the show as the floor general when Golden State became defined by fast breaks and high scoring.

At six-feet tall, Hardaway was undersized by the NBA's standards but his stature only fed the Chicago native's desire on the court.

"Just like when I was a kid, I felt if I got a chance I could show people what I could do," Hardaway told the *Chicago Tribune* in 1990. "It was like that in college and then coming out of college."

The Warriors selected Hardaway 14th overall in the 1989 Draft out of the University of Texas El Paso (UTEP). With Chris Mullin and Mitch Richmond already lighting it up for the team, Hardaway would complete the trio of perimeter studs. He was short but stocky, muscular and tough with a Midwestern drawl that complemented his quickness on the court.

Due to his handle and tenacity, Hardaway could get anywhere he wanted on the court but his specialty was breaking down his defender one-on-one off the dribble. He had an uncanny ability to start one way and then zip back the opposite direction and his crossover was almost impossible to stay in front of. Hardaway was so quick, defenders were still reacting to his initial movement when he would jerk the other way and disappear.

Despite being the third point guard taken in his draft class behind Pooh Richardson and future Warrior Mookie Blaylock, Hardaway immediately became a starter for Don Nelson. That first season, he averaged 14.7 points and 8.7 assists while earning a spot on the All-Rookie first team. Hardaway proved to be perfect for the Warriors' fast pace and, with Mullin and Richmond, lit up the scoreboard enough to eventually earn the nickname Run TMC. While the 1989–90 team did not make the playoffs, they showed the possibility of much brighter days ahead.

Hardaway's second season, everything came together. He stepped up his game, averaging 22.9 points, 9.7 assists, and 2.6 steals, and was selected to his first All-Star game. At the same point, the team took off, winning 44 games and finishing second in scoring at a massive 116.6 points per game.

That 44–38 record was good enough to get the Warriors back in the playoffs and, led by Hardaway, the seventh seeds pulled off one of the franchise's most notable upsets. He averaged 23.3 points, 9.3 assists, and 2.3 steals while toppling the highly touted and second-seeded Spurs. While Magic Johnson's Lakers ended up defeating the young team in the next round, the Warriors had captivated the basketball world and were on the precipice of something special.

When it looked like Run TMC was about to take it to another level, Nelson traded Richmond to Sacramento for big man Billy Owens. While that move had devastating long-term implications, Hardaway had a very strong season with 23.4 points and 10 assists per game as the point guard made the All-Star team and the All-NBA second team. On top of that, Golden State actually improved their record without Richmond, winning 55 games and leading the league in scoring. Then in the playoffs, the team felt the impact of trading Richmond when the sixth-seeded Sonics easily handled the third-seeded Warriors in the first round. It would be the last time Hardaway saw the postseason as a Warrior. While he averaged 24.5 points, Hardaway shot just 40 percent from the field and saw his assists decrease noticeably to 7.3 per game.

In Hardaway's first three years, the Warriors went from 37 wins to 44 to 55 as they made the playoffs in back-to-back seasons for the first time since the mid-70s.

However, Hardaway's tenure with the Warriors was about to get much rockier. While the point guard reached personal success with another All-NBA appearance in 1992–93, Golden State missed the playoffs and then a knee injury cost Hardaway the 1993–94 season. The tornado that was the 1994–95 season—which saw the team trade Chris Webber in-season and Don Nelson resign months later—affected Hardaway because he clashed with eventual replacement Rick Adelman. While Hardaway averaged 20.1 points and 9.3 assists in 1994–95, he did not dominate in the same way he had as a younger player and before the knee injury. His shooting percentage dropped to a then-career low 42.7 percent and the Warriors won just 26 games.

With Adelman at the reins the next season, Hardaway struggled to his worst run as a Warrior then reportedly demanded a trade. The front office obliged, shipping him to Miami with Chris Gatling in exchange for Bimbo Coles and Kevin Willis.

Hardaway revitalized his career with the Heat, making the playoffs each of his six seasons there. After turning 30, he finished fourth in the MVP voting for the 1996–97 season after averaging 20.3 points and 8.6 assists per game, leading Miami to a 61–21 record. Following his time in Miami, Hardaway finished his career with short stints for the Mavericks, Nuggets, and Pacers before retiring in 2003.

Despite playing in only six seasons for the Warriors, Hardaway made two consecutive All-NBA teams and three consecutive All-Star teams and remains in the top five for assists, three-pointers, and steals in franchise history.

21 Franklin Mieuli

A deerstalker cap will forever be associated with the Warriors because of Franklin Mieuli.

For 24 years, he owned the Warriors and brought a free spirit to the executive ranks. He sported a full beard beneath a plaid Sherlock Holmes cap and was more likely to be found in a leather bomber jacket, jeans, and Hawaiian shirt than a business suit. Mieuli often traveled via one of his many motorcycles, which he was known for forgetting to drive back home. When Mieuli did drive his convertible, he could be spotted riding with the 1975 NBA championship trophy in the back.

Jim Fitzgerald, who bought the Warriors from Mieuli in 1986, summed up Mieuli perfectly in a 2004 *San Francisco Chronicle* article:

"Larry O'Brien, who had been in the Kennedy administration, was the commissioner and we were having a meeting of the league television committee," Fitzgerald was quoted saying. "Both Franklin and I were members. O'Brien said he wanted us to go to the 21 Club for lunch, and all eyes turned to Franklin. He was wearing a Hawaiian shirt, with his chest hair sticking out. He said, 'I'll be alright.' When we get there, the owner comes to the front door. Looks at us, looks right past Larry O'Brien, right past me, and right at Franklin. He says, 'Franklin! Come on in and bring your buddies.'"

The San Jose product was pivotal to the Warriors' growth as a franchise. The local marketing mogul and media pioneer bought a stake in the Warriors in 1962 when they moved to the Bay Area from Philadelphia. A year later, poor attendance prompted most of the investors to back out, so Mieuli bought off the other owners to become the sole owner.

In 1965, with the team struggling financially, Mieuli traded Wilt Chamberlain back to Philadelphia. That same year, he drafted Rick Barry—an obsession of his—out of the University of Miami.

Despite Barry's status as the player he coveted, Mieuli allowed him to leave the Warriors twice. In 1967, Barry—who felt he was being cheated out of incentive money—signed with the ABA's Oakland Oaks. In 1972, Barry returned after a district court judge ruled the only NBA team Barry could play for after his ABA contract ended was the Warriors. Six years later, Barry signed a free-agent deal with Houston and finished his career with the Rockets.

Mieuli was known for marching to the beat of his own drum. In 1971, he moved the Warriors to Oakland and changed the name to the Golden State Warriors. He opposed the merger of the NBA and ABA, which eventually happened in 1976, and the three-point shot, which was instituted in 1979.

While Mieuli opposed those league reforms, he supported and played an active role in diversifying the NBA. Al Attles, who was Mieuli's head coach for 14 seasons, said he only ever saw Mieuli extremely angry twice. The first was when Attles initially refused to take the head coaching job during the 1969–70 season and the second came five years later. In a slowly integrating league, many owners were worried about whether fans would support a heavily black team, so Attles went to Mieuli's office to tell him, "I just want to alert you that I'm keeping only two white players, Barry and [Jeff] Mullins." As Attles tells it, Mieuli "slammed his fist down like a crazy man and said, 'Why would you even mention that to me? You take the 12 best players, period!'"

That season, the Warriors won the 1975 championship with ten black players.

"Franklin Mieuli was one of the most instrumental figures in my life," Attles said in a news release after Mieuli's death. "Both from a basketball standpoint and simply life in general. He was always there for me and my family and provided me with so many wonderful opportunities. He was one of the most unique and eccentric individuals that I have ever met, and I'm not sure there will ever be anyone like him again."

In the 24 seasons Mieuli owned the team, the Warriors experienced 11 winning seasons. They won the 1975 championship, made the NBA Finals three times, and twice lost in the Western Conference Finals.

Mieuli, who maintained his courtside seat at Oracle until his health deteriorated, died of natural causes at the age of 89 on April 25, 2010, in San Francisco.

22 Wilt Chamberlain

Wilt Chamberlain was already an icon and a phenomenon known around the world when he entered the NBA at 23 years old.

Still, there was a hint of doubt when he came to the Philadelphia Warriors. Chamberlain stood 7'1" and combined shocking athleticism and uncanny skill for someone of his size, but still needed to prove himself in the best professional basketball league in the world.

The uncertainty added to the drama of his debut on October 14, 1959. Also, it was at Madison Square Garden, the mecca of basketball.

That night, Chamberlain scored 43 points and grabbed 28 rebounds.

It was a fitting start for what would be an astonishing career, as Chamberlain became one of the most dominant players in sports history.

Almost 60 years after his debut, basketball fans are still grappling with Chamberlain's excellence and dominance, while the concept of Chamberlain's size and skill coupled with today's technology and sports-centered culture continues to boggle the mind. He spent about a third of his career with the Warriors and yet he is easily the greatest player in franchise history.

Astonishingly, Chamberlain did not begin playing basketball until high school. His first love was track and field.

Even with that passion, Chamberlain—who was 6' at age 10 and 6'11" in high school—became a basketball sensation at Overbrook High School in Philadelphia, winning two city championships and averaging 37.4 points per game his senior year.

He went on to dominate at the University of Kansas, even before he was allowed to play. While NCAA rules prevented freshmen from playing varsity, Chamberlain led the freshman team to a win over the varsity team. "We whipped 'em, 81–71," Chamberlain told the *Philadelphia Daily News*. "I had 40 or 42 points, about 30 rebounds, about 15 blocks. I knew I had to show them either I could do it or I couldn't."

Finally eligible as a sophomore, Chamberlain led the Jayhawks to the NCAA title game in 1957, averaging 29.6 points and 18.9 rebounds per game. As a junior, he was named an All-American and increased his scoring average to 30.1 points per game.

Up for a new challenge, Chamberlain was ready to become a professional instead of spending his senior year at Kansas. NBA rules prevented him from entering their draft before his class graduated, so Chamberlain took $50,000 to go on tour with the Harlem Globetrotters in 1958. He was an incredible draw, even selling out a tour in Russia.

In 1959, Chamberlain was finally able to enter the NBA draft. The fledgling league used a process known as the Territorial Draft that allowed teams to claim a local college player in exchange for giving up its first-round pick in the hopes that franchises would be able to increase attendance with college stars who had already built strong local followings.

Philadelphia Warriors owner Eddie Gottlieb claimed Chamberlain as a territorial pick, arguing that the established star had grown up in Philadelphia and was popular there as a high school player. Plus, since there were no NBA teams in Kansas, the Warriors were not stepping on another franchise's argument. The league agreed, marking the only time in NBA history that a player was made a territorial selection based on his pre-college roots.

According to a 2010 *Los Angeles Times* article, Gottlieb made his argument for Chamberlain before the 1955 Draft, while Chamberlain was in high school. He wanted to draft Chamberlain, a star in Philadelphia, in 1955, even if it would take four years for him to play. Four years before he was eligible, the league determined that, per the *Times'* research, Chamberlain's rights belonged to the Warriors unless Chamberlain went to college in the territory of another team. Gottlieb reportedly urged Chamberlain to attend Stanford while Boston's legendary Red Auerbach tried to talk Chamberlain into attending Harvard so the Celtics could secure his rights.

Gottlieb's plan worked and he was willing to pay the price for his young star. Chamberlain made $30,000 as a rookie, the highest salary in the league. Seven years earlier, Gottlieb bought the Warriors for $25,000.

His investment paid off immediately. In Chamberlain's rookie season, he averaged 37.6 points and 27 rebounds per game and won both the league MVP and Rookie of the Year honors, a feat that has only been matched once since. On top of those accolades, he was also the MVP of that season's All-Star game, tallying 23 points and 25 rebounds in 30 minutes.

The Warriors made it to the Eastern Conference Finals that year, taking on Boston. Auerbach sought to take advantage of Chamberlain's inexperience, hoping to get under Chamberlain's skin and frustrate him. A notoriously bad free throw shooter, the Celtics intentionally fouled the Big Dipper and deployed future Hall of Famer Tom Heinsohn as the primary nuisance.

The Celtics ran a play where legendary big man Bill Russell, who would become Chamberlain's greatest rival, would sprint down court immediately after free throws. Boston would get the ball in quickly to point guard Bob Cousy and Cousy would get it

Wilt Chamberlain laughs with Warriors owner Eddie Gottlieb at the Philadelphia Sports Writers Association Basketball Club banquet where Chamberlain received the group's trophy as the NBA's outstanding player. (AP Photo)

to the streaking Russell for a layup before his defender could catch up. Chamberlain was an incredible athlete capable of running with Russell, so Auerbach assigned Heinsohn to set a screen on Chamberlain whenever he tried to chase Russell. It made for a brutal collision.

"After a couple of games, Wilt says to me, 'You do that to me again, I'm going to knock you on your ass,'" Heinsohn told the *Philadelphia Inquirer* in 1999. "So he did. I slid from the top of the key to midcourt. He goes to level me with a punch, lets it fly, and I'm saying, 'Did I leave a will?' But he hits Tom Gola in the back of his head, and he breaks his hand. He kept playing with the broken hand."

After struggling in that contest and Game 4, Chamberlain scored 50 points in Game 5, but Heinsohn clinched the series for the Celtics by tipping in the game winner at the buzzer in Game 6. Chamberlain contemplated retiring after the series over concern he might have to deal with how the Celtics played him regularly.

Fortunately, he decided to keep playing and two years later he scored 100 points against the Knicks on March 2, 1962, in Hershey, Pennsylvania.

The summer after Chamberlain's 100-point game, the Warriors moved across the country to San Francisco. He averaged an eye-popping 44.8 points and 24.3 rebounds per game that inaugural season but both were below his standard from the prior campaign. Now on a Western Division team, Chamberlain and Russell met in the 1964 NBA Finals. The rivalry was rekindled and Chamberlain averaged 29.2 points and 27.6 rebounds in the series, but the Celtics were loaded and controlled the Warriors, winning the series in five games.

Despite his status as a dominant figure in basketball and the team's success, Chamberlain did not prove to be a draw in the Bay Area. While Oscar Robertson credited Wilt the Stilt with saving the league, noting that "people heard about Wilt scoring a hundred, averaging 50 a night, and they wanted to see the guy do it," that often came in the opposing team's arena.

Strapped for cash and frustrated that even a winning team with Chamberlain could not bring in fans, owner Franklin Mieuli told head coach Alex Hannum when he left for All-Star Weekend that his star would be "traded before I go home." Mieuli followed through on his word, sending Chamberlain back to Philadelphia, where the Syracuse team had just moved. In 1967, Chamberlain reunited with Hannum, won the league MVP, and faced his former team in the NBA Finals. At 30 years old, he averaged 17.7 points, 28.5 rebounds, and a team-high 6.8 assists per game as the 76ers defeated the Warriors in six games, giving Chamberlain his first NBA championship.

In total, he played four seasons with the 76ers and another five with the Los Angeles Lakers, winning a second championship in 1972.

Chamberlain was inducted into the Naismith Memorial Basketball Hall of Fame in 1979 and his No. 13 is retired by all three of his former teams. Over the course of his 14-season career, he amassed over 31,000 points, won four MVP Awards, made 10 All-NBA teams and 13 All-Star teams, and led the league in scoring seven times and rebounding 11 times.

Despite only playing 429 games for the Warriors over five and a half seasons, Chamberlain is still the franchise leader in points scored and behind only former teammate Nate Thurmond in rebounds.

23 Tom Meschery

Tom Meschery, then with the Seattle SuperSonics, just started swinging at former teammate Wilt Chamberlain.

The 6'6" forward threw punch after punch at the 7'1" center, none of them landing, as Chamberlain asked, "Tommy, what are you doing?" The legendary big man practically laughed and, as Meschery would later describe, Chamberlain stretched out his arm and planted his hand on Meschery's forehead, keeping the smaller guy at bay.

Meschery was being "the Mad Russian."

"I knew that in order to make it in the NBA, I had to be tenacious," Meschery, who led the league in personal fouls his rookie season, told NBA.com. "I had to have more energy and work harder on the court. I think that translated into being tough, and to a certain extent I was. I wasn't about to let anybody intimidate me."

His temperament was just one of the reasons Meschery was such a distinctive player in the NBA. The child of Russian immigrants who fled their home country in 1917, Tomislav Nikolayevich Meshcheryakov was born in Harbin, Manchuria, a city in the northeast part of China. His family moved around a lot after his birth because of World War II and he, his sister, and mother were interned in a Japanese internment camp near Tokyo. After the war, they immigrated to the U.S. and settled in San Francisco, changing their name to Meschery due to the anti-Communist environment in America.

Meschery had a difficult time assimilating to the American culture but basketball helped with the transition. He also watched American movies, which taught him English and connected him with kindred spirits John Wayne and James Cagney. He went to

Lowell High School in San Francisco and then played college ball in the hills of the East Bay at Saint Mary's College, where he was an All-American in 1961.

The Philadelphia Warriors drafted Meschery seventh overall in 1961, making him the first Russian and the first China-born player in the NBA. His rookie season was highlighted by Chamberlain's 100-point game. "That's being part of history," Meschery would later say. "I don't think very much can top that."

He had his best postseason performance as a rookie in the 1962 playoffs, averaging 20.1 points and 11.5 rebounds as the Warriors made the Eastern Conference Finals. He set his playoff high with 32 points in Game 7 at the Boston Garden.

When the team moved to San Francisco in 1963, Meschery made the All-Star team and finished the season averaging a career-high 16 points per game. The next season, he played in his first NBA Finals, a second showdown against Boston, and averaged 16.8 points and 7.3 rebounds in those playoffs, which included both the Finals and their preceding series win over the St. Louis Hawks, where Meschery scored 15 points in San Francisco's Game 7 win at home.

The next season, the Warriors traded Chamberlain to Philadelphia and Meschery played a key part in keeping the team afloat until they were ready to be competitive again. He, Nate Thurmond, and Guy Rodgers formed the team's core as the franchise transitioned from Chamberlain to Rick Barry, who they drafted in 1965.

Just a few years later, Meschery helped get the Warriors back to the NBA Finals in 1967, though by then he was playing a lesser role thanks to the brilliance of Barry. As he put it, Meschery went from "scoring forward" to "power forward" when Barry joined the team. Following that 1966–67 season, the Seattle SuperSonics selected him in the 1967 NBA Expansion Draft, where Meschery played four seasons before retiring.

Hanging up his basketball sneakers allowed the Mad Russian to adopt another nickname: "Renaissance Man." He pursued his passion for literature and earned his Masters of Fine Arts from the University of Iowa in 1974. After a stint coaching the Carolina Cougars of the American Basketball Association, Meschery became a high school English teacher. He has published six books, including three of poetry.

In six seasons with the Warriors, Meschery averaged 12.9 points and 8.5 rebounds while participating in three playoff runs. He became the first Warrior to have his jersey retired when his No. 14 went up to the rafters on October 13, 1967, just months after his departure in the expansion draft and four seasons before his retirement from professional basketball. Meschery holds a unique Bay Area distinction as his jersey is also retired at Lowell High School and St. Mary's College.

24 Draft Busts

The 1996 NBA Draft was one of the greatest of all time. The amount of talent in the first round rivals just about any year. It featured Kobe Bryant, Allen Iverson, Ray Allen, and Steve Nash, who are all surefire Hall of Famers.

The first round also included several more All-Stars in Antoine Walker, Jermaine O'Neal, Stephon Marbury, Peja Stojaković, Shareef Abdur-Rahim, and plenty more longtime NBA players, such as Marcus Camby, Zydrunas Ilgauskas, and Derek Fisher.

With the 11th pick in a draft with that remarkable collection of talent, the Warriors came away with Todd Fuller, a 6'11" North Carolina State product. Golden State drafted Joe Smith first overall the season before and were desperate for a true center. In an ominous sign, general manager Dave Twardzik cited Fuller's 3.95 GPA as an attribute that made him draft-worthy.

Three of the next four picks were Bryant, Stojaković, and Nash.

Fuller played the fewest NBA games of anyone in the top 20. Of the 58 players drafted in 1996, he ranks 30th in career minutes. He lasted just two seasons with the Warriors and ended up a high school calculus teacher in his hometown of Charlotte. He wasn't the inside presence the Warriors needed, instead a soft, high-post big man who could shoot pretty well but would overthink on the court.

It worked out to be one of the worst picks in Warriors history, in NBA history. And it was not the first time.

Like most NBA teams, the Warriors' draft history is full of swings and misses. However, their particularly shoddy draft résumé explains why the franchise spent so much of their first 50 years in the Bay Area as a frustrating perennial underachiever.

The list of players they could have drafted or selected but traded is mind-blowing. The Warriors even passed up a chance to draft Larry Bird. While Purvis Short played nine strong seasons for Golden State, Bird was a college star who became an icon.

When the Warriors hit big in the draft, they usually do really well, including Nate Thurmond, Rick Barry, Chris Mullin, and Stephen Curry. However, they also missed big too, often leaving Warriors fans thinking "What if?" While Fuller stands as the Warriors' greatest draft blunder, there are many other strong contenders.

Joe Barry Carroll

Calling a player who averaged 20.4 points, 8.3 rebounds, and 1.7 blocks over seven seasons with the Warriors a bust is strange but there is no other way to describe the first overall pick in 1980, whose initials became an acronym for Joe Barely Cares. The franchise banked on Carroll elevating the franchise and he had immense talent but played in only one playoff series with the Warriors.

What makes matters worse is that Golden State had to move up from the third pick to number one in order to draft Carroll. The price for doing so was center Robert Parish and Red Auerbach chose another All-Star, Kevin McHale, with the Warriors' No. 3 pick.

Chris Washburn

Washburn is one of the great draft tragedies in a draft remembered for tragedy. Selected third overall in 1986—one pick after Len Bias, who died from a drug overdose before he could play in the NBA—Washburn was another super-talented player coming out of the Atlantic Coast Conference.

The high school prodigy played for a loaded North Carolina State team and was expected to be the big-time player the struggling Warriors needed.

By the following January, Washburn checked into a drug rehabilitation clinic to address his cocaine addiction and he never came close to fulfilling his potential. In total, he played 43 games for the Warriors before they traded him to the Atlanta Hawks for forward Ken Barlow and that was Washburn's last season in the NBA because he received a lifetime ban in June of 1989 after three failed drug tests. Chuck Person, Ron Harper, John Salley, and Dell Curry were all selected after Washburn and went on to have long, productive careers.

Russell Cross

The Warriors had the sixth overall pick in 1983 and chose a center who scored 166 points in a 354-minute NBA career that consisted of 45 games for Golden State.

To make matters worse, University of Houston star Clyde Drexler was on the board. Imagine a backcourt with Eric "Sleepy" Floyd and Drexler.

It would have been fine even if the Warriors took the next shooting guard drafted, Dale Ellis, who had a strong career and would have helped the team, particularly since they had traded guards World B. Free and Michael Ray Richardson during the prior season.

Bob Portman

In the 1969–70 season, the Warriors had Nate Thurmond at center and traded for Jerry Lucas at power forward. They also had Jumpin' Joe Ellis at small forward and stalwart Jeff Mullins at shooting guard. All they needed was a point guard.

Unfortunately, they drafted Creighton guard Portman with the seventh overall pick. He underwhelmed for four seasons with the Warriors when two of the next three picks were future Hall of Fame point guard Jo Jo White and Butch Beard, who eventually played a key role on Golden State's 1975 championship team.

Barry Kramer

In 1963, the Warriors used their first pick after moving to San Francisco on Nate Thurmond, despite already having Wilt Chamberlain on the team. The two played together for that 1963–64 season and it was clear they did not need another big man as long as they intended to keep both towering figures on their roster.

With that in mind, they turned to swingman Barry Kramer out of NYU, who played just 276 minutes for the Warriors and 563 in his career.

That desire to avoid a big man led to the passing on both Willis Reed and Paul Silas, who went in the next four picks. On top of that frustration, the team traded Chamberlain to Philadelphia eight months later, so even that rationale was short-lived.

Joe Smith

In 1995, the Warriors won the NBA Draft lottery and the first overall pick. Joe Smith turned out to be a solid NBA player for many years, but he only played two and a half seasons with the Warriors. While less painful than Chris Webber's opt-out two years before, Smith's three-year contract gave him the power to work his way back to the East Coast during that third season after rejecting an extension offer. Eventually, the Warriors only received expiring contracts Jim Jackson and Clarence Weatherspoon for the far more productive Smith.

Beyond losing Smith so quickly, the next three picks, Antonio McDyess, Jerry Stackhouse, and Rasheed Wallace, went on to combine for seven All-Star appearances and superior careers.

Even with their comparative success, the prize of the 1995 Draft became fifth pick Kevin Garnett. He played the same position as Smith and clearly had a higher ceiling but was seen as a risk since he was jumping from high school. Incidentally, Smith and Garnett would become teammates in 1999, when Smith joined Minnesota as a free agent.

Mike Dunleavy Jr.

The Duke product was the consolation prize after Golden State, owners of the worst record in the league, did not end up with the first pick in the 2002 Draft lottery. Houston then drafted the player the Warriors coveted: 7'6" Chinese center Yao Ming.

They got the third pick and took Dunleavy. While his versatile game made him a good complementary player, he could not become the savior the team so desperately needed.

On top of that, the Warriors missed on another high-risk, high-reward star in Amar'e Stoudemire.

Adonal Foyle

The Colgate product is still Golden State's all-time leader in blocks and was one of the best role models a team could expect from a professional athlete, but the team needed much more from the eighth overall pick in 1998.

Once again, the Warriors' desperation for a big man and aversion to risk prompted them to pass up a prep-to-pro star. This time, Hall of Famer Tracy McGrady went one pick after Foyle.

Ekpe Udoh

Entering the 2010 Draft, the Warriors had hit rock bottom just three years after pulling off an historic playoff upset. However, there were promising signs that season since they had drafted their point guard of the future, Stephen Curry, a year earlier and possessed the cap space they eventually used to sign David Lee. A successful selection would have gone a long way to pushing things forward.

Unfortunately, the Warriors missed. Udoh, a defensive specialist, brought a skill the Warriors needed but was older and limited on offense. Future All-Stars Paul George and Gordon Hayward and more successful center Greg Monroe were all chosen in the next four picks.

Other Misses

Fred Hetzel is an amazing piece of Warriors trivia, as the Davidson Wildcat was chosen over Rick Barry with the first pick of the 1965 Draft. While Hetzel made the All-Rookie team and played three productive seasons in San Francisco, two-time All-Star Jerry Sloan and Hall of Famer Billy Cunningham were two of the three players chosen immediately after Barry.

The San Francisco Warriors selected San Jose State's Darnell Hillman eighth overall in the 1971 Draft. While Hillman had a successful pro career, it came with the ABA's Indiana Pacers instead of the Warriors. Power forward Curtis Rowe went three picks later and made the 1976 All-Star Game for the Pistons.

In 1987, Golden State drafted power forward Tellis Frank 14th overall and he played just two seasons for the team before they traded him to Miami for a second-round pick. The Knicks selected future All-Star and Warriors head coach Mark Jackson four choices later.

In 2003, the Warriors drafted French swingman Mickael Pietrus at No. 11. Fellow Frenchman Boris Diaw went 10 spots lower and had a vastly superior career, while longtime contributors Nick Collison and future Warrior David West went in the next seven picks.

While some may argue with his inclusion on this list, Latvian center Andris Biedrins was chosen in 2004 instead of talented American high schoolers Al Jefferson, Josh Smith, and J.R. Smith.

In 2005, the Warriors selected Pac-10 Player of the Year Ike Diogu with the ninth pick but high school center Andrew Bynum and talented New Mexico forward Danny Granger could have become difference-makers.

In 2006, Golden State drafted seven-foot project Patrick O'Bryant ninth overall. Duke sharpshooter J.J. Redick went just two picks later but was the only significant contributor in that range in a notoriously bust-filled lottery.

In 2007, they traded Jason Richardson for the eighth overall pick right after the We Believe team's stunning playoff run. While Brandan Wright became a serviceable big man for other franchises after an injury-plagued three and a half seasons with the Warriors, two-time All-Star Joakim Noah could have been the long-term solution at center.

In 2008, the Warriors took LSU freshman Anthony Randolph No. 14 overall. Stanford product Robin Lopez went with the next pick and both Cal power forward Ryan Anderson and center Roy Hibbert would have fit in well too.

In 2013, the Warriors bought their way to the 26th pick in the first round but traded down to 29th and then 30th to save some additional money and selected guard Nemanja Nedovic. The Serbian guard played in just 24 games before being cut and the Utah Jazz selected French center Rudy Gobert 27th overall.

25 Unanimous

Stephen Curry finished the 2014–15 season on top of the basketball world. In the span of 12 months, he started on Team USA's gold medal team in the 2014 FIBA Basketball World Cup, then won his first Most Valuable Player Award after propelling the Warriors to the league's best record, and secured a place in history by leading Golden State to their first championship in 40 years.

When someone bursts onto the scene with that degree of urgency and brilliance, the inevitable question that follows is what they will do for an encore. Curry's newfound superstardom took him all over the world during the summer of 2015, but he also retained the ability to work on his game since he did not have to grapple with recovering from any lingering injuries like so many other off-seasons.

Opening Night served as an omen, as the reigning MVP scored 40 points on New Orleans and less than a week later he dropped 53 on the same Pelicans in their arena. During the Warriors' historic 24-game win streak that started the season, Curry averaged 32.5 points, 6.1 assists, and an incredible 5.2 made three-pointers. In those 24 contests, Curry eventually tallied 125 made threes, a number only 37 other players reached over that entire season.

Curry's most indelible performance came almost four months later. While the Oklahoma City Thunder had never been a playoff opponent to that point, Russell Westbrook and Kevin Durant's team became a regular season rival with a multitude of competitive games. He scored 15 points in the first half before rolling his left ankle early in the third quarter. After missing about five and a half minutes, Curry nailed three three-pointers in 2:42 and then helped the Warriors send the game to overtime. With nine overtime points already, the ball found Curry with exactly five seconds remaining and a tie score after an Iguodala rebound. He dribbled down the court and then pulled up from about even with the Oklahoma City logo despite having another two seconds on the clock. Thirty-seven feet later, Curry both won the game and broke his own NBA record for made three-pointers in a season with 24 contests still to go.

From that point on, it only became a question of what Curry's MVP margin would be. He ended the season with career highs in scoring and rebounding while also posting a more efficient season despite taking even more shots, almost an impossibility for someone who had just won the MVP. His Player Efficiency Rating (PER) of 31.5 is eighth all-time and the Warriors' offense was among the best in league history as well on their way to breaking the NBA record for wins in a season with 73.

Curry's final numbers are awe-inspiring: a league-leading 30.1 points per game, 6.7 assists per game, 5.4 rebounds per game, a league-leading 2.1 steals per game, and 402 made three-pointers, surpassing his own NBA record by 116.

The NBA has given out 62 Most Valuable Player Awards, one every season since Bob Petit in 1955–56. While both LeBron James and Shaquille O'Neal finished just one vote short, no player had ever received every single first-place vote from the media.

26 Nellie Ball

Two principles that arose out of necessity now have a massive imprint on basketball at all levels, becoming more ubiquitous since Don Nelson's retirement. One, speed kills. Two, put your best players on the floor.

While the concepts are simple and their effects have become remarkably commonplace, Nellie Ball was revolutionary, partially because it stands in such stark contrast to the traditional style of play. Height has always been coveted in basketball, especially in the NBA. After all, the core of the game is to put the ball in the basket and stop the other team from doing so. It intuitively follows that most of the strategy and scheming centers on creating the highest percentage chances to score and limiting those same opportunities for opponents. Plus, it also follows that the closer a potential scorer is to the basket, the more likely the shot is to go in.

To that end, tall players make a ton of sense. They can get closer to the basket and possess superior physical tools to limit the other team from doing the same. For decades, big men dominated basketball, and the Warriors, with Wilt Chamberlain and transitioning to Nate Thurmond, kept them firmly ensconced in this tradition for more than a decade.

Nellie Ball inverted this pattern. His quest to be faster and put his best players on the floor often called for Nelson to replace his taller players with smaller ones. Nelson himself said, "When I had good teams and big teams, I didn't play small ball." The NBA typically possesses more capable guards and forwards. The tall guys are the anomalies but there are rarely shortages of perimeter players. Plus, since they are not planted right at the rim, smaller players have to develop their skills to get closer to the basket or score further away from it.

While Don Nelson did not invent this style of play, he popularized it during his coaching stints with the Bucks, Warriors, and Mavericks. He credits his former Celtics coach Red Auerbach for the concept. In practices as a player with those legendary teams, Nelson said the skilled perimeter players, led by John Havlicek, would consistently beat the bigger players, led by Bill Russell.

Inspired by those Celtics practices, Nellie Ball became about attacking size with speed and skill. Absent a dominant big man, which are rare, it is much more feasible to find players who can run circles around the big men.

While it can create intractable challenges for the opposition, the pitfall of going small has always been on the defensive end. Unsurprisingly, smaller players are vulnerable against bigger, stronger players and can struggle to deny them position. This reality seemed to always put a ceiling on Nelson's small ball teams.

In 1980–81, his Milwaukee Bucks won 60 games in the Eastern Conference. They averaged 113.1 points, second in the NBA, but finished sixth in points allowed, becoming the first Nelson squad that flourished on offense and held its own defensively.

During the playoffs that season, Milwaukee ran into Philadelphia, who had even better perimeter players, led by Julius Erving and Maurice Cheeks, and quality big men in Bobby Jones and Darryl Dawkins. In the series opener, Milwaukee scored 122 points but gave up 125. They eventually lost in Game 7 of the series when they fell behind in a rough second quarter and ended up falling just short. However, the blueprint proved viable because of an added wrinkle: a mobile big man.

Nelson did not need a seven-footer if he could have a 6'8" or so big man with some guard skills, since that could give Nellie Ball enough grit and toughness. Terry Cummings, a 6'9" forward out of DePaul, was the prototype: tall, physical, and tough, while also able to dribble and score in a variety of ways.

Tim Hardaway in 1992, pushing the pace versus the Heat in Miami. (AP Photo/ Al Messerschmidt)

In 1983–84, the only thing stopping the Bucks was Nelson's former team, as the Celtics featured two Hall of Fame big men in former Warrior Robert Parish and Kevin McHale, and overwhelmed Nellie Ball in the Eastern Conference Finals.

Nelson brought his scheme to the Warriors in 1987 when he became president of the franchise and started coaching in 1988. By 1989, he had a trio of perimeter players who could dominate with skill and quickness: Chris Mullin, Tim Hardaway, and Mitch Richmond. Nellie Ball took off.

The Warriors racked up points by playing fast, which worked against most big men because they tired trying to keep up with the faster pace. Golden State made the playoffs in three of Nelson's first four seasons and won 55 games in 1991–92, but they never conquered the defensive end. Giving up size for scoring prowess left them vulnerable defensively and in the postseason when they would get punished on the boards and in the paint by the most talented teams in the league.

Despite Run TMC's burgeoning popularity, Nelson's desire to find another Terry Cummings type drove him to trade Richmond for Billy Owens, a 6'9", ball-handling forward. Eventually, Nelson would find out that while Owens had the right size and an intriguing skill set, he was not the player who could provide the Warriors' defense and rebounding needs. Unfortunately, the Warriors gave up one of their best players in Richmond for him.

The answer to Nelson's quandary seemed to arrive in 1993. The Warriors drafted Chris Webber, a 6'9" big man with size and strength who could also dribble and pass like a guard. He was the perfect center for Nelson's vision—big enough to compete on the interior and rebound with the skills and quickness to play at the Warriors' pace.

The Warriors won 50 games in Webber's rookie season despite Hardaway missing the entire year with a torn ACL. While the Suns swept them in the first round as Hall of Famer Charles Barkley schooled the Warriors inside, the future for the Warriors looked bright if Webber and Nelson could resolve their tension. They could not, and things fell apart during the next season as the team traded Webber early on and months later Nelson resigned and took a job with the New York Knicks.

At that point, it seemed as if Nellie Ball would be written off as a gimmick, inexorably doomed in the playoffs when the game slowed down and size became even more impactful. Amazingly, long after Nellie Ball fizzled out with the Warriors with Nelson at the helm, the concept returned, revitalized thanks to the prowess of the three-pointer.

By taking advantage of the extra point, Nelson's style could make the opponent pay even more. The extra possessions from the rapid pace gave those teams more opportunities to rack up points, putting pressure on the opponent to match them. Those that could not keep up would end up following Nelson's lead and taking out their big man to go small.

While both the Dallas Mavericks, featuring Nelson draft pick Dirk Nowitzki, and the San Antonio Spurs, coached by former Nelson assistant Gregg Popovich, won championships with elements of Nellie Ball, its biggest triumph eventually came from the team Nelson coached for 865 games. Two years after his retirement, the Warriors drafted Draymond Green, who became the perfect Nellie Ball big man, and in 2015 Golden State won their first championship since 1975 by shifting to a lineup where the multitalented Green started at center. Even though the Nellie Ball impact and reputation went far outside the bounds of its namesake's creative approach in a way that distorted public perception of his impact, the Warriors' championship vindicated both his vision and legacy by proving a small team who played strong defense while also running and shooting could succeeded on the largest stage.

27 The Cocktail Napkin

In 1991, media entrepreneur Chris Cohan purchased 25 percent of the Warriors for approximately $21 million, but owner Jim Fitzgerald and his group maintained control of the franchise.

For a few years, that equilibrium held and the Warriors enjoyed a nice run of success from the Run TMC teams in the early '90s to the surprising 1993–94 squad that made the playoffs behind Latrell Sprewell and Chris Webber despite Tim Hardaway missing the season.

In November of that 1993–94 season, Cohan filed suit against the other Warriors owners (the main ones being Fitzgerald and Dan Finnane) claiming that his 1991 deal for one-quarter of the team also came with the ability to purchase the team in full three years later, which was rapidly coming due.

While it mostly lurked under the radar during that 1993–94 season, the issue came to a head almost a year later, when a hearing in San Francisco Superior Court was scheduled for October 1994. Cohan was certainly litigious in his business dealings but a minority owner suing for full control of a team was not exactly a common course of action when it came to NBA ownership.

The scheduled hearing was news enough, but the story became substantially more shocking when the sides settled before it occurred and Cohan bought the team for a reported $119 million, $34 million more than Leslie Alexander paid for the Houston Rockets one year before. What's more, after the dust settled Cohan was one of only six people with 100 percent ownership of an NBA team.

Considering Fitzgerald was actually a rare multi-time NBA owner with prior experience owning the Milwaukee Bucks before selling to Herb Kohl and buying the Warriors, the whole situation and its surprising resolution was jarring to fans and the Bay Area sports community.

However, a big part of the reason the lawsuit and ownership struggle ended the way it did was because Cohan had an ace in his back pocket: proof that the 1991 deal had gone down the way he claimed.

That evidence was a cocktail napkin.

With the pre-hearing revelation that Cohan had evidence of what he was claiming, it makes sense that the rapid settlement and sale went down in that fashion.

While no one knew it at the time, that cocktail napkin would be the bane of Warriors fans' existence for 15 years as Cohan established himself as one of the worst owners in professional sports before finally selling the team in 2010.

28 Chris Cohan

It was a wet and gloomy day in Oakland on February 13, 2000, as the rain mixed with the East Bay's grunge to make for a mucky setting at the 2000 NBA All-Star Game. However, the outside weather was pristine compared to the dark clouds inside what was then known as The Arena in Oakland because of the presence of Warriors owner Chris Cohan.

Michael Jordan, then president and part owner of the Washington Wizards, took to center court and Cohan joined him, with his five-year-old son Dax. The All-Star game has a torch-passing moment between the current host and the next year's host, which is typically presentational filler in the grand scheme of the

NBA's big weekend, but became a significant moment in Warriors history.

After the crowd cheered for Jordan, the announcement of Chris Cohan's name sent boos cascading down onto the hardwood. Six years after he gained control of the team, the fans were fed up with him and expressed their frustration on an incredibly public stage.

Cohan, though, was not even halfway through his tenure.

In 1991, Cohan bought 25 percent of the Warriors and he bought the remaining interest in the team through the settlement of his 1994 lawsuit against then-majority owner Jim Fitzgerald and his group.

In the first four full seasons of Cohan's tenure, the Warriors went 36–46, 30–52, 19–63, and 21–29 in the lockout-shortened 1998–99 campaign. When he took center court at All-Star Weekend, his team was 12–35 and on their way to another 19-win season.

Amazingly, the next season turned out even more disastrously, as the Warriors' 17–65 record was the worst since the team moved to the Bay Area.

In Cohan's first seven full seasons as an NBA owner, the Warriors had five coaches and went 163–379, a win percentage of .301. Even worse, there was little hope in sight. After years of missing on many opportunities to add talent and then driving the few successes away, there was no bright young potential star to carry the team forward. On top of that, no top free agents would take the Warriors' money and no credible NBA powerbroker would come turn the franchise around.

Cohan, who already kept a low profile, went into full-on hiding after getting jeered on his home court. Behind the scenes, he developed a reputation as a litigious businessman who soured as many relationships as he gained. A 2002 article on Cohan in the *San Francisco Chronicle* painted the picture of an owner who would rather win in court than on the court, even suing friends who were close enough to be in his wedding.

Unlike Donald Sterling of the Clippers, Cohan was not a notoriously cheap owner. After all, he doled out big contracts, including a maximum extension to Antawn Jamison that made the rest of the NBA scratch their heads. He also spent $110 million on the renovation of Oracle Arena and the team's practice facility in downtown Oakland, according to the Warriors.

However, spending money did not lead to success, as Cohan never seemed to find the right people to run the organization.

In June 2003, Cohan gave the reins of the franchise to a friend. He had close ties to San Luis Obispo, and that connected him with Robert Rowell, an alum who worked in the athletic department. In 1995, Rowell was hired fairly low on the totem pole as an assistant controller. A year later, he was the team's director of finance, handling the daily operations and the finances for the renovations. By 1998, Rowell was promoted to vice president of business operations and he was elevated to COO in 2001. Two years later, Cohan made Rowell team president, and with Cohan becoming a recluse of an owner, that left Rowell as the most powerful man in the franchise.

Rowell's rise made sense from a business perspective since the Warriors were bringing in corporate sponsors and doing well at the turnstiles despite being poor on the court. While an intense local fan base played a major role in their continued profitability despite consistently putting a horrendous product out on the floor, Rowell's marketing and business savvy helped the Warriors set attendance records and add season ticket holders.

The problems came when Rowell's power began reaching over to the basketball side. With Cohan's blessing, Rowell became the effective head of both business and basketball operations. At the time, Chris Mullin was the team's vice president of basketball operations and supposedly responsible for the Warriors' roster.

However, he frustratingly found out that power was far from absolute. Rowell nixed Mullin's attempt to trade for Kevin Garnett, who went to Boston instead and won a title that season. He also went against Mullin's wishes by disciplining Monta Ellis harshly for his scooter accident that tore a ligament in his left ankle. At the end of that season, Mullin worked out an agreement to keep star point guard Baron Davis but Rowell did not like the terms and issued a counter offer and Davis departed for the Clippers, leaving the Warriors without a point guard or compensation.

Almost exactly two years after Davis' departure, Cohan sold the team through a bidding process to Joe Lacob and Peter Guber for a then-record price of $450 million, a tidy return since Cohan paid a reported $119 million for the team a decade and a half earlier.

While Cohan's departure happened immediately, Lacob and Guber took a year to evaluate the existing front office personnel. After that process, the new owners decided to clean house and only a few top executives stayed with the team.

One of those who did not was Rowell, effectively ending the Cohan era.

29 Latrell Sprewell

For a long time, Latrell Sprewell was the best thing the Warriors had going.

Selected 24th overall in the 1992 NBA Draft, Sprewell proved to be a steal fans could cling to after the Warriors broke up Run TMC by trading Mitch Richmond. At 6'5", 190 pounds, with springs in his calves and an aggressiveness to his game, Sprewell looked like a player immediately. He was a starter from the jump, a slashing athlete who fit right into the Warriors' scheme. His energy was impossible to ignore.

Sprewell became the first Warriors rookie to record at least 1,000 points, 250 rebounds, 250 assists, 100 steals, and 50 blocks in a season and was also chosen for a spot on the All-Rookie second team.

The next season, drafting Chris Webber gave the Warriors a legitimate duo, as Sprewell was ready to lead the team. Even though Tim Hardaway missed the season with a knee injury and Chris Mullin was winding down his storied career, the Warriors looked like a team on the rise. They were back in the playoffs and Sprewell led them there—averaging 21 points, 4.9 rebounds, and 4.7 assists. He made his first All-Star game in his second season and went from second team All-Rookie to first team All-NBA while also making the All-Defensive second team.

The next fall, Golden State traded Webber after he feuded with Don Nelson and Nelson left too before the end of that season. Less than a year after winning 50 games, Sprewell was the lone hope for the future. Paired with aging stars Mullin and Hardaway, he became the face of the franchise.

Two seasons later, Sprewell had a breakout year. The Warriors were mired in irrelevance, playing in San Jose while their arena was being remodeled and squeezing out a mere 30 wins, but Sprewell's game took off. He averaged 24.2 points, 6.3 assists, and 4.6 rebounds per game and even had a career-best 19.7 Player Efficiency Rating that season. Sprewell's 1997 All-Star Game appearance would be the Warriors' last until 2013.

After a spectacular early rise and fall due to circumstances beyond his control, Sprewell emerged as a star rising up the tiers. His outside shot was improving and he was also a workhorse who led the league in minutes his second season and was not bothered by averaging 40 minutes per night. In addition to his rugged knack for scoring, Sprewell was a good defender coming out of the gate and, when he was focused, could really lock down.

The Warriors' record was declining as the pieces around him faded, but they had their centerpiece in Sprewell. He was an impressive story considering his route to NBA stardom.

Raised in a broken home in Milwaukee, Sprewell and his mother were abused by his father, per an ESPN biography. His parents split up when he was six years old; by seven he was living with his grandmother in Flint, Michigan. He returned to Milwaukee in time for his junior year of high school, joined the Washington High School basketball team and dominated immediately. He had his first child at 17, before he even graduated, and did not get any scholarship offers despite his basketball prowess. Sprewell went to Three Rivers Community College in Missouri, where he earned a Division I scholarship, choosing the University of Alabama over prestigious basketball powerhouse University of Kansas. He was part of a trio of Alabama stars that would go pro, with Robert Horry and James Robison. Horry produced a legendary career as a reserve star known for making clutch shots on championship teams, but Sprewell was the most talented of the three.

Three All-Star appearances in his first five years. Second team All-Rookie. First team All-NBA and second team All-Defense in his second season. Sprewell was on his way to becoming one of the greats in franchise history.

And then everything came apart.

The Warriors returned to their refurbished arena with dismal prospects for success. They traded Mullin to Indiana two years after shipping Webber to Washington and hired a new coach, P.J. Carlesimo, who had just been fired by Portland.

The Warriors squad that looked so promising just three years earlier was back in the doldrums and it got far worse.

During a practice session, an angered Sprewell attacked Carlesimo and put his hands around his coach's neck. Sprewell was soon

Latrell Sprewell dunks on the Sacramento Kings in 1996. (AP Photo/Steve Castillo)

separated from Carlesimo by his teammates and staff but the damage was done. The Warriors had reached a new low—a player choked his coach. In a shock that extended far beyond the world of professional basketball, Golden State became a supermodel of dysfunction.

"More surprise, not shock," Carlesimo told the YES Network in 2013, recalling what he felt. "Again, I mean, there were so many people around. It was, you know, it's a practice, and things happen at practice, but no, there was nothing that led up to it. So it was more surprise."

Sprewell would never play for the Warriors again. After unsuccessfully attempting to void his contract, the league suspended him for the remaining 68 games of the season and Golden State traded him to New York before the start of the next season. The Warriors received little in return due to the circumstances—John Starks, forwards Chris Mills and Terry Cummings, though there was a rumored offer involving Dan Majerle and Brent Barry that never came to fruition.

He returned from suspension and served as a sixth man for the Knicks in the lockout-shortened 1998–99 season. The Knicks roared into the playoffs and he was on the court when Allan Houston hit the famous game-winner to knock out Miami, making New York the second No. 8 seed to knock out a No. 1 seed. In the second round, Sprewell scored 62 points in the first two games of their sweep of Atlanta, became a starter in Game 4 of the Eastern Conference Finals, and posted a team-high 29 points in a pivotal Game 5 in Indiana. The Knicks went on to the NBA Finals and Sprewell, 18 months after being everything that was wrong with the NBA, was on top of the NBA world as a star on one of the NBA's legacy franchises.

After four more seasons on the Knicks, Sprewell was traded to the Minnesota Timberwolves and again helped his new team reach playoff success, this time starting and averaging 16.8 points per game as Kevin Garnett and the Timberwolves made it to the

Western Conference Finals before losing to the Los Angeles Lakers. Sprewell's knack for drama returned when, after that playoff run, Minnesota owner Glen Taylor offered the 34-year-old a three-year, $21 million contract extension. That marked a pay cut from his prior salary and Sprewell responded, "I have a family to feed…. If [Timberwolves Owner] Glen Taylor wants to see my family fed, he better cough up some money." That ended up being his final season in the NBA after spurning less lucrative contract offers from various franchises over the next few years.

After a stunningly strong start, Sprewell wound up being the next in a long line of Warriors stars that got away.

30 Phil Smith

Along with Tom Meschery, Phil Smith stands out as a Bay Area native who made it big with his hometown team.

Smith attended George Washington High School in San Francisco before becoming an All-American his senior year at the University of San Francisco in 1973–74. Without the benefit of territorial selections like the Philadelphia Warriors used to add Wilt Chamberlain, Guy Rodgers, and others, Smith went into the general draft pool and the Warriors selected him with their second-round pick (29th overall) in the 1974 Draft.

Both Smith and first-round pick Jamaal Wilkes entered the rotation immediately on a team with serious expectations after winning 44 games the season before. While Wilkes started at forward, Smith became an indispensable bench piece, scoring 7.7 points per game in 14.3 minutes. While his role did not increase in the bright lights of the playoffs, Smith scored 20 points in Game

1 of the 1975 NBA Finals and the Warriors' six-point win in Washington sparked a massive upset and the team's first championship since moving to the Bay Area.

After being a key piece on his hometown team's first championship, the local product's star grew significantly the next season, as Smith averaged 20 points per game and earned a place on both the All-NBA second team and the All-Defensive second team in just his second season. At just 23 years old, the young guard also made his first All-Star game, giving him the added thrill of playing with teammates Barry and Wilkes. Smith upped his game in the 1976 playoffs, averaging 24 points, 4.7 rebounds, and 4.6 assists per game, but the Warriors fell to the Suns in a seven-game Western Conference Finals, depriving them of a shot at repeating as NBA Champions.

Smith stayed at that high level for three more seasons as the team changed around him, averaging between 19 and 20 points per game from 1976–77 to 1978–79 while making another All-Star team in 1977. The Warriors were one of the five best defensive teams in the league all but one of Smith's first five seasons, even as the key players from the 1975 championship team headed elsewhere.

Unfortunately, the shooting guard's bright career took a turn before the 1979–80 season when he injured his Achilles' tendon in a preseason practice. Coach Al Attles said, "If that injury hadn't occurred, we'd be talking about him as one of the greatest guards ever to play this game."

Rick Barry added, "Had he not gotten hurt, he could have been a really outstanding player. But he had a terrific career anyway." It's hard to argue, considering Smith's passion for the game and work ethic. While he played another four NBA seasons after the injury, Smith never reached the heights of his early-to-mid twenties and retired at 31 years old.

The San Francisco product retired to San Diego and stayed connected with Attles and the Warriors while working as a stockbroker. Smith passed away in 2002 at just 50 years old after an extended battle with multiple myeloma. His USF coach, Bob Gaillard, called Smith "the best of competitors and the best of human beings."

31 Move to Oakland

For the longest time, Oakland was Raiders country. As one of the original American Football League teams, the Raiders had a monopoly on professional sports in Oakland when the franchise was created in 1960. In 1968, baseball's Athletics moved from Kansas City to Oakland, bringing Major League Baseball to the East Bay.

In 1966, the National Hockey League purchased the San Francisco Seals, who then moved from the Cow Palace to the Oakland Coliseum Arena and became the California Seals. In 1967, they changed their name to the Oakland Seals. This grungy stepsister city next to the major metropolis of San Francisco now had three professional sports teams.

So in 1971, with the San Francisco Warriors—who split home games between the Cow Palace in Daly City and the San Francisco Civic Auditorium—struggling at the gate and looking to flee the basketball apathy in "The City," Oakland became a natural destination.

Franchise owner Franklin Mieuli worked his marketing genius behind the scenes. He set up the Warriors to be California's team. The Warriors played 15 of their 41 home games in Oakland during the 1970–71 seasons, and another two in San Diego.

So Mieuli came up with a new plan: play 29 games in San Diego and televise them in Oakland, and play the remaining games in Oakland while televising them in San Diego. And he changed the name of the franchise to the Golden State Warriors.

Was this a real plan? Or was this a ploy by Mieuli to get a sweet deal? Whatever the case, it worked. In 1971, the Warriors moved into the Oakland Coliseum Arena full time. That year, Oakland was one of only six cities in the country with a team in all four major professional sports.

The Oakland Oaks of the ABA were previously tenants at the Arena and even with star Rick Barry on the roster, the Oaks drew poorly. The scarce professional basketball interest in the area was concentrated on the San Francisco Warriors, but now the NBA was coming to Oakland.

Forty years later, Oakland and the East Bay are a hotbed of basketball, a renowned and required stop for any NBA fan looking for a special experience.

It was not always that way.

The Warriors failed to crack the 500,000 attendance mark for the team's first 17 seasons in Oakland, including the 1974–75 championship season. Around the same time, the Oakland Athletics were also having trouble drawing, despite winning three straight championships in the early '70s.

Attendance picked up around the time of Run TMC. The Warriors drew 587,820 fans for the 1988–89 season and that number steadily increased. The high-scoring era featuring Tim Hardaway, Mitch Richmond, and Chris Mullin brought an identity to the team and their frenetic pace created an energy that made basketball in Oakland unique. At that point Warriors basketball created and nurtured passion in its fans, often in spite of the team.

The Warriors' competitiveness dipped drastically starting with the 1994–95 season after a clash between head coach Don Nelson and budding star Chris Webber led to Webber being traded and

Nelson resigning. They went from 50 wins in 1993–94 to 26 wins the following season.

Golden State would fail to win even half their games each of the next 12 seasons. They maxed out at 38 victories and won 21 games or fewer five times during that span. However, attendance dipped below 500,000 only once during that time and that was during the lockout-shortened 1998–99 season when teams only had 25 home games.

The team left Oakland temporarily for the 1996–97 season due to arena renovations, spending a year in San Jose. In 2007, the loyal, long-suffering fans were finally rewarded with a return to the playoffs, which had not happened since Webber departed. In a season that will forever be known for the "We Believe" signs that filled the arena, the Warriors made history, becoming the first No. 8 seed to beat a No. 1 seed in a seven-game series, upsetting the Dallas Mavericks in six games, and the crowd provided a special atmosphere for those raucous playoff games.

The very next season, attendance skyrocketed to 800,000 for the first time in franchise history. The total attendance for that 2007–08 season (804,864) was more than even the Warriors' 2014–15 championship season (803,436).

Mieuli, the man who brought the Warriors to the Bay Area and then to Oakland, had the chance to experience his initial vision successfully manifest. Before he died in 2010, he was a regular courtside at Warriors games, witnessing an NBA fanaticism that did not match the product on the court. The Warriors finished the 2016–17 regular season with a sellout streak of 239 games and no end in sight, considering the waiting list for new season ticket holders is over 42,000.

32 Joe Lacob

While Joe Lacob taking over the Warriors from the disastrous reign of Chris Cohan in July 2010 thrilled a long-suffering fan base, his earliest steps did not exactly inspire significant optimism.

After Don Nelson's retirement, the new owners decided to give his assistant Keith Smart the first shot at the job while also keeping an eye out for a long-term fit. Despite the team winning 10 more games that season, coupled with development from their young players, Lacob fired Smart after that season, citing a desire for a coach with "experience," though he did not specify experience as a head coach.

That logic faced a challenge when they decided to bring former player and ABC announcer Mark Jackson on, since he had never coached at any level. Around that time, Lacob sent a letter to season ticket holders promising to freeze prices for the 2012–13 season if the team did not make the playoffs that season.

That lockout-shortened season ended up becoming rockier than they expected and playoff hope was almost extinguished when March 19, 2012, rolled around. That night, Lacob continued his well-intentioned and well-executed effort to reconnect the franchise with its history by retiring Chris Mullin's jersey. The crowd was intense but the team had pushed that frustration to another level the week before by trading fan favorite Monta Ellis to the Milwaukee Bucks for injured center Andrew Bogut.

When Lacob took the mic at center court, the Oracle Arena crowd let him have it.

Twice.

The response was so filled with vitriol that both Mullin and Warriors legend Rick Barry implored them to calm down, but they would not let up.

Thirty-eight months later, Lacob was back as the center of attention, but in front of a significantly larger crowd. This time, he was on a stage at the Henry J. Kaiser Convention Center, overlooking Lake Merritt and a sea of fans being showered with applause.

"I'm not sure many people can say they've been booed by 20,000 people," Lacob said in his speech, "and cheered by a million people all in the span of three years."

While there were many reasons why Lacob had been booed, there was wide consensus why he was cheered. It was because the trade worked, he made good on his proclamations and delivered a championship.

Warriors owner Joe Lacob speaking next to the Larry O'Brien Trophy during the 2015 rally. (AP Photo/Jeff Chiu)

Less than five years after he won the franchise in a blind auction by outbidding Oracle billionaire Larry Ellison, Lacob had accomplished what he said he would do. He pulled off what he dreamed of as a daydreaming child of a working poor family who grew up in Massachusetts during the Boston Celtics' glory years.

Lacob, the venture capitalist turned NBA owner, is really a rags to riches story.

He grew up in New Bedford, Massachusetts, a port city with a history of whale hunting and manufacturing. His mother worked at a local supermarket and his father worked at a paper products company. They worked so hard Lacob said he hardly saw them.

When Lacob was 14, his dad's company was sold and he was transferred to Orange County, California. Lacob considers that move one of the greatest breaks in his life.

Upon graduation from high school, Lacob enrolled at UC Irvine, where he received a bachelor's degree in biological sciences. He made money as a vendor at California Angels games selling peanuts and soda. He went on to get a master's degree in public health from UCLA and an MBA from Stanford.

"I was a very poor kid," Lacob said. "Had nothing. I paid every dime of my education through college. Every single dime. I was the first person to graduate from college in the history of my family. Ever. I came from nothing."

In 1987, he became a partner at the venture capital firm Kleiner Perkins Caufield Byers. As a venture capitalist, his job was to weigh the potential of companies and decide whether to invest in them. If he chose to invest, he would then have to establish the infrastructure of the company and ensure its growth. Lacob says he built 70 companies and his firm is responsible for financing giants like Amazon, Google, and Snapchat. Lacob was the front man for the development of Autotraders and Invisalign braces. If he stopped there, his story would qualify as the American dream.

Lacob's skills as a venture capitalist helped him shape the Warriors. His philosophy of finding the best people to work with—mandatory for success at his day job—led to him securing a high-quality front office staff. Building companies from the ground up gave him experience in creating a productive work environment, which he employed in changing the culture of the Warriors from the toxicity that preceded him.

That transition involved firing most of the team's executives and instituting several elements to make the work environment pleasurable, from bringing a massage therapist some days to give the staff a 15-minute treat to having buffet-style lunch delivered. During the NBA Finals, he flew the entire office to a game in Cleveland on a charter plane.

His experience in venture capital also led Lacob to forming an unusual but extremely effective front office. In May 2011, he brought in legendary player and architect of the Shaq and Kobe Lakers, Jerry West, as an executive board member reporting directly to ownership. West became an important voice in the room for key decisions, including drafting Klay Thompson and refraining from trading the talented shooting guard in a massive deal for Kevin Love in 2014, where he reportedly threatened to resign if the trade went through. That same year, Lacob hired Bob Myers away from his job as a powerful player agent to become the team's assistant general manager. That faith was rewarded when Myers took over the head job a year later and continued his work building a powerhouse on his way to Executive of the Year Awards in both 2015 and 2017.

Lacob's philosophy is to get the best people and make them happy. It turned the Warriors' franchise from what was widely known behind the scenes as a mess to one of the best-run and most-successful franchises in the NBA.

33 Jeff Mullins

Jeff Mullins, fresh off winning a gold medal with USA Basketball at the 1964 Olympics in Tokyo, had no idea what he was doing in St. Louis. The 1964 ACC Player of the Year for Duke, who played in two Final Fours, wound up stuck on the bench behind established guards Lenny Wilkens, Richie Guerin, and Chico Vaughn.

He expected to go to a team where he could have an immediate impact, like the Warriors.

"I asked Marty Blake, who was the [general manager], 'Why did you draft me?'" Mullins recalled back in 2007. "He said, 'So S.F. couldn't get you.' Everybody knew all San Francisco needed was a guard. I ended up in St. Louis for the wrong reason. That was a tough team for a rookie. It was a veteran team."

Mullins lasted just two seasons with the Hawks and averaged a little over five points per game. During the 1966 off-season, they sent Mullins to the expansion Chicago Bulls, who in turn traded him—along with Jim King, a draft choice, and cash—to the Warriors for All-Star guard Guy Rodgers.

Bill Sharman, a Hall of Fame player who broadcasted for the Hawks and became close with Mullins during that time, took over as coach of the Warriors and helped get Mullins to the Bay Area. Sharman used to shoot around with Mullins after Hawks practices, so he knew exactly what he was getting in the third-year guard, which is why Sharman immediately named the 24-year-old newcomer a starter.

"Bill was great for my career," Mullins said. "When I got to the Warriors, he said, 'I want you to play just like you did in college. When you're open, I want you to shoot.'"

Mullins, playing with swingman Rick Barry, big man Nate Thurmond, and guard Paul Neumann, hit the ground running and the Warriors reached the NBA Finals in his first season, losing in six games to the Wilt Chamberlain–led Philadelphia 76ers.

Following that season, Barry left to play for the Oakland Oaks of the ABA, which allowed Mullins to have an even bigger role on the team. He flourished following Barry's departure, making three straight All-Star teams from 1969–71, while averaging 21.2 points, 5.4 rebounds, and 4.8 assists during the five seasons Barry was gone.

After Barry returned in 1972 and the team added new talent over the next few years, Mullins became a role player for the 1974–75 Warriors and the three-time All-Star accepting coming off the bench helped set the tone for an unusually deep team. Those Warriors would win the 1975 championship as he contributed with 8.1 points in 18.4 minutes per game during those playoffs. Even in his diminished role, after coming up short many times before, Mullins said winning the title was the defining moment of his entire basketball career.

During his final injury-riddled season of 1975–76, Mullins worked alongside legendary broadcaster Bill King for a number of Warriors broadcasts.

In 10 seasons with the Warriors, Mullins averaged 17.5 points per game, appeared in three All-Star games, and made the playoffs eight times.

34 Bad Signings

While not as infamous as some of their trades or draft picks, one of the other trademarks of the Warriors' lean years was horrendous contracts that limited the team's flexibility and potential.

Jason Caffey (1999) Seven years, $35 million

The Warriors acquired Caffey from the Bulls at the 1998 trade deadline and he averaged 10.9 points and 5.9 rebounds in 29 games after the trade, primarily coming off the bench. After the lockout, they signed him to this monstrous deal with general manager Garry St. Jean saying, "He demonstrated during his brief stint with the Warriors last season that, when presented with the opportunity, he can be a very special player in this league." Caffey appeared in 106 more games as a Warrior before being traded to Milwaukee in a three-team deal that netted them Billy Owens, Bob Sura, and Vinny Del Negro. That contract was Caffey's last in the NBA.

Derek Fisher (2004) Six years, $37 million

Already 30 when the Warriors signed him, Fisher was coming off three championships and four NBA Finals in five years with the Lakers. Even before Baron Davis supplanted Fisher later that same season, Speedy Claxton was already starting over him regularly. After two seasons, the Warriors traded Fisher to the Jazz for filler contracts (Keith McLeod, Devin Brown, and Andre Owens) and almost exactly a year later, Fisher and the Jazz shockingly mutually terminated the rest of his contract so he could better help in his daughter's battle with retinoblastoma, an extremely rare form of eye cancer. He re-signed with the Lakers two weeks later.

Stephen Jackson (2008) Three years, $27.6 million

Different from the others but remarkable in its own way. A remaining piece from the We Believe team, Jackson negotiated directly with team president Robert Rowell and received a maximum extension with two seasons remaining on his existing contract. Almost exactly a year later and still a season before that extension kicked in, Jackson agitated and the Warriors traded him to the Charlotte Bobcats with Acie Law for Raja Bell and Vladimir Radmanovic.

Erick Dampier (1999) Six years, $48 million

Acquired from the Pacers for Chris Mullin in 1997, Dampier started 132 games for the Warriors before hitting the market after the Warriors refused to give him an extension that February. The center missed 100 games over the next two seasons as the team floundered and his lucrative contract being on the books was part of what prevented the Warriors from having the salary flexibility to re-sign Gilbert Arenas in 2003. After having the best year of his career in 2003–04, Dampier opted out of the final two years of this contract and then was traded to the Mavericks, who gave him seven years and $73 million.

Corey Maggette (2008) Five years, $50 million

After Baron Davis left for the Clippers, the Warriors tried to sign Gilbert Arenas (five years, $100 million) and Elton Brand (five years, $90 million), both of whom turned them down. Another former Clipper ended up taking their money and Maggette put up solid statistics and little else on two massively disappointing Warriors teams before being traded to Milwaukee for Dan Gadzuric and Charlie Bell in the 2010 off-season. He was traded each of the next two summers as well, playing for four teams on that five-year contract.

Troy Murphy (2004) Six years, $58 million

The Warriors announced extensions for Murphy and Jason Richardson on the same day but the two deals went in massively different directions. Murphy had played a much larger role in 2002–03, but injuries limited him to just 28 games in 2003–04. Despite that missed time, the forward still received an extension worth almost $10 million per season. While Murphy started 143 games in the next two seasons, he failed to live up to his promise and was included in the massive eight-player trade with the Pacers during 2006–07, which sparked the We Believe team. Amazingly, after playing for three franchises, Murphy returned to the Warriors at the 2011 trade deadline on the final year of that extension along with the 2012 second-round pick that became Draymond Green. The team bought Murphy out before he played another game for his original team.

Antawn Jamison (2001) Six years, $79.3 million

At the time it was signed, Jamison's extension was the most lucrative contract in Bay Area sports history. The talented forward had impressed in 2000–01 despite the team's futility by averaging almost 25 points per game and the team rewarded him with the deal that kicked in after the 2001–02 season. While he stayed healthy for the next two seasons, Jamison's Warriors career stagnated at about that level and in 2003 the team traded him to Dallas in a massive nine-player deal that included guard Nick Van Exel. Jamison won Sixth Man of the Year the following season and the Mavericks traded him to Washington for a significantly better return than the Warriors had received 10 months earlier. He played another 11 seasons in the NBA and made two All-Star teams with the Wizards.

Adonal Foyle (2004) Six years, $41.6 million

While other teams were hoping to get the shot-blocker for the mid-level exception (about $5 million per season then), the Warriors vastly exceeded that number while also giving him six seasons starting at age 29. Foyle played three seasons and 203 games on the contract before agreeing to a buyout after the 2006–07 season. He is still the franchise leader in blocked shots with 1,140.

35 The City Uniforms

The Warriors players were warming up at Madison Square Garden, set to take on Walt Bellamy, Willis Reed, and the Knicks on November 3, 1966. Tip-off neared and then–point guard Al Attles noticed his players still had on their warm-ups.

"I don't know if it was intentional or not," Attles said some 35 years later, "but nobody wanted to be the first to take the jacket off."

It was the ninth game of the season. The Warriors had already played in Boston, Chicago twice, Baltimore, and Cincinnati, but this was the Warriors' first time in New York City with their new uniforms.

"It had the bridge on the front with the words 'The City' and a cable car on the back," Attles recalled. "Imagine, we're in New York, people from New York consider it the Big Apple, The City…. Finally, we take the jackets off and I'll be darned if we don't get a standing ovation from the New York crowd."

The appeal of the jersey the Warriors debuted for the 1966–67 season has only grown over the years. It has become an iconic piece of sports fashion, universally regarded as one of the best uniforms in basketball history.

Attles said at the time he and the rest of the team were worried about how people would react to the uniform change.

On the front of the blue road jersey was a big yellow circle featuring an outline of the Golden Gate Bridge. Hovering above the bridge was each player's jersey number. On top of the circle— where it would normally read the team's home, San Francisco, it read CITY in big letters with a smaller "The" in script above the "C." The back had a cable car, a popular staple of San Francisco, with the player's number in it.

They became an instant hit. Even the All-Star jerseys were themed after The City jerseys when the game was held at the Cow Palace in 1967.

The original outfit even featured warm-up suits with the cable car on the back of the jackets and the SF logo in the middle. The team only wore the jerseys for five seasons, from 1966–67 until 1970–71, because the move to Oakland necessitated changing to uniforms featuring their new name: Golden State Warriors.

The Warriors brought the jerseys out of retirement during the throwback jersey craze of the early 2000s. The blue jerseys returned during the 2005 season for the NBA's Hardwood Classic Nights, while the yellow home jerseys returned during the 2006–07 run featuring Baron Davis, Jason Richardson, and the crew now known as the "We Believe" Warriors and then returned again for a four-game stint during the 2010–11 season.

The jerseys were so popular that they inspired the Warriors' current jerseys. When new ownership took over in 2010, they brought back the previous Warriors colors—the franchise had ventured off to navy blue, orange, and gold—and a new logo spun off The City jerseys. The big circle on the front of the jerseys returned but the Golden Gate Bridge was replaced with a rendering of the new eastern span of the Bay Bridge.

Even after the change, the Warriors brought The City jerseys back for the 2015–16 season and redesigned the hardwood for those throwback games, putting the beloved logo at half court of

Oracle Arena. The reaction from the young Warriors illustrates how impactful those uniforms have been over the years.

"I think that's gonna be pretty dope," Draymond Green said of wearing The City uniforms. "Since I've been here, I've wondered when we're going to wear them."

"Just look at the greats who wore them up on the wall," Klay Thompson said. "Like Alvin Attles, Rick Barry, Nate Thurmond. It's an honor to wear them."

With the Warriors' upcoming return to San Francisco for the 2019–20 season, there is renewed interest in The City jerseys making a broader return, but the team has not made any announcements about their future.

36 Jim Fitzgerald

Jim Fitzgerald stood out among both Warriors owners and NBA owners in general through his approach and story.

He built a fortune in his hometown of Janesville, Wisconsin, through various ventures, including gas stations, shopping centers, and eventually pieces of banks and cable television networks. In 1975, at just 50 years old, Fitzgerald and other backers purchased the Milwaukee Bucks in the wake of the team trading Kareem Abdul-Jabbar to the Lakers, though he had already been on their board of directors for two years. Fitzgerald ascended to president and chairman of the board, leading the Bucks in some of the best seasons in franchise history.

Ten years later, Fitzgerald and his business team sold the Bucks to future-Senator Herb Kohl and then bought the Warriors from Frank Mieuli the next season, with Fitzgerald taking the majority stake.

One of Fitzgerald's most significant contributions to the Warriors came a few seasons later when he brought over his long-time coach and general manager from the Bucks, Don Nelson. Fitzgerald and Nelson distinctively relied on handshake deals instead of written contracts, though Fitzgerald associate John Steinmiller clarified, "It started out as a handshake, but later it became a handshake on a piece of paper."

Still, the level of trust and respect between the two men led Nelson to stay with Fitzgerald during his Bucks tenure, despite offers from the Celtics in 1983 and Spurs in 1984, and then inspired him to join the Warriors as head coach and vice president in 1988. After the fact, Nelson said, "Looking back, I was a loyal guy because Jim Fitzgerald was so good to me, so I don't really regret not going." That reflects a very different kind of connection for an owner and coach in professional sports.

Remarkably, Fitzgerald's other principal coach as owner of the Warriors eventually became a Hall of Famer as well, though George Karl's season and a half in Oakland was decidedly less smooth than Nelson's despite Golden State making the playoffs in his first season at the helm.

In 1992, Chris Cohan purchased 25 percent of the team and eventually sued, claiming his original deal came with the expectation that he would own the team in full in time. Shortly before hearings would have taken place, the sides settled and Cohan bought the team for $119 million, ending Fitzgerald's tenure as the successful and popular steward of the team.

In the eight years Fitzgerald owned the team, the Warriors made the playoffs five times and had a 325–331 record (.495 winning percentage). In the eight years before and after his tenure, Golden State never made the playoffs and won 35.5 percent of their games.

When Fitzgerald passed away in June 2012, Al Attles paid tribute to him as "Simply a terrific man of incredible character and high standards who was a model owner for the Warriors and the NBA." He said, "[Fitzgerald] always put the needs and concerns of others ahead of himself and was one of the most giving and caring individuals I have ever met."

37 Purvis Short

Stephen Curry had just put on a show in Houston, scoring 40 points as the Warriors took a 3–0 lead in the 2015 Western Conference Finals. It was a splashy 40, marked by deep threes as the Warriors routed the host Rockets in Houston.

After the game, the Warriors' locker room was abuzz with excitement as they were a win from reaching the NBA Finals. Standing quietly on the side, his arms folded, a smile on his face, was Purvis Short. He just watched the celebration and soaked up the energy. He was waiting for a chance to speak to Curry.

When he saw his opening, he walked across the locker room to Curry, and he leaned over and whispered into Curry's ear.

"It's unbelievable," Short said. "I sit on the edge of my seat every time he gets the ball."

If anyone can appreciate Curry's shooting prowess, it's Short. The Warriors' franchise has a rich history of shooters, from Paul Arizin, the inventor of the jump shot, to Stephen Curry, the master of the three-pointer. Rick Barry and Mark Price to Chris Mullin and Mitch Richmond. That list is incomplete without Short, who was a mid-range expert, but the 6'7" forward was known for his high-arching outside shot. They called him Rainbow Man because his jumper would kiss the sky before descending into the hoop.

Short, one of the greatest players never to make an All-Star game, bridged the gap between Barry and Run TMC. At the height of his career, he was a top-notch scorer capable of taking advantage of his size and manipulating the spectacularly soft touch on his shot. Short averaged 20 points per game in four straight seasons, including 28 in 1984–85. In November of that season, against the visiting New Jersey Nets, he scored 59 points on just 28 shots, two more than the 57 he tallied against San Antonio the year before.

Not bad for a player from a small school in Mississippi. Short starred at Jackson State University and was named Southwest Athletic Conference Player of the Year in both 1977 and 1978. He was also college basketball's second-leading scorer in 1978.

Even with all that, Short's legacy still has a bit of infamy attached since the thing he may be most remembered for is his draft position. The Warriors selected Short with the No. 5 overall pick in the 1978 NBA Draft, one pick before the Boston Celtics selected Larry Bird. Short was far from a bust, but Bird turned out to be a Hall of Famer and centerpiece of multiple championship teams.

That reality set the stage for one of the greatest feats in Short's career and it had nothing to do with shooting. On January 2, 1981, the Warriors hosted the Celtics and Short drew the assignment of defending Bird. In 37 minutes of action, Bird missed all nine of his shots. It was the first time in his career he had been held scoreless, in college or the pros, as the Warriors snapped the Celtics' 12-game win streak.

With a proven elite scorer in Bernard King on the roster, Short started his career as a reserve. He was one of the most potent scorers off the bench his first three years in the league before becoming a starter during the 1982–83 season and his scoring average jumped to 21.4 points per game.

Short then began working with basketball legend Pete Newell, who helped him improve his jump shot and started stretching his range out to three-point territory. He took 72 three-pointers in

1983–84, then 150 the following season. He made 31.1 percent of his attempts during that two-year binge from three-point range and never took more than 49 in any of his other 10 seasons.

In his ninth season, Short finally made it to the playoffs. He played only 34 games that year because of knee and thigh injuries but he averaged 14.6 points in 25.3 minutes, mostly off the bench. That year, the Warriors upset the Utah Jazz before getting outclassed by the Lakers in the Western Conference Semifinals.

The following season, the Warriors traded Short to Houston for a first-round pick and center Dave Feitl. He spent two seasons with the Rockets before closing his career with one season as a New Jersey Net. Short remained in the NBA following his playing career, spending decades with the National Basketball Players Association before becoming director of player programs in 1999. He is currently the eighth-leading scorer in Warriors' franchise history and seventh in the time since they moved to the Bay Area.

The 2012 Draft

In the NBA, the best teams make the most of their draft picks. It is where franchises are built. It is where holes are filled.

After years of futility, the Warriors had been getting better at drafting. The fate of the franchise changed in 2009 when Stephen Curry fell to them in the seventh slot and they did not squander the opportunity. While 2010 first-round pick Ekpe Udoh eventually failed to live up to his defensive potential, they followed that up with Klay Thompson in 2011.

During the 2011–12 season, Golden State finally secured their white whale: a quality center. The team had disappointed in the lockout-shortened campaign and swapping Monta Ellis for Andrew Bogut also made it easier for the team to retain their first-round pick, which had been traded away years before in the ill-fated Marcus Williams deal. The Warriors would only keep that choice if it ended up in the top seven and that late season tumble put them in a tie for seventh with the Toronto Raptors. After winning a coin toss, Golden State narrowly held on to their lottery selection.

All of that set the stage for the 2012 Draft. If the Warriors were going to be a contender, it would require another successful draft. Since they still were not attractive enough to attract a top-notch free agent, the front office had to continue building through the draft.

Bob Myers, who the team had recently promoted to general manager, entered his first draft as the head man, knowing he had a point guard in Curry, a shooting guard in Thompson, a power forward in David Lee, and a center, he hoped, in the recovering Bogut.

He also had three picks in the 2012 draft: No. 7, No. 30, and No. 35.

The team's most pressing need was a fifth starter, small forward per traditional lineups. There were two in the draft who were expected to be really good: Kentucky's Michael Kidd-Gilchrist and North Carolina's Harrison Barnes, but most experts did not expect either to be on the board when it was the Warriors' turn.

They also needed a backup center in case Bogut did not work out, a long-term backup point guard behind Curry, another scorer off the bench, and anyone who was actually good at defense.

Heading into draft night, the signs pointed to the Warriors selecting Dion Waiters, a guard out of Syracuse who drew comparisons to Dwyane Wade. Consultant Jerry West, who advocated strongly for Thompson the year before, liked Waiters. Barnes and

Kidd-Gilchrist were expected to be off the board. The best big man likely remaining on the board, Andre Drummond of Connecticut, was a project who likely needed time to develop. The Warriors wanted someone more ready to play with such a high pick.

There was an outside chance Kidd-Gilchrist would fall to the Warriors, mainly due to his poor shooting, but he was a great defensive player who had the skills to mesh with the Warriors' other four starters, making him a fit for the team.

As can happen in the draft, things shook up quickly after clear top pick Anthony Davis was taken first overall. While many expected Barnes to go to the local Charlotte Bobcats, they chose Kidd-Gilchrist instead.

While Washington stuck with its expected pick of Bradley Beal, a guard to pair with point guard John Wall, Cleveland completely changed Golden State's plans by taking Waiters at four.

Myers had wanted Barnes all along and placed the forward second on the team's draft board, but they did not see a scenario where they could actually get him until Cleveland chose Waiters.

Since Portland was a guarantee to take Oakland product and eventual 2013 Rookie of the Year Damian Lillard with the sixth pick to fill their void for a point guard, all the Warriors needed was for Sacramento to draft someone else at number five. The Kings obliged by taking power forward Thomas Robinson.

Thrilled, Myers and the Warriors were able to get their man in Barnes.

However, they were just getting started. In the Bogut for Ellis trade, Golden State acquired former We Believe standout Stephen Jackson but moved him to San Antonio for swingman Richard Jefferson, with the Spurs giving the Warriors their first-round pick since Jefferson had an additional year remaining on his sizable contract. That pick ended up being the final selection of the first round, and the front office had their eyes on a sleeper.

When it was their time to choose, they had a few players in mind and opted to go for size by selecting Festus Ezeli, a center out of Vanderbilt. He was the kind of big, strong athlete they needed on both ends of the floor and the Warriors could afford to develop him since they were banking on Bogut playing.

The front office was thrilled with their first round. After all, they were able to pick two players they wanted who also filled important needs. While the Warriors had traded their own second-round pick in the 2010 sign-and-trade for Lee, they ended up with a superior pick from when they traded Brandan Wright and Dan Gadzuric to the New Jersey Nets for Troy Murphy the year before. Just five spots after Ezeli, one of their first-round possibilities was still on the board. Following the path for both Barnes and Ezeli, the front office was thrilled to pick Draymond Green, a senior out of Michigan State who played defense and was known for winning.

While draft experts praised the Warriors' night, it ended up surpassing even the front office's most lofty expectations.

Barnes and Ezeli became immediate starters since Bogut was not healthy to start the 2012–13 season. With a strong supporter in head coach Mark Jackson, Green became a factor off the bench as a rookie. The three developed together and eventually became an excellent supporting cast for Curry and Thompson.

That season, the Warriors made their first postseason appearance in six seasons and all three rookies started at least one playoff game. Barnes shifted from small forward to power forward when Lee went down with an injury as Golden State shocked the Denver Nuggets, then Green started in their Game 2 win in San Antonio a round later.

After another successful campaign in 2013–14, the trio all played significant roles in Golden State's 2015 championship, with Barnes and Green starting in every appearance while Ezeli provided some pivotal minutes off the bench in the decisive Game 6.

The next season, Green, Barnes, and Ezeli were all major factors when the Warriors won an NBA-record 73 regular season games, though Ezeli and Barnes battled injuries during the year. While the Warriors failed to win the championship, all three members of the 2012 Draft class had become essential components of two history-making teams.

Green's status as a second-round pick allowed him to hit free agency first and the soon-to-be All-Star signed a five-year, $82 million contract to stay with the Warriors in 2015. Due to the four-year contract structure for first-round picks, Barnes and Ezeli had to wait a year and neither secured an extension that same off-season. When the Warriors secured the services of Kevin Durant right as Barnes and Ezeli hit free agency, they had to let both of them go in order to clear salary cap space for the new star, leading Barnes to join the Dallas Mavericks and Ezeli to go north to the Portland Trail Blazers.

While Green's continued dominance puts his impact far ahead of his fellow 2012 rookies, the trio of Green, Barnes, and Ezeli made the playoffs all four seasons together and helped the Warriors win their first championship in 40 years.

39 Andre Iguodala

While David Lee was the first prominent free agent to join the Warriors from a different team in the current era, Andre Iguodala helped mark and create the transition to title contender.

After spending eight seasons in Philadelphia, including one All-Star appearance, one All-Defensive team selection, and three seasons averaging more than 18 points per game, the 76ers traded

Iguodala to the Denver Nuggets as a part of the massive four-team blockbuster that sent Dwight Howard to the Lakers. His season in Denver proved to be a massive success as he helped lead them to a 57–25 record and the No. 3 seed in the Western Conference. Despite a strong performance on his part, Iguodala and the Nuggets were upset in six games by the sixth-seeded Warriors.

That summer, Iguodala faced unrestricted free agency for the first time and had a bevy of interested suitors. Interestingly, he took a meeting with the Warriors despite their insufficient salary cap space and pursuit of fellow free agent Howard following his rocky season in Los Angeles. After Iguodala committed to signing in early July, the Warriors were able to send three expiring contracts to the Utah Jazz to clear the space, with two first-round picks as the necessary sweetener.

Iguodala immediately stepped into the starting lineup at small forward and combined with Andrew Bogut to instill a defensive edge on the young team. They jumped from 14th to fourth that first season but Iguodala ended up on the losing end of a first-round series for the second season in a row, this time to the Clippers.

After Steve Kerr replaced Mark Jackson as head coach, he made an unusual decision that required a massive buy-in from one of his team's best players. Iguodala had started every single game of his 806-game professional career and played a significant part in the team's success the prior season, but Kerr wanted to see Harrison Barnes' fit with the starting lineup. Iguodala's acceptance of the change helped set the table for fellow starter David Lee doing the same after Draymond Green succeeded in his role while Lee recovered from a strained hamstring to start the season. While Iguodala's minutes declined, he still played an integral role on the surprisingly dominant squad and finished fourth in Sixth Man of the Year voting.

In the playoffs, the veteran's responsibilities and playing time both increased since his ability to fit in with starter-heavy groups while still anchoring the second unit made him a natural bridge between the two units. Over the first three rounds, a lineup with Iguodala in place of Bogut that put Draymond Green at center succeeded in limited minutes, including some significant stretches against Memphis after falling behind in the series.

After LeBron James and the Cavs took a 2–1 series lead in the NBA Finals, at the prompting of assistant Nick U'Ren, Coach Kerr decided to make a major change. Iguodala had been the team's best defender on James to that point and Green at center opened up new offensive possibilities. The shift paid off on both ends of the floor and Iguodala provided a surprising scoring punch with 22, 14, and 25 points as the Warriors won three straight games and the NBA championship. Iguodala was named the Finals MVP and crystallized the "Strength in Numbers" mantra of the remarkable season. That night, Green reflected on the veteran's sacrifice and significance, remarking, "I always said Andre's a pro's pro. He's a professional guy and it showed, and that's why he's MVP of the series and that's why we're champions."

Over the following two seasons, Iguodala maintained a similar role and workload to 2014–15, finishing second in Sixth Man of the Year voting for 2015–16 and 2016–17. During the 2016–17 season, he stepped up when Kevin Durant missed time due to injuries with some of his best play as a Warrior. He was also healthy for the 2017 NBA Finals and was a major factor in the decisive Game 5, scoring 20 points in a whopping 38 minutes. That summer, Iguodala spurned other offers and decided to return on a three-year contract, helping keep the team and the dominant Hamptons Five lineup of Curry, Thompson, Iguodala, Durant, and Green together.

40 Jason Richardson

It had been more than seven years since Jason Richardson played for the Warriors when he announced his retirement in November 2015, but his connection to the franchise was clear as he sat courtside at a Warriors game.

He choked up after a rousing ovation met him at half court. He shared a few words with the sellout crowd as another ovation followed.

The relationship between Warriors fans and Richardson cannot really be explained, only felt.

"I don't understand it," Richardson said about his popularity. "It amazes me. It really does. Why me? I didn't win many games. I wasn't an All-Star. I never guided them to the promised land. But Warriors fans have always shown me incredible love. Even when I was on other teams.... So much love. So much."

Although he was never a part of any Warriors teams with sustained success, few players are as popular in the franchise's history as Richardson. He will not be a Hall of Famer and his jersey will not be retired but he is a legend for a generation of Warriors fans.

During the dark time that was Warriors basketball in the early 2000s, Richardson brought a sense of pride to the Warriors. Selected fifth overall in the 2001 NBA Draft out of Michigan State, his arrival came on the heels of the worst season in the franchise's Bay Area history, the 17–65 debacle. Looking at it with some added hindsight, Richardson was at the tail end of a long line of Warriors futility.

In 2002, Richardson gave the Warriors rare positive recognition on a national scale when he blew away the field in the 2002 NBA Slam Dunk Contest in Philadelphia, giving Golden State

Jason Richardson winning the 2002 slam dunk competition.
(AP Photo/Gene J. Puskar)

a meaningful presence on the NBA's biggest weekend. It had been five years since the Warriors had an All-Star and eight since they made the playoffs, so Richardson's performance in the dunk contest served as a major highlight for Warriors fans. Facing off against Gerald Wallace in the final round, Richardson needed a 45 on his final dunk to win it. He lobbed the ball in the air, caught it off the bounce, and went up for what looked like a traditional windmill dunk but in mid-air Richardson contorted for a two-hand backward dunk, sending the arena into a frenzy and clinching the title.

As the defending champ, Richardson returned for an encore in the 2003 contest in Atlanta and he did not disappoint. In the final round, on the heels of a highlight-reel dunk from SuperSonics leaper Desmond Mason, Richardson needed a 48 to win it.

"He's got to show me something I haven't seen before," Kenny Smith, a judge and former dunk contest winner, said during the broadcast as Richardson collected the ball. "He can't do a dunk that I've seen."

Richardson tightened his shorts and walked to the right corner of the court, backing up into the bench filled with All-Stars in street clothes. He threw the lob to himself, but it wasn't right so he tried it again.

"I don't think throwing it in the air is going to do it," Smith said, seconded by his cohosts. "People have seen that."

Richardson tossed it high in the air and ran behind it as it bounced near the rim, then jumped, caught it, whipped it backwards between his scissoring legs, and dunked it backwards with his left hand.

As the arena went crazy—All-Stars running around, fans at Philips Arena screaming, announcers hyperventilating—Richardson stood calmly right where he landed under the basket. With both arms raised in the air, and the Warriors logo across his chest, Golden State fans had a reason to be proud. Finally.

"I've seen something," Smith screamed on the TNT broadcast, "I've never seen before."

Richardson was finally able to top that moment by helping bring the Warriors glory where it really matters. He was a central figure on the 2006–07 Warriors squad that finally broke their postseason drought. Known among Warriors fans as the We Believe season, Richardson played a big part in Golden State's upset of the top-seeded Dallas Mavericks in the first round, the first time a No. 8 seed advanced in a seven-game series. He was the star in the return of the NBA playoffs to the Bay, scoring 30 points in the Warriors' emphatic Game 3 win.

He was the happiest of the Warriors when they clinched the series in Game 6 at Oracle.

A month after his career highlight, Richardson had his heart broken. The Warriors traded him to the Charlotte Bobcats on draft day in exchange for the draft rights of eighth overall pick Brandan Wright. The Warriors lost 58.1 percent of their games in Richardson's six-year tenure but Richardson wanted to stay. His departure is still one of the more frustrating front office mistakes in Warriors history even if the trade was originally intended to be part of a larger deal for star Kevin Garnett that never materialized.

To this day, Jason Richardson jerseys can be seen at Oracle Arena and all around the Bay Area.

"They respected my play," Richardson said. "Not my talent, but that I brought it every night. For a losing team, that's all they wanted and that's how I played. I think that's why they really have love for me."

41 Favorite Underdog

For almost 30 years, the Warriors occupied a rare, special niche in NBA fandom: the favorite underdog.

While the franchise started their time in the Bay Area far closer to traditional power than also-ran and even boasted one of the league's top young stars in Wilt Chamberlain, they became less threatening and more accessible after missing the playoffs for nine straight seasons starting just three years after their NBA championship in 1975.

Another central element to the Warriors' status was their special, engaging teams during the seasons they were actually good. While other franchises have long bouts of trouble and disappointment with a few seasons of success, no one else produced Run TMC, We Believe, and the amazing 1993–94 team. Even without their underdog status, those three squads had all the hallmarks of a fan favorite: talented young players, colorful characters, cool uniforms, and the freewheeling style of Nellie Ball. Those teams were interesting enough to keep an eye on whenever they received the national TV spotlight during the regular season and then produced fascinating playoff series when they made it.

During that time period, the Warriors were also able to maintain a broad base of appeal by not scarring too many rival fan bases. From the start of Run TMC in 1989–90 until the championship season in 2014–15, the Warriors made the playoffs six times but only won three series and all of them were memorable upsets: the We Believe team downing the top-seeded Mavericks in 2007, Run TMC over the No. 2 seed Spurs in 1991, and the first Curry/Thompson/Green playoff team shocking the third-seeded Nuggets in 2013.

Two other great examples of this are Sleepy Floyd's 51-point game that was the Warriors' only win of that 1987 second-round series against the Lakers and Baron Davis' iconic dunk on Andrei Kirilenko that came in the We Believe team's only win of the series after their upset of the Mavericks. Bluebloods like the Lakers and Celtics are hard-pressed to generate broad-based enthusiasm even for theoretical fan favorites because of their frequent success, consistent star power, and long histories with so many other franchises.

As strange as it sounds, one of the other reasons the Warriors successfully maintained their status as a favorite underdog was the seemingly perpetual turmoil the franchise dealt with during that time. Trading Robert Parish and Kevin McHale for Joe Barry Carroll, losing Chris Webber after one year due to his feud with Don Nelson, and the disastrous Cohan years elicited well-earned sympathy around the league, especially since even in down years, devotees flocked to the Oakland Coliseum Arena/Oracle and produced a special environment that affected opposing players and rival fans alike.

Another element of the Warriors' appeal was that while the Bay Area is and was significant as an overall metropolitan area, it never gained the big-market label of Los Angeles or New York. Before their recent run of success, Bay Area teams were able to operate in the gray area between the monoliths and small markets without drawing too much resentment from either camp.

While recent success has changed this dynamic, basketball enthusiasts around the world still have a unique relationship with the Warriors due to their decades as an engaging underdog with intensely devoted fans.

42 Steve Kerr

By the fall of 2010, new Warriors owners Joe Lacob and Peter Guber—months after they'd won the bidding war for the franchise—knew they were moving on from Don Nelson. The Hall of Fame–bound head coach had burnt out on the gig and was not who they wanted to lead the team into uncharted waters.

With that in mind, they tapped assistant coach Keith Smart to run the show while they got their bearings as NBA owners. By the end of that first season, they were ready to hire the leader of their franchise.

Their first call was to Steve Kerr.

Kerr had long been a friend of Lacob. Kirk Lacob, son of the Warriors' new CEO, was set to do an internship under Kerr with the Phoenix Suns before he stepped down as the general manager. Lacob knew Kerr's basketball mind, understood his pedigree, and was convinced he was the perfect fit despite a lack of head coaching experience.

However, Kerr was not ready to get back into the grind. Just a year removed from a rigorous stint with the Suns, he was enjoying himself as a color commentator for TNT. Kerr knew he wanted to coach at some point but needed more time to recharge and get his philosophy down.

"He told me to call him in three years," Lacob said. "I said, 'Well Steve, I'm going to have to hire somebody. This job won't be available in three years.'"

Lacob was wrong. The job was open in three years, but again Kerr was not available.

Before the Warriors' job become vacant when the team fired Mark Jackson, Kerr had already started down the road to becoming the coach of the New York Knicks. Phil Jackson, Kerr's former coach with the Chicago Bulls, took the job as Knicks team president and tapped Kerr as his guy. Their relationship was such that it was just a matter of working out the details. Kerr was loyal to Jackson.

The Warriors were so convinced Kerr was going to the New York Knicks, they went after Stan Van Gundy after kicking the tires on then-college coach Fred Hoiberg and veteran coach Lionel Hollins, to name a few.

Then Kerr called. While working the Western Conference Finals, he let the Warriors know he was interested in hearing their pitch. It was the inkling the Warriors needed and they dropped everything to fly to Oklahoma City to interview Kerr.

Steve Kerr, Kevin Durant, and GM Bob Meyers enjoy Durant's introductory press conference on July 7, 2016. (AP Photo/Beck Diefenbach, File)

When they got there, he blew them away. Kerr had already drawn up an advanced offense and prepared plans for both what to do with the Warriors and how he would take them to another level. Plus, since he had already known Lacob and general manager Bob Myers for years, they knew they would all work well together. Kerr topped the Warriors' list all along and the interview confirmed that conclusion.

This confidence was critical because the Warriors had won 51 games the previous year and, despite having two injured centers, nearly upset the Los Angeles Clippers in the first round. They were coming off two consecutive postseason appearances, something the franchise had not done since the 1990s. Plus, the firing of Mark Jackson polarized the fan base and upset star point guard Stephen Curry.

That complicated context meant the Warriors absolutely had to nail this hiring and the results prove they did. Kerr turned down the offer from his friend and mentor to resurrect the lowly Knicks and accepted the Warriors' five-year, $25 million offer to maximize their rising franchise.

Kerr may have been the perfect coach to elevate the Warriors to another level. He won five championships in his 16 NBA seasons. He played alongside some of the game's greatest players in Michael Jordan, Tim Duncan, and Scottie Pippen, which gave Kerr credibility with players despite his lack of coaching experience.

Along the way, Kerr had also been coached by two of the greatest ever in Phil Jackson and Gregg Popovich, plus his stint as Phoenix's general manager had him working closely with offensive wizard Mike D'Antoni. That diverse experience gave Kerr plenty to draw from in terms of game planning, player development, and motivation.

His stint as general manager, overseeing the run-and-fun Suns led by Steve Nash, gave him experience in the front office, a perspective most head coaches do not have. That understanding also helped the Warriors specifically since their previous regime was marred by a rift between the front office and the coaches.

Kerr's NBA connections landed him two big guns as assistant coaches. Alvin Gentry, the former head coach of the Phoenix Suns and a bright offensive mind, left the Los Angeles Clippers to become Kerr's top assistant, while Ron Adams, one of the most respected defensive coaches in the NBA, left the Boston Celtics to serve as the Warriors' defensive coordinator. Jarron Collins and Luke Walton, two former players and bright young coaches on their way up in the ranks, also joined the staff. Kerr had all the support a rookie head coach would ever need.

He began by winning over Stephen Curry, the star who was vocal about his support for Mark Jackson. The two played golf together and talked about his plans for building on what they had started under Jackson.

Kerr wound up winning over the entire locker room by maintaining key elements of the Jackson era. He did not ditch their team slogan "Just Us" or drastically change how they operated. On top of that, Kerr consistently praised Jackson publicly and behind the scenes, while also validating what they had accomplished.

Kerr also upgraded the elements of the team that were holding the Warriors back. Their offense transitioned to a motion style emphasizing movement, passing, cutting, and getting out in transition instead of relying heavily on isolations and post-ups. In Jackson's final year, the Warriors ranked 12th in the NBA in Offensive Efficiency at 105.3, which marked an improvement over 104.2 the year before. In the first year with Kerr's offense, they finished second in offense, averaging 109.7 points per 100 possessions.

While Kerr's incorporation of analytics and advanced concepts catapulted the Warriors' offense, the bigger concern was whether he could keep the Warriors playing the defense Jackson inspired. During his three seasons, Golden State become a reliably stout defensive team, something the franchise had not been able to pull off for decades.

As it turned out, Kerr's emphasis on offense did not take away from defense. The Warriors got better on that end, too. Golden State finished a strong third in defense during Jackson's final season and actually improved to first in the league the next season and stayed in the top four each of Kerr's first three seasons.

Beyond the x's and o's, Kerr had to work hard to maintain or even improve the great chemistry the team built under Jackson. He got Andre Iguodala to take a reserve role and deftly managed the transition of Draymond Green replacing David Lee in the starting lineup during and after Lee's hamstring injury. Late in the season, and pivotally in the NBA Finals, he experimented with lineups where Green played center while keeping both young center Festus Ezeli and veteran Andrew Bogut on the bench.

The storybook season ended in appropriate fashion, with an NBA title, the first for a new head coach since Pat Riley with the Lakers in 1982.

That off-season, Kerr decided to undergo two surgeries on his ailing back and the complications from those created an unusual challenge for the reigning champions. After the title, Gentry departed for the head job in New Orleans and Kerr's complications forced him to miss an unforeseen amount of the regular season. He decided to give young Luke Walton the reins, keeping Adams in a stable role as defensive coordinator and reliable advisor. The team responded with a league-record 24 straight wins to start the season and a remarkable 39–4 record when Kerr returned to the sideline on January 22, 2016. Amazingly, the Warriors kept on their historic pace even after the changeover and broke Kerr's 1995–96 Bulls record with 73 regular season wins. Despite missing the first three months of the regular season, the league honored Kerr with the 2016 NBA Coach of the Year Award.

After that summer's successful trip to the Hamptons, Kerr had to integrate former MVP Kevin Durant and a massively turned-over team with their 73-win core. It took some adjustments early but the Warriors still finished the 2016–17 season with the best record in the NBA, marking a different kind of three-peat during Kerr's first three seasons as head coach.

During the 2017 playoffs, Kerr surprisingly had to leave the sideline again to deal with more complications from his 2015 back surgeries, this time handing the reins to former Cavs head coach Mike Brown. The team went 9–0 while he recovered but Kerr was able to return for Game 2 of the NBA Finals and then coached the Warriors to their second championship in three years. That success was a wonderful reflection of Kerr's impact on the franchise since his system, staff, and players can survive and even thrive when he cannot be on the sideline, which is a truly remarkable achievement.

43 StephVP

It was early evening on May 3, 2015. Stephen Curry found a quiet spot in his Orinda home. He had broken away from his family as his wife, Ayesha, daughter Riley, parents, Dell and Sonya, and siblings, Sydel and Seth, continued partying in another room.

Meanwhile, Curry found a chair of perspective.

He took a seat in a quiet room, a place where he could stare at nothing and be captivated by the cinematography of his memories. Before long, tears were streaming down his face. His lips moved slightly as whispered prayers seeped from his heart. He shook his head slowly in disbelief.

Curry was the MVP.

The frail kid from Charlotte who was scarcely recruited out of high school and could only muster a walk-on invitation from the college where his father starred was the Most Valuable Player of the best basketball league in the world.

The one-trick pony who was too small, too weak, and not athletic enough to thrive at the NBA level, who was only good for his shooting and did not possess the skills or mentality to master the point guard position, was the MVP.

The injury-prone guard who was supposed to become the next star doomed by injuries, whose fragile ankles could not hold up, was the MVP.

What Curry pulled off was enough to blow his mind in this moment. His family had surprised him with the news before it went public. They revealed it to Curry in personalized t-shirts—Ayesha's said, "Wife of the MVP," Sonya's said, "Mom of the MVP," and so on—he had beaten out Houston's James Harden for the NBA's most-coveted award.

Curry's 23.8 points and 7.7 assists were not even career highs since he had averaged 24 points and 8.5 assists the year before. Even so, his 2014–15 season was his most special yet because he spent the entire 82 games debunking all the previous slights levied against him while leading the Warriors to the best record in the NBA.

He shed the label of a poor defender.

Coach Steve Kerr stopped hiding Curry on that end of the court and he improved significantly. Quick hands, improved strength, and better grasp on how to maneuver and attack weaknesses turned Curry into an asset on defense. He not only set a career high for steals per game (2.0), but advanced stats reflected the improvement as well.

The Warriors gave up 101 points per 100 possessions when Curry was on the floor, three fewer than the previous season and

11 better than his worst defensive season. Curry actually finished second among point guards in Defensive Real Plus-Minus, ESPN's statistic that attempts to measure on-court impact by incorporating elements including performance and teammate quality.

"I knew he was better defensively than people gave him credit for," Kerr said. "But what he's done this year at that end is remarkable."

He became more efficient.

Curry's 48.7 percent shooting was his best since his third season, when he played just 26 games because of ankle injuries.

He eclipsed his own NBA record for most three-pointers in a single season with 286, making them at a remarkable 44.3 percent clip. At the same time, he increased his usage rate to a career high while significantly lowering his turnover rate from the prior season.

The result was the most proficient and productive season in Curry's career. He finished the season third in Player Efficiency Rating at 28.06, a massive leap from 10th, 19th, tied for 25th, 32nd, and 92nd in his previous seasons.

He dominated.

Harden had a strong contingent for MVP with a frequently argued narrative that he was doing more with less and carrying injury-riddled Houston. Curry, on the other hand, was playing on a loaded roster and had an easier time.

While it had many proponents, that analysis was too superficial and undervalued Curry's impact. Curry played 80 games that season but he only appeared in 60 fourth quarters because he and his team were so dominant that many games were over by the end of the third quarter. In a way, Curry could not show his clutch bona fides because the opportunities rarely presented themselves. The Warriors outscored opponents by 9.4 points over the first three quarters when Curry was on the court, which led the league.

If the games did get close, the Warriors leaned even heavier on Curry. That explains why he ranked fifth among qualified players in scoring average down the stretch of close games, as Golden State went 21–5 in games that were within five points in the final five minutes.

On top of that, when he was not breaking defenses with his own shots, Curry drew so much attention it freed up his teammates to thrive.

Statistics only painted part of the picture. The eye test also showed Curry had reached another level.

He became a Vine sensation.

Over that season, Curry became one of the reasons the NBA has become the favorite sport of social media types. In an existence centered on short-burst sensationalism, Curry is the perfect athlete. He wows in a blink. The flashiness of his game is perfectly captured in six- and 15-second intervals, and the jaw-dropping nature of his work requires being rewound multiple times—convenient on the likes of Vine and Instagram.

Nobody knows that better than Chris Paul.

The Los Angeles Clippers point guard, who used to dominate Curry, became the victim in two of Curry's most viral highlights.

The first, on March 8, 2015, was a dribble move that would've made Curly Neal chuckle. He crossed over left to right to evade Matt Barnes on the left wing at the three-point arc, a move that took him into a triple team, then dribbled it back through his legs into his left hand, freezing Clippers center DeAndre Jordan, who was at the left elbow of the free throw line, blocking Curry's path to the paint. In a blink, Curry whipped the ball back to his right hand just under the swipe of Paul, who was closing in behind Curry, then one more detour eluded Clippers big man Spencer Hawes, who was waiting at the free throw line. Headed back out toward the three-point line, Curry turned, fired, and drilled the three-pointer.

Coach Steve Kerr famously was on the sidelines with his hands in the air and a "What are you doing?" look on his face. After Curry made the three, Kerr walked back to his bench shaking his head. "Chagrined to gratified within like three seconds," Kerr said after the game. "That pretty much sums it up."

The next Curry special that sent the Internet into a frenzy came 23 days later with Paul reprising his role as the victim.

This time at Staples Center, Curry dribbled down the middle of the lane where Jordan was waiting, so he passed through without taking a shot and dribbled toward the right corner with Paul chasing Curry the whole way. On the baseline, Curry suddenly changed directions, dribbling behind his back like he was about to drive back into the paint, so Paul had to stop on a dime. While the perennial All-Star and former nemesis was still adjusting to the first move, Curry shifted back the other way with *another* behind-the-back dribble. Paul buckled to the hardwood, the Warriors' bench went crazy, and social media exploded.

Over the course of the 2014–15 season, Curry became a sensation. While winning the MVP cemented his status as a dominant force in the league, that season's playoff run and the Warriors' championship turned him into a global superstar.

44 Baron Davis

Boom Dizzle. Too Easy. B. Diddy.

The sheer number of nicknames could have made it clear that the Warriors acquired a star when they traded for Baron Davis on February 24, 2005. For a Warriors squad in a decade-long rut, he was exactly what they needed.

Davis was an elite talent with a flair to his game that proved engaging for fans and teammates alike, making him an instant injection of hope and excitement into the Warriors. Trading for Davis was the signature move in Chris Mullin's tenure as general manager as they acquired a two-time All-Star while only sending back part-time starting guard Speedy Claxton and aging big man in Dale Davis.

Five years after the Hornets drafted him, Davis missed most of the first half of the 2004–05 regular season and his clashes with coach Byron Scott and the organization fueled the team's desire to move the unquestionably talented point guard. That desire opened the door for Mullin and the Warriors to make a deal, particularly at that astonishingly low price.

Davis came off the bench the first nine games, while Derek Fisher—signed away from the Lakers the prior off-season—held the starting role. In his 10th game with the Warriors, he took over as the starting point guard and never looked back.

Led by Davis, the Warriors started to turn the season around in March. He scored 33 in a showdown with Steve Nash that produced a rare Warriors victory in in Phoenix, immediately followed by a road win against the playoff-bound Sacramento Kings. The improbable back-to-back wins gave life to the thinking the Warriors were on their way.

Later that season, Davis averaged 24.4 points and 11.4 assists during an eight-game win streak, including 40 points, 13 assists, five rebounds, and five steals in a home upset of the Houston Rockets.

The Baron Davis era was officially blooming.

After that season, the Warriors drafted Monta Ellis. While Davis only played 54 games the next year due to various injuries, by the end of the 2005–06 season the Warriors had two critical pieces in place beyond franchise stalwart Jason Richardson. The third came in August 2006, when the Warriors fired Mike Montgomery and brought back Don Nelson, the last coach to lead the Warriors to the playoffs.

Nelson had been a point guard whisperer in his coaching career, with Tim Hardaway and Steve Nash among his greatest works. It made sense that the unconventional coach and Davis could become a productive duo, even if the pairing had the potential to be combustible due to their personalities.

While Davis flourished the first two months in Nelson's system, averaging 21 points and 8.5 assists, the team was only 16–16 at the end of 2006, so Mullin looked to give Davis some help. A trade for Stephen Jackson and Al Harrington brought some players for Davis, Richardson, and the steadily improving Ellis to run with but it took some time, particularly since Davis had to undergo in-season arthroscopic knee surgery that caused him to miss almost all of February. A six-game losing streak without Davis to end the month had the season spiraling to another playoff-less season but the team still had not spent much time at full strength.

That turned in a road game at Eastern Conference power Detroit on March 5, 2007, where Davis returned to the lineup and outplayed Chauncey Billups in the blowout Warriors win. That sparked the Warriors to dig in for one last push, which ended up changing the season.

The Warriors won seven of their next 11 to get back into the playoff picture, then closed the season by winning 9 of 10 to sneak into the playoffs. During that run, Davis had 34 points, 15 assists, and nine rebounds in a showdown with Washington All-Star point guard and former Warrior Gilbert Arenas, and another strong 25 points and 10 assists in Houston. In a win-and-in game on the final day of the season, he notched a triple-double with 12 points, 14 assists, and 10 rebounds in Portland, clinching the Warriors' first playoff appearance in 13 years.

That late push earned the Warriors the No. 8 seed and a first-round matchup with top-seeded Dallas Mavericks, who had won

67 games. Davis immediately flexed his dominance with one of the greatest postseason performances in Warriors playoff history. He totaled 33 points, 14 rebounds, eight assists, and three steals as Golden State picked up a massive upset win in Dallas that set the tone for the series. Davis averaged 25 points, 5.7 assists, and 6.2 rebounds in the six-game upset.

Davis continued to produce in their second-round series against the Utah Jazz. He scored 17 points in the second quarter of Game 1 as the Warriors narrowly lost and added 36 points in Game 2 but missed a free throw down the stretch that helped Utah send it to overtime, where the Jazz won it and took control of the series.

In Game 3, at Oracle Arena, Davis provided the signature moment of the We Believe playoff run. The Warriors were up 20 in the final minutes and the game was all but over. In fact, Ellis was at the scorers table ready to take out Davis, who would finish with 32 points and nine assists in a crucial game.

Before the next dead ball, Davis dribbled the ball on the left wing. A hesitation allowed him to get past Jazz point guard Deron Williams with a clear lane to the basket. Jazz defensive wizard Andrei Kirilenko rotated over to contest the shot but Davis exploded and threw down a one-hand tomahawk dunk over Kirilenko that nearly turned Oracle Arena into a Roman coliseum.

"I shocked myself on that dunk," Davis said after the game. "Knowing we were up, I just tried my luck."

"It was the greatest dunk I have ever seen with my eyes in person," added teammate Jason Richardson, a two-time dunk contest champion.

The Warriors went on to lose the series in five games but it was clear they were going places with Davis. However, it would all end soon.

After a surprisingly tumultuous off-season for the franchise, Davis played all 82 games of the 2007–08 season, something he had not done since 2001–02, and averaged 21.8 points, 7.6 assists,

4.7 rebounds, and 2.3 steals in 39 minutes per game. While the Warriors won 48 games, their highest win total since 1993–94, they did not make the playoffs in a daunting Western Conference. That is still the most wins by a team that did not make the playoffs.

Behind the scenes, Davis' relationships in the franchise were eroding. He was a divided star, as his off-the-court interests were taking off and he had a business-savvy, Hollywood side to him. Raised in South Central Los Angeles, Davis played high school ball in Santa Monica, where he was friends with Kate Hudson and frequently spent the night at the home of Goldie Hawn and Kurt Russell. His best friend growing up was Cash Warren, son of actor Mike Warren, best known from the hit TV series *Hill Street Blues*. Davis went to play college ball at UCLA, where his Hollywood connections increased. When he started his NBA journey, Davis was already developing his mogul side. In 2008, he released a documentary called *Crips and Bloods: Made in America*.

While Davis sought to increase his endorsement deals while hobnobbing in the entertainment world, he also clashed with Nelson. Team president Robert Rowell didn't like that Davis' interests were divided and he carried himself like a star.

The night after the Warriors won at Milwaukee to cap a four-game winter road trip in January, Davis was in Park City, Utah, for the showing of his documentary at the Sundance Film Festival. The next afternoon, he played 39 minutes as the Warriors lost at home to lowly Minnesota. Two months later, the Warriors beat the Lakers in Los Angeles, then flew home and lost to the same Lakers at Oracle in overtime. After the game, Davis headed back to Los Angeles for a celebrity-filled birthday party in West Hollywood, which Ellis also attended. A few weeks later, with the Warriors in the heat of the playoff chase, Davis had another party on his actual birthday, April 13, in Arizona. The next night, he was 2-for-13 in the first half at Phoenix. Nelson benched him for the second half even though the Warriors were hanging on for their postseason lives.

Heading into that off-season, Davis held a $17.8 million player option, meaning he could become a free agent. Rowell, among a few others in the organization, believed Davis was not fully committed to the Warriors. Mullin disagreed, or felt his talent superseded those potential issues, so he and Davis worked out a deal where the star would pick up his $17.8 million player option and then the two sides would add a three-year, $39 million contract extension on top of it, meaning four years and $56.8 million in total.

Rowell nixed the agreement, so Davis opted out of his contract and signed a five-year, $65 million deal to play for the Los Angeles Clippers. Just like that, after Davis had finally breathed life into the Warriors, it was over.

45 Mitch Richmond

Mitch Richmond was driving left but New York Knicks point guard Mark Jackson was waiting with the help, so Richmond spun back to his right and looked to launch into a turnaround jumper from just right of the free throw line. Knicks guard Gerald Wilkins, a defensive specialist once dubbed the Jordan Stopper (to his own demise), was all over Richmond. That turnaround jumper proved to be a pump fake, but it was the second pump fake that sent Wilkins flying into the air, allowing Richmond to duck under him for a clean look. Knicks seven-foot center Patrick Ewing was coming, so Richmond, with Wilkins coming down on his back, lofted his shot over Ewing's outstretched arm and rimmed it in.

That shot counted for two of Richmond's 37 points that night, on 14-for-21 shooting. Richmond was a rookie making his

Madison Square Garden debut against a Knicks squad that was 23 games over .500 and headed for the No. 2 seed in the East.

As impressive as the final numbers were, how Richmond scored was what stood out. It was his smoothness and instinctiveness. The soft touch on his jumper. The variety of angles he could get his shot off and make it. The mastery in the way he used his frame—he was 6'5", 215, and strong enough to be nicknamed "the Rock"—to impose his will.

Richmond won the 1989 NBA Rookie of the Year after averaging 22 points per game. It was clear he was a gem, a natural scorer who would pose problems for NBA defenses for years to come. That season, Richmond had nine 30-point games, including a 47-point outing against Sacramento. In all but one of those contests, he shot better than 50 percent from the floor. The Warriors had nailed their pick in the 1988 Draft with the shooting guard from Kansas State.

"Being drafted by the Golden State Warriors, my first team, I really, truly loved the area, I loved the teams, I loved how we played," said Richmond, who won a bronze medal in the 1988 Summer Olympics. "I just had an opportunity to come in right away and start and get familiar with the offense. With Chris [Mullin] and some of the guys on that team, it really helped me and propelled me to win the Rookie of the Year. It was definitely a team effort."

Not many players can spend just three years with a team and be considered a legend of that organization. Richmond did just that.

His three-year run in Oakland, 1988 to 1991, produced some of the greatest memories in Golden State Warriors history at a time when the fans were desperate for something to feel good about.

Richmond was a superb scorer who, with Chris Mullin, gave the Warriors a potent offensive player on both wings. Mullin was a lights-out shooter while Richmond, who could also stroke it well, could score in just about any fashion. Michael Jordan, widely considered the greatest to ever play the game, said Richmond was the toughest shooting guard he ever had to defend.

After winning 20 games the season before, the Warriors finished 43–39 and made the playoffs in Richmond's rookie season. That would have been enough on its own but with Mullin and Richmond leading the way, the seventh-seeded Warriors swept the No. 2 seed Utah Jazz, who boasted future Hall of Famers John Stockton and Karl Malone, in the first round of the Western Conference playoffs. Richmond's averages during that series were incredible: 25.7 points on 58 percent shooting with 8.3 rebounds and 6.3 assists. In the next round, the Warriors lost to the Phoenix Suns in five games, but their promise was obvious. Richmond was a cornerstone for something special coming. A month later, the Warriors drafted Tim Hardaway to complete their perimeter.

The fast-paced, high-scoring trio would transform the Warriors into the highest-scoring team in the NBA that season. They missed the playoffs that season, though Richmond increased his scoring despite taking fewer shots than his rookie season.

1990–91 was when Run TMC blossomed and Richmond's dominance played a major part in both their success and resonance around the basketball world. His 23.9 points per game, on 49.4 percent shooting, was his highest scoring average over his first eight seasons and the Warriors returned to the playoffs with a 44–38 record.

In the postseason again, the Warriors pulled off another upset by taking down the second-seeded Spurs led by David Robinson in the first round. Yet again, Golden State lost in the second round, but in encouraging fashion. They lost to the Lakers largely because the Warriors' frontcourt was still an issue, but it was clear the Warriors were going somewhere with their fantastic young core if they addressed the issues.

Unfortunately, before Run TMC could really get going and before Richmond could fully maximize his obvious potential, he was gone.

Just before the start of the 1991–92 regular season, Don Nelson remembered the team's issues in the frontcourt against the Lakers and stunningly decided to trade Richmond to the Kings with Les Jepsen and a second-round pick for Billy Owens, a 6'9" power forward who, on paper, fit perfectly in Nelson's up-tempo system. Richmond said, "That was a tough call to get." And while he remembers his time as a Warrior fondly, he notes that Nelson "broke up something special that could have went on for a long time."

Richmond became a star in Sacramento, playing seven seasons for the Kings and leading them in scoring each year. He made five consecutive All-NBA teams, six straight All-Star teams, and won an Olympic gold medal in 1996. Richmond spent three years of his twilight on the Washington Wizards, then finally won a championship in his final NBA season as a member of the 2001–02 Lakers.

While Warriors fans were thrilled when Richmond was enshrined in the Naismith Memorial Basketball Hall of Fame in 2014, that joy also came with some anguish since more of his seasons should have come in a Warriors uniform.

46 Wilt's 100

Al Attles likes to brag about that night in Hershey, Pennsylvania, on March 2, 1962. Then a starting guard for the Philadelphia Warriors, his version of events from this historic night in basketball has a different twist.

"I tell people all the time," Attles says in his trademark gravelly voice, "me and Wilt Chamberlain combined for 117 points that night."

He is right. Attles made all eight of his shots and his only free throw attempt. He finished with 17 points in the 169–147 win over the New York Knicks.

Chamberlain had 100.

It's one of the holy grail record in sports, right up there with Joe DiMaggio's 56-game hit streak and UCLA's 88-game win streak. It is the landmark moment for a legendary sports figure whose talent and athleticism still mystifies to this day.

The game was not televised and there is no video footage. Only 4,124 spectators attended the game at the Hershey Sports Arena, though the number claiming to have been there is much, much larger. Perhaps the best account of this game is Gary Pomerantz's 2006 book *Wilt, 1962: The Night of 100 Points and the Dawn of a New Era*.

The Warriors were clearly the superior team, coming in with a 46–29 record and headed to the playoffs. With four games left in the season, the 27–45 Knicks were playing out the string and they were without starting center Phil Jordan, who officially missed the game with the flu, but his backup, Darrall Imhoff, confirmed in a 2012 *Los Angeles Times* article that the team suspected Jordan had a hangover.

The game was all but over after the first quarter, with the Warriors ahead 42–26. The Knicks cut the deficit to 11 at halftime but the Warriors were never in real danger. In the locker room at halftime, according to the book, future All-Star Warriors guard Guy Rodgers suggested the Warriors keep dumping it down low to Chamberlain and see how many points he could get. First-year Warriors coach Frank McGuire obliged.

The Knicks had no chance of denying Chamberlain—who was 7'1", 275 pounds, with world-class athleticism—or stopping him once he got the ball. Chamberlain, who had 41 points at halftime, put up 28 points in the third quarter even as the Knicks triple-teamed and fouled him unabashedly. The Warriors pushed their lead back up to 19 and Chamberlain was on the heels of breaking his career high of 78 points.

The once-sleepy crowd was fully into the game when Chamberlain scored his 79th point at the 7:51 mark of the fourth quarter. In the book *Tall Tales: The Glory Years of the NBA* by Terry Pluto, Chamberlain recalled hearing the fans yell for 100 points once he reached the 80-point plateau. Chamberlain said he was tired and thought he had aptly satiated the lust for a record by getting to 80, which no player had ever done before.

"I got 80," Chamberlain turned to Attles and said. "What's the difference between 80 and 100?"

The public address announcer was now counting Chamberlain's points over the sound system. With six minutes left in the game, the Knicks' main goal was stopping Chamberlain from getting to 100. They began milking the clock and intentionally fouling Chamberlain's teammates.

The Warriors, wanting to get Chamberlain to 100, started intentionally fouling the Knicks to stop the clock and give the Warriors more possessions. McGuire even brought in four bench players to play with Chamberlain so his key players would not foul out.

Inside the final minute, with Chamberlain on 98 points, the drama intensified. The audio of the last 90 seconds of Bill Campbell's call on WCAU radio is available on YouTube, immortalizing teammates Joe Ruklick and Ted Luckenbill with Chamberlain.

"Rodgers throws long to Chamberlain. He's got it. He's trying to get up. He shoots. No good. The rebound Luckenbill. Back to Chamberlain. He shoots. Up. No good.

"The rebound Luckenbill. Back to Ruklick. Into Chamberlain. He made it! He made it! He made it! The Dipper Dunk! He made it! The fans are all over the floor.

They stopped the game. People are running out on the court. One hundred points for Wilt Chamberlain!

"They stopped the game. People are crowding, pounding him, banging him. The Warriors players are all over him. Fans are coming out of the stands. Forty-six seconds left. The most amazing scoring performance of all time. One hundred points for the Big Dipper."

Chamberlain played all 48 minutes and converted 36 of his 63 field goal attempts. A career 51.1 percent free throw shooter, Chamberlain went 28-for-32 from the free throw line and scored 31 points in the fourth quarter.

Before he died in 1999, Chamberlain often ended the retelling of his 100-point game with a story about having to ride home with some Knicks players. And when he got out of the car of Willie Naulls, who had 31 points that game, Chamberlain said he apologized for the hundred.

47 Old-School Gear

While being a Warriors fan has been hard for much of the last 30 years, one perk then and now is the team's amazing selection of old-school gear.

The Warriors have used a series of different uniforms and logos since their move to San Francisco and just about all of them carry significant visual appeal. More amazingly, despite the team's struggles, they have produced quality memories in just about all of the variations, so fans have plenty of quality options worthy of consideration.

1962–63 and 1963–64: The Warriors' first uniforms in San Francisco worked as a bridge from their Philadelphia style, with drop shadowed lettering and the same color set. The 1963–64 team, which included Wilt Chamberlain, Guy Rodgers, Nate Thurmond, Al Attles, and Tom Meschery, donned these on their way to the 1964 NBA Finals.

1964–65 and 1965–66: A short-lived shift with a bold-script "WARRIORS" on the front only had two seasons in circulation but they encompassed both Wilt Chamberlain's final season with the Warriors and Rick Barry's rookie year.

1966–67 to 1970–71: The City. Some of the most popular uniforms in NBA history were worn by giants in franchise history, including Rick Barry, Nate Thurmond, Al Attles, and San Francisco native Tom Meschery in his final season with the team.

1971–72 to 1974–75 and 1975–76 to 1983–84: While the Warriors kept most of their signature jersey elements throughout the '70s and early '80s, they did change the home color from gold to yellow while shifting the text on the front of the jersey from "Golden State" to "Warriors" after the 1975 championship. That 1974–75 team is full of great options (Rick Barry, Jamaal Wilkes, Phil Smith) but there are a slew of others, including Nate Thurmond, World B. Free, Bernard King, and Jim Barnett.

1984–85 to 1986–87 and 1987–88 to 1988–89: The team maintained the general style of their 1970s jerseys but changed their home color from yellow/gold to white for the late '80s. Fan favorites Chris Mullin, Sleepy Floyd, Mitch Richmond, Larry Smith, and Manute Bol wore these during their Warriors tenures.

1989–90 to 1996–97: The classics popularized by Run TMC were still worn by the surprise 1993–94 team with Chris Webber and Latrell Sprewell. Fans interested in inflicting pain on their brethren could also consider sporting a Billy Owens, Todd Fuller, or Joe Smith jersey from this era.

1997–18 to 2001–02 and 2002–03 to 2009–10: Two similar styles in the Cohan era, with the biggest difference being the earlier version's emphasis of lightning bolts on the side of the jersey and pants. The We Believe team is the headliner but these squads boast a wealth of "wait, him?" players who would be fun, including Gilbert Arenas, Donyell Marshall, Brian Cardinal, Muggsy Bogues, Larry Hughes, Jamal Crawford, and Anthony Randolph.

2010–11 to 2013–14 and 2014–15 to 2016–17: Many worthwhile options from the time after the most recent ownership change, particularly considering their recent success.

Of course, there are plenty of other non-jersey options, including shooting shirts, jackets (the mid-90s warmup jacket is a personal favorite), hats, and socks.

48 "Sleepy Floyd Is Superman!"

Sleepy Floyd scores again!
Sleepy Floyd is Superman!

"And he was," former Warriors forward Tom Tolbert said in a Fox Sports Bay Area interview. "There was no kryptonite that day. It didn't matter what he did, the ball was going to go in the hoop."

Legendary Bay Area voice Greg Papa shouted those memorable words on May 10, 1987, when Eric Floyd—nicknamed "Sleepy" after getting called out for sleeping on the court during a fourth grade basketball game—pulled off one of the greatest performances in NBA history.

Nearly 28 years before Klay Thompson set a new mark with 37 points in a single quarter, Floyd established a place in Warriors' history with 29 points in a quarter. The 6'3" point guard from

Georgetown, who made one All-Star game in his career, played the quarter of his life.

Amazingly, Floyd's indelible moment came in the fourth quarter of a nail-biter of a playoff game against a Los Angeles Lakers squad featuring three future Hall of Famers, while being guarded by one of the best defenders of his time in Michael Cooper.

The Warriors were on the verge of getting swept in the second round of the 1987 playoffs, down 102–88 entering the fourth quarter of Game 4 in Oakland. However, Floyd had gotten hot toward the end of the third quarter and it kept rolling into the fourth.

Floyd, a scoring point guard at his best, was a great penetrator. He had a jerkiness to his game that made it hard for defenders to keep him in front and he knew his way around the rim. With an arsenal that included finger rolls, pull-ups, and bank shots, if Floyd got into the lane, he could make it happen.

That night, pushed to the brink by the Lakers' dominance—and trash talk, he would later reveal—Floyd had everything clicking.

After a finger roll to open the fourth quarter, he converted a three-point play that changed the tide of the game. He slipped past Cooper, spun away from Mychal Thompson, and scooped a finger roll that Kurt Rambis goaltended—plus the foul. The Warriors were suddenly down just nine.

That dropped to seven after Floyd's breakaway dunk, then five after he drove right around Cooper for a baseline layup. Floyd taking Cooper off the dribble at will became a theme of the quarter despite Cooper's almost permanent status on the NBA's All-Defensive team. Cooper made the first team that season but Floyd had his way with him.

Next up was Byron Scott, the Lakers' other defensive stopper. He did not stand a chance either. Floyd lost Scott easily with a crossover, leaned into Kareem Abdul-Jabbar, and banked in a floater off the glass, capping a run that put the Warriors up by three.

The next time down, Floyd blew by Scott again down the right side of the lane, then jumped to his left across the rim and scooped in a left-handed layup off the glass.

At one point, Floyd seemed to be toying with Cooper. Isolated at the top, he jabbed like he was about to drive and Cooper flinched in reaction, but Floyd pulled back. He did it again, and Cooper reacted again, and Floyd pulled back. This happened two more times before Floyd eventually pulled up for a jumper that rattled in.

"Everything slowed down for me," Floyd told the *Mercury News* during a 2013 visit to Oracle Arena. "It felt like I was wide open. But when I look at the tape and see the difficult shots I made, I see most of them were contested. It was just a perfect storm of events."

For this one game, Floyd had the Warriors in the role of the superiors. For a franchise and a fan base that had mostly known heartbreak and disappointment, Floyd gave them 12 minutes of feeling like the universe was on their side.

For one quarter, Superman wore blue and gold.

49 Jamaal Wilkes

Jamaal Wilkes was a part of historic success before joining the NBA and that continued during and after his time with the Warriors. His game also fit in with that reputation since he worked hard on defense and passed willingly despite being a capable scorer. Wilkes' unusual shot inspired a unique description from Lakers coach Paul Westhead: "Snow falling off a bamboo leaf." It's worth watching clips on YouTube to fully appreciate it.

Wilkes attended UCLA for four years and his college teams won their first 93 games, including an undefeated freshman campaign alongside Bill Walton when freshmen could not play varsity and two undefeated NCAA championship seasons after that. Nicknamed "Silk" by a member of the UCLA band due to his playing style, Wilkes was a consensus first team All-America twice as a Bruin and made the NCAA All-Tournament team in 1972.

Despite all that success, Wilkes fell to the 11th pick in the 1974 NBA Draft and joined a Warriors team that had just missed the playoffs after three straight years in the postseason. He took on a starting forward role immediately and won Rookie of the Year, averaging 14.2 points and 8.2 rebounds per game as the Warriors finished first in the Western Conference. He then scored 20-plus points in five Western Conference playoff games, including 23 in their Game 7 win over Chicago, which put Golden State in the NBA Finals.

Facing the 60–22 Bullets, who had just taken down the Celtics in six games, Wilkes had the task of defending Elvin Hayes, who was first team All-NBA after finishing fifth in the league in both scoring and rebounding. The rookie was up to the task on both ends, scoring 11.5 points per game while making life hard on Hayes as the Warriors completed the shocking sweep and won the NBA Championship.

Wilkes continued to have a large role on the next two Warriors teams, making the All-Star Game in 1976 while increasing his scoring to 17.8 and 17.7 points per game. His reputation on defense also grew, leading to All-Defensive team selections in both 1975–76 and 1976–77. While the Warriors made the playoffs both of those seasons, they fell in their second series each time, meaning they were never able to make a return trip to the NBA Finals. Wilkes averaged just under 19 points per game in their seven-game series loss to the Lakers in 1977.

That summer, Wilkes hit free agency for the first time and decided to return to Southern California and join those same Lakers who had just knocked out the Warriors, becoming an integral support player around Magic Johnson and Kareem Abdul-Jabbar. In a turn that is both haunting and reflective of the league at the time, Wilkes wanted to stay with the Warriors but, as he put it years later, "This was at a time when the NBA was changing from owners who owned a team as a hobby to big business. Our owner was a well-intentioned guy, but I don't think he had the funds."

Wilkes got his chance to play for the NBA title again in 1980 and again came up big in the decisive game. With Abdul-Jabbar out due to an ankle injury, he scored 37 points and added 10 rebounds in a performance that was overshadowed by Johnson starting at center and hitting the iconic "Junior Sky Hook." Appropriately, one of the league's best support players made a massive contribution to a championship but stayed in the limelight.

After his second title, Wilkes stayed with the Lakers for another five seasons and won rings in 1982 and 1985, though he missed the 1985 playoffs due to tearing ligaments in his left knee that February. That injury functionally ended Wilkes' career, as he played just 13 more NBA games as a member of the L.A. Clippers before retiring.

Wilkes became a successful motivational speaker and financial planner after retirement and was enshrined in the Naismith Memorial Basketball Hall of Fame in 2012.

The 1966–67 Season

The 1966–67 Warriors provided the template for success after Wilt Chamberlain, but ended up as more of an anomaly than expected.

After trading Chamberlain during the All-Star break of the 1964–65 season, San Francisco went 35–45 while incorporating Rookie of the Year Rick Barry and allowing Nate Thurmond to spend a majority of his time at center. That off-season, they built around the Thurmond/Barry core by trading aging Hall of Fame point guard Guy Rodgers to the Chicago Bulls for guards Jim King and Jeff Mullins, both of whom would become All-Stars for the Warriors. Head coach Alex Hannum ended up following Chamberlain to Philadelphia, so the team replaced him with NBA legend Bill Sharman.

As it turned out, the Warriors' offense actually improved despite replacing Rodgers with Paul Neumann. As prior coach Hannum had advised owner Franklin Mieuli, improving the team's shooting helped create space and different players shouldered the playmaking burden, with six Warriors averaging between 2.5 and 4.5 assists per game. Thurmond flourished in the new system, averaging 18.7 points and 21.3 rebounds and finishing second to former teammate Chamberlain in MVP voting. Barry led the league in scoring at 35.6 points per game in just his second season and finished fifth in MVP voting himself. That foundation fueled the Warriors to a 20–9 start and when San Francisco hosted the All-Star Game that year, the West starting five included Thurmond, Barry, and Rodgers. Even with a lackluster end to the regular season, San Francisco won the Western Division by five games at 44–37 and was the only team over .500 due to the strength of the 76ers and Celtics in the Eastern Division.

Since four of the five teams in each division made the playoffs in those days, the Warriors faced off with the 36–45 Lakers in the first round. Los Angeles had to play without star Jerry West due to injury and never really threatened, losing two of the three games by double digits. Barry scored 37 points in the sweep-clinching Game 3 and averaged 28 per game in the series as a whole.

That win put them in the Western Division Finals against the second-place St. Louis Hawks, who would win 56 games the next season and featured a talented collection, including guards Lenny Wilkens, player/coach Richie Guerin, forward Lou Hudson, and big men Bill Bridges and Zelmo Beaty. The Warriors won Games 1 and 2 at home by single digits as Barry scored 85 points combined in the two games, but St. Louis followed suit by winning their two home games narrowly as well despite Mullins pouring in 40 points in Game 4. Needing another victory to retain control, the Warriors took a 32–22 first quarter lead in Game 5 and never looked back, putting the Hawks' backs against the wall. Like San Francisco the game before, the Hawks stormed out to a massive first-quarter lead but the Warriors chipped away at the massive 39–21 deficit and actually led by the end of the third quarter. Twelve minutes later, they were on their way to their second NBA Finals since moving in 1962.

Unfortunately, they were staring down a true giant in NBA history. The Philadelphia 76ers set league records for wins (68) and margin of victory (9.44 points per game) in the regular season before eliminating the eight-time reigning champion Celtics in five games. Chamberlain won the MVP and was a dominant figure, but the 76ers were a deep team, including Billy Cunningham, Chet Walker, and Hal Greer.

Despite those vastly different profiles, the Warriors forced overtime in Game 1, though Philadelphia eventually prevailed 141–135. In Game 2, the 76ers dominated from start to finish, winning 126–95. When the series returned to San Francisco, Barry scored 55 in a Game 3 triumph but Philadelphia bounced back with a 122–108 road win that largely sealed the series. Even with championship aspirations fading away after the loss, the Warriors rebounded with an astonishing 33–13 fourth quarter that forced a Game 6 in San Francisco. There, the Warriors took a narrow halftime lead and held it through the third quarter but a big fourth-quarter run and clutch Chamberlain free throws followed by a put-back gave Philadelphia a lead. After Barry missed a tough shot, the 76ers secured the jump ball and made two free throws to seal a championship that was both their first in Philadelphia and the first in Chamberlain's illustrious career.

With a 25-year-old Nate Thurmond and Rick Barry just 23, even with the series loss it looked like the Warriors were on their way to becoming a league power. However, that game at San Francisco Civic Auditorium was the last Rick Barry would play in a Warriors uniform for five years and the franchise would not make another NBA Finals until 1975.

51 Number One Picks

Since the end of territorial selections with the 1966 NBA Draft, the Warriors have started or finished the draft process with the No. 1 overall pick three times. That history has been dotted with successes but also shows the amazing missed opportunities for the franchise.

1980

The Boston Celtics landed the first overall pick through a 1979 trade with the Detroit Pistons and ended up dealing the selection the night before the draft to the Warriors in a deal that dramatically affected the fortunes of both franchises. The Celtics traded the No. 1 and No. 13 selections in the 1980 Draft to the Warriors for the No. 3 pick and center Robert Parish, who had just finished his fourth season and averaged 17 points and 10.9 rebounds per game at 26 years old.

What makes this move so devastating is how those draft choices turned out. The Warriors took center Joe Barry Carroll No. 1 and he had a somewhat underappreciated career (20.6 points, 8.3 rebounds, and 1.7 blocks per game in seven seasons with the team and made the 1987 All-Star team). He failed to elevate the franchise, which only made the playoffs once during his tenure. At No. 13, Golden State took another center, Rickey Brown, who played low-end rotation minutes and spot starts for two and a half seasons before being traded to the Atlanta Hawks for a future second round pick. Boston selected Kevin McHale third overall and he put in a Hall of Fame career entirely in a Celtics jersey. McHale and Parish helped Boston win three championships while combining for 16 All-Star appearances in Green and White.

1993

Thirteen years later, both the Orlando Magic and Golden State Warriors had massive jumps in the lottery: the Warriors went from the seventh worst record to the No. 3 pick while the Magic took the best non-playoff record and a 1.52 percent chance of winning the lottery all the way to the No. 1 pick. Those unlikely leaps ended up inspiring significant changes to the lottery process, but that had to come the next season.

Those two teams then swapped their picks on draft night, with the Warriors moving up to No. 1 in order to secure Chris Webber at the cost of their No. 3 overall choice and first-round picks in 1996, 1998, and 2000.

Chris Webber won Rookie of the Year that season, becoming a central figure in the Warriors' surprising 16-win improvement and playoff berth. Unfortunately, Webber's contract included an opt-out after his first season and the talented big man wielded that to leverage a trade after that single season.

Orlando selected guard Anfernee "Penny" Hardaway third overall and he combined with Shaquille O'Neal to form one of the NBA's most exciting young duos. However, after beating the Bulls and making the 1995 NBA Finals, O'Neal left for the Lakers in 1996 and Hardaway's career derailed due to injuries after spectacular 1995–96 and 1996–97 campaigns.

Amazingly, Golden State's 1996 and 1998 first-round picks included in the draft-night deal made it back to them, through

Chris Webber, left, of Michigan and Anfernee Hardaway, right, from Memphis State, shown with their new hats following a trade after they were selected in the 1993 NBA Draft. (AP Photo/Lennox Mclendon)

Orlando trading them to Washington for guard Scott Skiles the next summer and then Washington including them in the aforementioned Webber trade four months later. The Warriors then used those choices on Todd Fuller and Vince Carter, who was traded in another massive draft-night swap for Antawn Jamison. The other first round pick in the trade became Mike Miller (2000).

1995

Substantially more straightforward than the other two, the Warriors won the 1995 Draft lottery with the fifth worst record. They used their luck to select Joe Smith, a power forward from Maryland who had just won the Naismith College Player of the Year in his sophomore season. Smith started his entire rookie season and was first team All-Rookie after averaging 15.3 points and 8.7 rebounds. He maintained his starting spot for another season and a half before Smith encouraged the Warriors to trade him with just a few months remaining on his rookie contract, which they ended up doing by sending him and guard Brian Shaw to the Philadelphia 76ers for veterans Clarence Weatherspoon and Jim Jackson.

While Smith never reached his lofty expectations, he did have a 16-season NBA career.

What makes the Smith pick painful are the players chosen immediately after him: Antonio McDyess, Jerry Stackhouse, Rasheed Wallace, and Kevin Garnett, each of whom had a more productive career than Smith.

Interestingly, another five first overall picks since 1965 ended up playing for the Warriors during their careers: Andrew Bogut (2005), John Lucas (1976), Cazzie Russell (1966), Ralph Sampson (1983), and Kwame Brown (2001).

52 The 1993–94 Season

While the Warriors had a 20-year span full of disappointments and short-lived successes, there was no greater oasis than the 1993–94 season.

Unlike Run TMC or We Believe, the story of that season starts with what was taken away rather than what was built.

After a 55-win season in 1991–92, almost everything went wrong the next season. Chris Mullin, Tim Hardaway, Šarūnas Marčiulionis, and Billy Owens combined to miss 149 games due to injury and the team dropped all the way to 34–48, the seventh-worst record in the entire league.

That luck turned around on lottery night when the Warriors jumped from No. 7 to No. 3, though Orlando received more attention and actually generated reform to the process by jumping from No. 11 to No. 1. Those fortunate teams came together to create an absolute blockbuster of a trade: Chris Webber, the No. 1 overall pick, for Anfernee "Penny" Hardaway, the No. 3 selection, plus Golden State's first-round picks in 1996, 1998, and 2000.

Even with the addition of Webber, Don Nelson's team had a major challenge in front of them. Both Tim Hardaway and Šarūnas Marčiulionis would miss the entire 1993–94 season due to injuries after their absences helped fuel the prior season's swoon. With that in mind, the team signed Avery Johnson that summer to fill Hardaway's spot in the starting lineup.

While Johnson became the starting point guard, second-year swingman Latrell Sprewell took on more of the starring responsibilities. Mullin missed the first six weeks of the season and then mostly came off the bench until January, which opened up even more room for Sprewell, who scored 20 or more points nine times in 13 November games while also averaging more than four assists and five rebounds per contest. He kept that momentum going and made his first All-Star team that February before making the All-Defensive second team and first team All-NBA before his 24th birthday.

Webber maximized the opportunity in front of him as well, logging five straight double-doubles in his first month in the league. His first star-making moment came just four games into his NBA career, when the rookie blocked Danny Ainge's shot and then went behind the back and dunked on reigning MVP Charles Barkley, who was also Webber's favorite player growing up. His special combination of scoring, rebounding, and passing led to some amazing performances, including dropping 36 points, 13 rebounds, six blocks, four assists, and three steals on the Sacramento Kings in an early January win. He finished the regular season averaging 17.5 points, 9.1 rebounds, 3.6 assists, and 2.2 blocks per game and edged out Penny Hardaway for Rookie of the Year.

Even with those two massively positive stories, the Warriors spent November, December, and January around .500. There were also serious signs of the growing feud between Nelson and Webber, including a January film session with the guards where Nelson told them, "You don't give it to [Webber]" when the rookie would ask for it early in possessions. That information unsurprisingly made its way back to Webber and only escalated the tension. The two had a very public shouting match during their February 9 win in Charlotte and less than three weeks later the *San Jose Mercury News* reported that Webber was considering using his opt-out to become a free agent that summer.

Even with the Nelson/Webber drama, the team shifted into a new gear in February with a big six-game win streak that pushed the team to 31–20 and then caught fire in April with an eight-game run using a starting lineup of Sprewell, Mullin, Webber, Billy Owens, and former super-sub Chris Gatling where every player was

6'5" or taller. They finished the season with a 50–32 record, almost in line with the heights of the Run TMC team in 1991–92. On top of that, winning eight straight in April put the Warriors in the No. 6 seed in the West and set up a playoff series against the 56–26 Phoenix Suns.

While the young Warriors had plenty of momentum with strong play since February, the Suns came in with a seven-game win streak of their own, plus the drive to return to the NBA Finals and take advantage of the first playoffs after Michael Jordan's retirement. Led by Kevin Johnson, Cedric Ceballos, and the previously dunked on Charles Barkley, the Suns were certainly a major challenge for even the hot Golden State team.

The best-of-five series started with a 38–23 first quarter for the Suns and did not get significantly better from there for the Warriors. Other than Billy Owens' 27 points and 17 rebounds in Game 1 and a halftime lead in Game 2, the two contests in Phoenix mostly put Golden State in a massive bind against a capable, dangerous team.

Game 3 served as an elimination game due to the best-of-five first-round format and the Warriors started reasonably well, but Barkley took over with 38 points in the first half, which set an NBA playoff record. Despite that, Golden State actually carried a one-point lead into the fourth quarter and only trailed by two points with 2:07 left but could not hold on, losing 140–133. Barkley finished the game with 56 points, his career high and the third-most for a playoff game at the time.

Despite the season ending in a disappointing sweep, there were plenty of reasons for optimism in the Bay Area. Sprewell and Webber provided youthful energy and prodigious talent while Mullin was still performing at a high level when healthy and Hardaway would be able to return the following season.

Five months later, when Chris Cohan's purchase of the team went through before the start of the next season, he met with the players and emphasized continuity. Five weeks after that assurance, the Warriors traded Webber to the Washington Wizards after he exercised his one-year opt-out and Nelson resigned during that season.

What looked like an inspiring beginning to the next Warriors success story became the final playoff team for more than a decade, an oasis in the post–Run TMC desert.

53 The Choke

The frustration had been brewing for nearly two months. P.J. Carlesimo, hired in June 1997, was a raspy-voiced disciplinarian with a whip for a tongue. Latrell Sprewell, the rising star who had watched the franchise crumble around him in three years, clashed with Carlesimo immediately. Sprewell and Donyell Marshall received the brunt of Carlesimo's wrath.

On top of that, the Warriors were losing. Big.

According to a *New York Magazine* profile, Sprewell and Carlesimo were cursing at each other during warm-ups at Indiana— the second game of the season. The Warriors got swept on the four-game road trip to start the season and the team known for scoring twice failed to reach 90 points.

The Warriors lost by 35 to the Los Angeles Lakers, featuring Shaquille O'Neal and Kobe Bryant, in the sixth game of the season. Sprewell was benched for the rest of the game when Carlesimo caught him laughing with Bimbo Coles and Sprewell responded by calling Carlesimo "a joke." The next game, Sprewell did not start and the Warriors lost by 31, scoring just 71 points at home to a bad Detroit Pistons squad getting an off night from All-Star Grant Hill.

Sprewell requested a trade in November and was nearly shipped to San Antonio, but on December 1, he forced the Warriors' hand.

Carlesimo was barking at Sprewell about making crisper passes during a drill and Sprewell told his coach he was not in the mood that day, but Carlesimo continued demanding execution. Sprewell snapped, slammed the ball, and cursed at Carlesimo, who kicked him out of practice. Enraged, Sprewell charged at Carlesimo and put his hands around the coach's neck.

"I'll kill you," Sprewell reportedly shouted as teammates broke it up.

Sprewell was ushered out of practice but when it resumed, he came back shouting threats at Carlesimo and landed a glancing punch before being forcefully removed from practice.

Blow-ups were not new for Sprewell. In his second season, he fought bruising forward Byron Houston in practice and in 1995 he got into it with teammate Jerome Kersey before returning with a wooden beam, ready to rumble. Sprewell could get to his boiling point quickly.

That said, this was next level, a severe violation even greater than assault. Sprewell violated the sacred respect players are supposed to have for coaches and immediately became the preeminent example of how NBA players were out of control.

After the incident, according to a *Contra Costa Times* report, Sprewell went to the office of general manager Garry St. Jean and demanded to be traded. St. Jean was on the phone with Sprewell's agent, Arn Tellem, and Sprewell reportedly snatched the phone from St. Jean and ordered his agent to get him out of Golden State immediately.

The Warriors initially suspended Sprewell for 10 games. A day later, they voided his contract, erasing the remaining three years and nearly $24 million he was due.

The players' union filed an appeal and John Feerick, an independent arbitrator from Fordham University, concluded the punishment was excessive. Sprewell was ordered to be reinstated and the league then suspended Sprewell for the remainder of the season, 68 games.

Sprewell went on to play again. After the conclusion of the 1998–99 lockout, the Warriors traded him to the New York Knicks and Sprewell ended up becoming a key piece to the Knicks' run to that season's NBA Finals and later contributed on the 2003–04 Minnesota Timberwolves, who made the Western Conference Finals. Even with his success before and afterwards, for many people Sprewell's numerous accomplishments are overshadowed by the infamy of The Choke.

54 Bill King

For a generation of fans, Bill King was both the voice of the Warriors and their direct connection to the franchise. Due to the format, radio asks much more of announcer and listener alike and King excelled at conveying the intricacies, emotion, and beauty of the sport.

Born in Illinois, King grew up listening to Harry Caray and Bob Elson call baseball games in the Midwest and started broadcasting in the armed forces when he shipped out to Guam from San Francisco, falling in love with the city on his first visit. His transition to sports came out of the blue after he returned home when his small radio station desperately needed someone to cover after their normal sportscaster disappeared. After almost a decade honing his craft, King moved to San Francisco in 1958 and began calling San Francisco Giants games in 1959.

Being established in the local sports radio scene made King a natural fit for the Warriors when they moved to San Francisco in 1962. Owner Franklin Mieuli wanted King to do play-by-play on the television broadcasts but the station did not want the bearded King on camera, so Mieuli proposed that they use someone else for the on-camera pre-game and postgame work, which they agreed to.

One of King's famous moments as a Warriors broadcaster has become known as "Mother's Day." On December 6, 1968, King was doing radio for Warriors/SuperSonics in Seattle and became incensed at referee Ed T. Rush for a call shortly before overtime. King asked his engineer to cut his mic, then yelled "You motherfucker!" at Rush, but the crowd mic nearby caught his outburst. While a legend has grown that Rush called a technical on King, making it the only one ever called on an announcer, both King and fellow broadcasting legend Hank Greenwald denied it and Rush said he never even heard the expletive. A few years later, Rush hand-delivered King a Mother's Day card on the anniversary with the note, "You don't know how hard it is to find a Mother's Day card in December."

King's favorite team he ever broadcast was the 1974–75 Warriors, who won the franchise's first NBA championship in California by upsetting both the Chicago Bulls and Washington Bullets in stirring fashion. King kept a notebook that entire season with stories and insights from each game and his family gave a copy of it to Rick Barry years later. His definitive call of the final moments of the clinching Game 4 ended with "Al Attles' Golden State Warriors are champions of the world, they are the unbelievable champions of the world, the Cinderellas of the sports world!"

Part of what makes King's legacy truly special is that he thrived in all three major sports, broadcasting the Warriors for 21 years, the Raiders for 27 years, and the Athletics for 25 years.

King passed away at age 78 in 2005 and was honored with baseball's Ford C. Frick Award, their highest honor for broadcasters, in 2017.

55 Klay's 37

Go to YouTube. Type "Klay Thompson 37." Pick the longest video with at least a million views. Make sure the sound is on.

The moment is more than one of the greatest performances in NBA history, it's a video game played out in real life.

January 23, 2015. Oracle Arena. At the 9:45 mark of the third quarter, Thompson hit a mundane turnaround in the lane. No one knew it at the time but that shot was the start of history. The Sacramento Kings certainly had no idea they would become the victims of one of the greatest shooting displays of all time.

Thompson scored 37 points in the quarter, more accurately in nine minutes and 40.1 seconds. It took down the former record of 33, shared by Hall of Famer George Gervin and Carmelo Anthony. Thompson made all 13 of his shots, tying an NBA record, and made nine three-pointers, the most ever in a quarter.

"That was crazy," said point guard Stephen Curry, who has plenty of his own mind-boggling performances. "I have never seen anything like that in my life."

The Warriors, who were sitting atop the Western Conference standings at the time, had their hands full with the struggling Kings as the game was tied at 58 when Thompson started to take over. He followed that pull-up in the lane with a steal and a three-pointer in transition at the 8:22 mark. They trailed by a point before Curry found Thompson on the wing for a three at the 7:15 mark. With just over six minutes left, Thompson punctuated a fast break with a one-handed dunk off a lob pass from Curry.

It became abundantly clear Thompson was feeling it about 30 seconds later, as he casually pulled up for a wing three and splashed the net. There was no doubt he was hot on the Warriors' next possession.

Thompson was trapped off the pick-and-roll and had to give the ball up. He got it back about 28 feet from the rim. He pointed to the floor, telling Draymond Green to come set a screen for him. Just as Green started to move, Thompson launched the three and

Klay shoots over the Sacramento Kings' Jason Thompson (34) and Ray McCallum (3) during his 37-point third quarter on Friday, January 23, 2015.
(AP Photo/Ben Margot)

it did not come close to missing. He curled off a screen and showed off his quick release on a three from the right wing with 4:19 remaining. Thompson finally hit the rim at the 3:04 mark but the ball bounced high off the backboard and rimmed in.

Thompson ran down court laughing.

With 2:30 left in the quarter and the Kings finally aware he was on fire, Thompson drove to the hole and dropped in a finger roll. Pandemonium ensued at Oracle 23 seconds later when Curry found Thompson with a cross-court pass in transition and Thompson stepped into another three from the right wing.

Nobody was sitting. The cheering was constant in the NBA's version of the Roman Coliseum and they were screaming for another kill.

"You don't get that hot in *2K*," Draymond Green said, referencing the popular *NBA 2K* video game series. "Those video games are real now. That wasn't real.... You can't even do that in a video game."

Thompson was not done. At the 1:37 mark, with several Kings chasing him, he pulled up at the elbow of the free throw line and sank the jumper. After another Warriors stop, Curry pushed it, looking for Thompson the whole way. Thompson, in the right corner, faked the cut to the basket and popped right back behind the three-point line. The split second he created was enough to catch the pass from Curry and drop in another three with 1:07 remaining. It was his eighth three-pointer. The Kings called a timeout as Oracle was in a frenzy. The once-tied game was now a 22-point lead for the Warriors.

He still was not done. Believe it or not, Thompson ended up wide open on the Warriors' next possession. They ran a double screen for him and he found himself alone at the top of the key. Even after a timeout specifically called to cool him off, Thompson made a layup.

The Kings finally gave up and intentionally fouled Thompson in the final seconds, and it turned out to be a smart move by Sacramento to just give Thompson the two free throws because even the three-pointer he hoisted after the whistle blew was all net.

"Even I'm shocked," Thompson said, grappling for words after the game. "I don't even know what happened. It's crazy."

The 1964 NBA Finals

Wilt Chamberlain went up for a shot in Game 1 of the 1964 NBA Finals and Bill Russell blocked it. Nate Thurmond, playing power forward, got the loose ball and went back up with it. Russell blocked that, too. The Boston Garden erupted.

That was the San Francisco Warriors' first appearance in the Finals, two years after the franchise moved from Philadelphia. In Game 1, it was clear they had met their match.

Under new coach Alex Hannum, the Warriors had won 48 games to finish first in the five-team Western Division. They survived a thrilling seven-game series over the St. Louis Hawks, led by Bob Pettit, Cliff Hagan, Lenny Wilkens, and Richie Guerin, but the Warriors' first Finals appearance since moving West was a rude awakening. Not even two big men in Chamberlain and Thurmond, or having All-Star Tom Meschery, was enough to overcome the dominance of the Celtics.

In that series, Russell reestablished the possibility that he was Chamberlain's kryptonite.

The Celtics led by 18 at halftime and cruised to a double-digit victory in Game 1. The next game, also in Boston, was even worse for the Warriors. They trailed by 30 entering the fourth quarter.

Russell had neutralized Chamberlain, keeping him to 54 points in the first two games combined, when Chamberlain had 50 in the pivotal Game 5 of the Western Division Finals.

Plus, the Celtics just had too many weapons. Sam Jones scored 59 over the first two games, while John Havlicek had 28 in Game 1 and Tom Heinsohn had 20 points in Game 2 as Havlicek struggled.

The series shifted to San Francisco and the Warriors won Game 3 easily. They finally held Jones in check and Chamberlain had his biggest game of the series. His 35 points were a counter-punch of sorts to Russell's defensive dominance.

Game 4 was a thriller. The Celtics trailed for most of the first half but surged in the third quarter to take a 12-point lead into the fourth quarter, but the Warriors made a late surge as the crowd became frenetic.

Guy Rodgers took over. He dropped in a left-hand floater in the lane to cut the deficit to six, then came up with a steal that led to a fast break, but Meschery missed the breakaway layup. A free throw by Rodgers cut the Celtics' lead to 92–87 and, after a stop, Chamberlain tipped in Rodgers' missed pull-up to get the Warriors within three with just over two minutes remaining.

With 1:25 left, the Warriors still trailed by three and Rodgers took an ill-advised shot. He got the rebound and Russell knocked the ball off him, giving the Celtics possession. On the other end, a driving Heinsohn appeared to be going for a running hook shot but when the defense came to him, he dropped it off to Russell for a dunk.

Warriors guard Gary Philips answered with a jumper, then the home team got the stop they needed inside of 30 seconds left. Chamberlain got the rebound and tossed it ahead to Rodgers, starting the break. Rodgers slithered his way to the rim for a lefty finger roll.

The Warriors were within a point and the crowd was ready to explode but Havlicek never made it back on defense. The Celtics inbounded the ball quickly and found him streaking toward the basket behind the defense. Philips had no choice but to foul Havlicek with 18 seconds left.

The Warriors' last attempt failed when Meschery's turnaround jumper missed and Boston got the rebound. Instead of evening up the series, the Celtics went back to Boston ahead 3–1 with a 98–95 victory.

The Celtics pulled out another close one in Game 5. Russell punctuated the victory over Chamberlain and the Warriors with a thunderous follow dunk. He then ran down court with one arm straight up in the air as the Boston Garden fans erupted.

That was the Celtics' sixth consecutive NBA championship in a streak that would get as high as eight. For the San Francisco Warriors, it was a rare foray into the NBA elite and an early taste of the ultimate prize that would make the franchise thirsty for a championship but disappointed more often than not.

The next season, the Warriors ended up trading Chamberlain to the Philadelphia 76ers during the All-Star break and released Hannum after that season. Hannum reunited with Chamberlain in Philadelphia and they ended Boston's championship streak in their first season back together. While Chamberlain and Hannum finally bested Russell and the Celtics and won their championship, the Warriors were still about a decade away.

57 Local Warriors

Although he was born in Memphis, Tennessee, on September 17, 1959, Lester Conner was a Bay Area guy through and through.

The 6'6" point guard grew up in Oakland, then attended Fremont High School before splitting time at Los Medanos College in Pittsburg and Chabot College in Hayward, playing basketball at both. He transferred to Oregon State, where he earned the nickname "Lester the Molester" for his relentless defense. After winning Pac-10 Player of the Year, the Warriors selected him with the 14th pick of the 1982 NBA Draft, so Conner came home.

Making it to the NBA is unlikely enough and it is genuinely rare for someone to have the opportunity to play for his hometown team.

"Especially to be drafted by your hometown team. Guys like LeBron James and myself, we're rare," Conner said, referring to the Cleveland star being a native of nearby Akron, Ohio.

Conner played four seasons with the Warriors from 1982 to 1986 before sitting out the 1986–87 season due to a contract dispute and joining the Houston Rockets the following season. He would go on to play for an array of different teams before becoming an assistant coach.

Those four years put Conner in a select class: Bay Area natives who got to play for the Warriors.

In the early years of the league, NBA teams had first rights to snatch up the local stars since it helped with marketing the team in that area. The territorial picks allowed the Philadelphia Warriors to secure the services of Wilt Chamberlain, a Philadelphia native.

Since the league moved away from that rule in 1966, a player landing on his hometown team happens far less. Even so, the Bay

Area has a nice crop of players who have donned the Blue and Gold.

East Bay

In the first year after the NBA eliminated territorial picks, the Warriors selected an Oakland native in Joe Ellis. The 6'6" McClymonds High product played college ball at USF and then all eight of his NBA seasons with the Warriors, including the year the franchise moved to his hometown in 1971. In his career, Ellis averaged 8.8 points and 5.1 rebounds per game.

Nate Williams, another McClymonds High star, played 10 seasons in the NBA, with his last two spent with the Warriors. He totaled more than 1,100 points in just over 2,100 minutes.

Former De La Salle star Jon Barry, son of Warriors legend Rick Barry, spent one of his 15 NBA seasons with the Warriors, and his brother Drew played eight games for Golden State as well.

The Warriors traded for Oakland's Brian Shaw, from Bishop O'Dowd, before the 1997–98 season. Less than four months later, they traded him to Philadelphia. Later a three-time champion with the Lakers, Shaw played 39 games at home.

Berkeley-native Phil Chenier ended his career with the Warriors, playing nine games in the 1980–81 season while Todd Lichti, who played prep ball at Mount Diablo High in Concord, received a 10-day contract to play for the Warriors and appeared in five games.

Jamaal Wilkes, the Hall of Fame forward who won a title with the Warriors in 1975, was born in Berkeley but grew up in Southern California.

Former Duke star DeMarcus Nelson went undrafted in 2008 but the Oakland native earned a spot on the Warriors' summer league team and worked his way onto the roster. With Monta Ellis recovering from his moped incident and back-up Marcus Williams failing to impress head coach Don Nelson, Nelson started on opening night for his hometown Warriors.

"It's been a dream come true, me getting the opportunity to play here," said Nelson, who was waived after 13 games and went to play overseas.

West Bay

Tom Meschery, the first Warrior to have with his number retired, was a San Francisco native. The Lowell High School product starred at St. Mary's College of California and was selected seventh overall in the 1961 Draft by the Philadelphia Warriors. He experienced a homecoming when the franchise moved to San Francisco the following year. The Russian forward (who was actually born in China) was an All-Star in 1963 and played six seasons with the Warriors until the Seattle SuperSonics selected him in the 1967 NBA Expansion Draft.

Phil Smith, a 6'4" shooting guard out of Washington High in San Francisco, was the Warriors' second-round pick in 1974 and played a key role as a rookie on the 1975 championship team. He went on to play six seasons in the Bay Area, making one All-NBA second team, two All-Star teams, and one All-Defensive team, averaging at least 19 points in four straight seasons.

Saint Ignatius star Bob Portman, after playing college ball at Creighton, returned home when the Warriors drafted him with the seventh overall pick in 1969. He appeared in 221 games over four seasons.

Golden State drafted Balboa High School's Willie Wise 64th overall in 1969 but he chose the ABA's Los Angeles Stars over the NBA. Marlon Redmond, another Balboa product, was drafted 60th overall by the Warriors in 1977, but they cut him before the season began.

Keith Erickson, the former UCLA star and Olympic volleyball player who spent his first of 12 NBA seasons with the Warriors, was born in San Francisco.

South Bay

Before Linsanity took over Madison Square Garden, Jeremy Lin starred at Palo Alto High School, where he and his teammates captured a 2006 state title in an upset victory over powerhouse Mater Dei. Incidentally, Lin played high school basketball against current Warriors assistant general manager Kirk Lacob. Kirk's father (team owner Joe Lacob) remembered Lin, which became relevant later on.

After four years at Harvard, Lin went undrafted in 2010. When he lit up the NBA Summer League that same year, many teams were interested in the Bay Area product, but he chose to sign with the Warriors. It was a dream come true for Lin.

Although he rarely played during the regular season and made numerous trips to Reno to play in the NBA Development League, Lin developed a cult-like following amongst Warriors fans and frequently received some of the loudest ovations of the night whenever he stepped foot on the court at Oracle Arena.

Even so, Lin's stint in the Bay Area would be short-lived, as after one season with the Warriors, the team cut the fan favorite on the first day of training camp in 2011.

Camden High's own Raymond Townsend was the Warriors' first-round pick in 1978. Taken at No. 22, he spent two seasons with the Warriors before the Dallas Mavericks selected him in the 1980 Expansion Draft.

Golden State signed San Jose native John Coughran, who attended Piedmont Hills, before the 1979 season. In two separate stints that season, Coughran totaled 68 points in his 24-game NBA career, all spent with his local team.

58 Becoming the Golden State Warriors

When the Warriors moved from Philadelphia to San Francisco in 1962, Franklin Mieuli, a local marketing guru, was part of the group that bought the team. After one year, and even with star Wilt Chamberlain on the team, San Francisco did not show much interest in the Warriors and the initial investors wanted out, which is how Mieuli ended up buying out the rest of the investors and becoming sole owner of the franchise.

The city's indifference for the Warriors continued, leaving the Warriors struggling financially. In 1965, during the team's third season in San Francisco, a frustrated Mieuli traded Chamberlain back to Philadelphia since he had not been the draw Mieuli expected.

"He's a good friend of mine. But the fans in San Francisco never learned to love him," Mieuli said after the trade. "I guess most fans are for the little man and the underdog, and Wilt is neither. He's easy to hate, and we were the best draw in the NBA on the road, when people came to see him lose."

The lack of interest in the Warriors continued. Before the 1971–72 season, reports leaked that the Warriors had a deal in place to play games in San Diego, where the NBA team had vacated for Houston. Mieuli was reportedly set to announce an arrangement where the Warriors would play 29 games in San Diego at the San Diego International Sports Arena and the games would be televised in Oakland. The remaining 12 games would be at the Pacific Auditorium in Oakland and televised in San Diego.

Whether it was a plot by the media-savvy Mieuli or real developments, the franchise announced a change of its name to from the

San Francisco Warriors to the Golden State Warriors, giving credibility to the talk. Either way, in August 1971, the Warriors worked out a deal to play all of their home games in Oakland.

In 1972, the team moved into the Oakland Arena, now known as Oracle Arena, exclusively. Although the Warriors decided to call Oakland their only home, the franchise stuck with "Golden State"—even though three other NBA franchises call California home—in a decision that also fueled the natural rivalry between the East and West Bay.

After winning the 1975 championship, the Warriors held their parade in San Francisco despite playing all of their regular season home games in Oakland. During the 2015 championship run, speculation abounded over where the Warriors would have a parade should they win it all. With the franchise set to move to San Francisco, the Warriors opted to have the parade in Oakland. Approximately 1 million people showed up in downtown Oakland and Lake Merritt.

The pending move back to San Francisco provides the opportunity for another name change. While a return to San Francisco branding would have made sense a few years ago, the franchise's amazing success and rapidly elevated profile seem to have put the brakes on changing back and owner Joe Lacob expressed a similar sentiment at the Chase Center groundbreaking in January 2017. As such, it looks like the Golden State Warriors moniker will be around for the foreseeable future.

59 Guy Rodgers

Guy Rodgers played a fascinating and pivotal part in the Warriors' transition from Philadelphia to San Francisco, becoming a linchpin in their early success after the move.

A Philadelphia native, the Warriors used a territorial selection on Rodgers in 1958 after he was Philadelphia player of the year in high school and a two-time all-American at Temple University.

At just 6 feet tall, Rodgers made his mark in the league as a passer and ball-handler. Celtics guard Bob Cousy faced off with him in the early part of Rodgers' career and talked about how he did not like going against Rodgers "because you knew you'd have to work both ends of the court."

Reportedly Oscar Robertson once said, "Guy was the greatest passer, dribbler, and ball-handler that he'd ever seen." Rodgers received a natural playing partner in Wilt Chamberlain one year later. The point guard had twenty assists in Chamberlain's legendary 100-point game two seasons later.

Unlike some of his older teammates, Rodgers followed the Warriors to San Francisco and reached new levels of success. He led the league in assists that first season with 10.4 per game while making his first of four All-Star games. In 1963–64, Rodgers was an All-Star again, orchestrating the Warriors' offense on their way to a 48–32 record and the 1964 NBA Finals. In total, Rodgers made three All-Star teams in his four seasons as a San Francisco Warrior.

In 1965–66, Rodgers averaged a then-career-high 10.7 assists per game but his persistent lack of shooting playing next to the Warriors' young talent (including rookie Rick Barry) drove coach Alex Hannum to advocate for trading Rodgers for a point guard who was a better stylistic fit, even as Rodgers finished second to

Barry in scoring with a career-high 18.6 points per game. While owner Frank Mieuli refused that season, he eventually followed Hannum's advice and sent Rodgers to Chicago for Jim King and Jeff Mullins in 1966. In Rodgers' only full season with the Bulls, he dished out a career-high 908 assists, which is still Chicago's franchise record by an astonishing 246.

Despite success in his previous two stops, Rodgers continued moving around the league, playing most of the next season with Oscar Roberston, Jerry Lucas, and the Cincinnati Royals after an early season trade before being selected by the Milwaukee Bucks in the 1968 Expansion Draft. In 1969–70, Rodgers played his final NBA season with rookie Kareem Abdul-Jabbar, an appropriate ending to a career that first flourished playing alongside Wilt Chamberlain.

At one point, Chamberlain said, "[Rodgers] was better than Cousy or Jerry West or Robertson or Walt Frazier or Peter Maravich or anyone." High praise considering the Big Dipper's history in the game and multitude of talented teammates.

Rodgers was enshrined in the Naismith Basketball Memorial Hall of Fame in 2014.

60 Mullin vs. Rowell

Who knows when it began behind the scenes, but the beef between top basketball executive Chris Mullin and team president Robert Rowell spilled into the public arena in 2008.

First, Mullin worked out a contract with star point guard Baron Davis. Mullin traded for Davis in 2005 envisioning the dominant-but-problematic point guard would lead the franchise somewhere.

Davis did, guiding the Warriors to the 2007 playoffs, snapping a 13-season postseason drought and shocking the top-seeded Dallas Mavericks. The two agreed on a three-year, $39 million contract extension, but Rowell, who owner Chris Cohan left to run the franchise, nixed the deal. He wanted Davis to opt out of the final year of his contract, set to pay him $16.4 million, before getting the contact. Davis indeed opted out, but left the Warriors to sign a five-year, $65 million contract with the Los Angeles Clippers.

That August, Warriors guard Monta Ellis tore the deltoid ligament in his ankle riding a moped but initially lied to the Warriors about it, saying he got hurt playing basketball. Ellis, who was supposed to pair with Davis to provide the one-two punch that would move the Warriors forward, put the coming season in jeopardy.

Mullin's approach was compassion. He drafted Ellis in 2005, a second-round pick who successfully made the jump from high school to pro. At the time, Ellis was just 23 and justifiably afraid because he had just signed a six-year, $66 million contract after three years near the NBA minimum. Mullin believed Ellis, who required surgery and would miss most of the season, was already paying a price and felt it would be better for Ellis' development if the organization put an arm around him. After all, the talented young guard would be going through serious rehab and working to make sure this injury did not ruin his career. If the Warriors supported him through that, it would forge a strong connection between Ellis and the franchise and that loyalty could then be a selling point to potential free agents.

However, Rowell wanted Ellis to be punished. In late October, the Warriors slapped him with 30-game suspension and Rowell's explanation to the media threw Mullin under the bus. "Chris Mullin made it perfectly clear to both Mr. Cohan and myself that he didn't think this was a big deal at the beginning, and we happen to think it's a very big deal," Rowell said. "We happen to think that it's a big deal for our fans, it's a big deal for our season ticket holders, it's a big deal for our business partners, it's a big deal for the Warriors."

Rowell's decision to suspend Ellis was not about taking games away since the injury would cause him to miss more than those 30 games. It did cost him $3 million and Rowell maintained the Warriors would still consider voiding Ellis' contract, which the franchise had the right to do because it prohibited riding mopeds. Ellis was obviously not happy with that decision but was most frustrated about the Warriors holding the contract over his head. After Ellis returned and showed he was the same player, the team announced they were relinquishing their right to void his contract.

At this point, everyone who followed the Warriors knew Mullin, who assembled the team that broke the franchise playoff drought, was not in control. Rowell's expertise was the business side, but his actions made it clear he could and would assert his authority whenever he wanted. Just in case it was not abundantly clear who was in charge, in November, Rowell fired assistant general manager Pete D'Alessandro, Mullin's right-hand man in the organization. Unsurprisingly, those cumulative actions effectively ended the Mullin era as general manager. He faded into the background and ran out the clock on his contract as Rowell became the de facto head of basketball operations.

While those other points of conflict are part of the story, perhaps nothing encapsulates the Mullin/Rowell conflict and the later years of Chris Cohan's tenure as owner better than Stephen Jackson's extension saga.

Just 18 months after the We Believe team eliminated the Mavericks, Jackson was already the final star left and one of the last vestiges of the high point for an entire decade of Warriors basketball.

However, Jackson still had two more seasons on his existing contract that paid him $7.14 and $7.65 million, respectively.

Thirty years old at that point, Jackson would not have hit the open market until after his 32nd birthday.

In the aftermath of the front office conflict over Ellis' suspension and the firing of D'Alessandro, Rowell and Jackson negotiated his extension directly while head coach Don Nelson was considering trading the mercurial forward, and still–general manager Mullin was already negotiating a deal that would send him to the Detroit Pistons.

Rowell ended up giving Jackson his maximum allowable extension, adding three years and $28 million to his contract and obligating the Warriors to pay him until after his 35th birthday.

Jackson's story becomes far more ridiculous and representative because of what happened after that. He played the 2008–09 season as a captain but the team struggled to a 29–53 record without so many of their key contributors from the prior seasons. Over that off-season, Jackson began to agitate for a trade and clashed both publicly and privately with Nelson.

Less than a year after Jackson agreed to that maximum allowable extension, Nelson said, "At some point, and I don't know when, we have to [trade him]. He asked to be traded, and we'd like to trade him. That's if we can." A week later, one day before the anniversary of his extension and a year before it kicked in, the Warriors granted Jackson's wish, though they traded him to the atrocious Charlotte Bobcats instead of a championship contender like he had hoped. After all of the drama surrounding extension negotiations and then the trade demand less than a year later, Golden State walked away with forward Vladimir Radmanovic and Raja Bell's expiring contract before Jackson's extension even kicked in.

The perfect kicker to the story came three years later. Jackson was still on that extended contract but Charlotte traded him to the Bucks in 2011 as part of a three-team deal that also included his teammate Al Harrington and future Warrior Shaun Livingston. After butting heads with Bucks head coach Scott Skiles, they traded

Jackson to the Warriors as a part of the larger deal sending Monta Ellis to Milwaukee and Andrew Bogut to Oakland. However, Jackson never suited up for the Warriors because they flipped him to San Antonio two days later for Richard Jefferson (who had an extra year remaining on his contract) and the first-round pick that eventually became Festus Ezeli.

While the Warriors were largely able to get out of the Jackson situation with their books unscathed a year later, Rowell and Cohan's meddling into Mullin's jurisdiction as general manager had already cost the team Kevin Garnett, three more seasons of Davis, a positive relationship with Ellis, and all of the goodwill engendered from the We Believe team.

61 The $450 Million Bid

The winning bid was $450 million.

In July 2010, the dysfunctional Warriors, who had been to one postseason in 16 years, were officially the most expensive franchise in NBA history. It was perhaps the best execution of Chris Cohan's tenure as owner.

News of Cohan looking to sell his 80 percent stake in the Warriors started in earnest in July 2009. By January 2010, billionaire Larry Ellison was sitting courtside at Oracle Arena for the first time, watching LeBron James dominate. Sixteen days after his debut at a Warriors game, Ellison confessed during a public event at Oracle headquarters that he was trying to buy the team.

"I'm trying. I'm trying," Ellison (who was discussing Oracle's acquisition of Sun Microsystems) replied to an audience member asking about him buying the Warriors. "Unfortunately, you can't have a hostile takeover of a basketball team."

And just like that, it was on, the most engrossing drama involving the team in years: Who would buy the Warriors?

On March 22, 2010, the Warriors announced Cohan would be selling the team and had hired Galatioto Sports Partners to execute the sale. Sal Galatioto had previously orchestrated the sale of the Phoenix Suns in 2004 for a then-record $401 million and had a similar game plan for the Warriors.

Galatioto accepted blind bids from any groups interested in buying the Warriors with what he said was a hard deadline for getting the bid in. After that process, the most serious bidders would get full access and the ability to kick the tires on the Warriors but still had to finalize their bid without knowing the offer of any other group. The highest bidder got the team.

This seemed to be a cinch for Ellison, who not even two weeks before the Warriors announcement ranked sixth on *Forbes'* list of the world's wealthiest people. They reported Ellison's net worth to be $28 billion, third among Americans behind Bill Gates and Warren Buffett.

He was clearly the fan favorite to buy the Warriors. In February 2010, Ellison captured the 33rd running of the America's Cup, completing a 10-year personal quest that saw him spend $100 million. It was America's first win since 1982 and Ellison was onboard the BMW Oracle when it won. That process and its success provided fans a glimpse into the relentlessness he would bring to the Warriors, along with endless pockets that could make the Warriors relevant in a changing, more expensive NBA.

Two days after the announcement, another big-pocket Bay Area icon publicly expressed interest in buying the team. Mark Mastrov, founder of 24 Hour Fitness, immediately went after the notion that Ellison's billions made him the best candidate. "I think

I can do just as well, if not better," Mastrov told Bay Area News Group.

On May 18, the bids start rolling in. As many as 12 groups made their pitches, according to reports. Ten days later, Galatioto trimmed the field to four viable bidders, with Ellison and Mastrov as the only two known bidders at the time.

It was not until June that it was reported Celtics minority owner Joe Lacob and Mandalay Entertainment CEO Peter Guber were one of the final four. They were discovered on a tour of the facilities, as was Wall Street financier David Bonderman, head of the fourth group, a week later.

All bids were due July 6 and all four bids topped $400 million, according to Galatioto. At this point, Ellison and the Lacob/Guber tandem were the two highest bids. While Warriors fans waited for a resolution, Lacob and Guber were behind the scenes finalizing the sale of the team.

Lacob was in Greece at the time. He was supposed to be vacationing with his fiancé, Nicole Curran, but he was down to the final hours before the deadline to finalize the sale. Lacob was on the phone waiting for the official word the deal was done. The pilot of the helicopter, on his last trip before his union was going on strike, pressured Lacob to get on board but he refused to get off the phone until he got the thumbs-up.

Finally, he did. He beat Ellison.

"We were going by helicopter to Delphi in Greece," Lacob said, "which is famous for the Oracle. The Oracle of Delphi. To which I then said, 'We're off to see the Oracle.' The irony, right?"

The Warriors officially announced the sale was complete to Lacob and Guber but the drama was not over. Ellison put out a statement that left Warriors fans a bit miffed. "Although I was the highest bidder, Chris Cohan decided to sell to someone else," Ellison said in a statement released by Oracle. "In my experience, this is a bit unusual."

According to insiders, Ellison's bid was higher but Galatioto said Ellison's binding bid was late and the Warriors had already informed Lacob's group that they won the bid. Galatioto said it would have been unethical to back out on Lacob's group because Ellison's late bid was slightly higher.

The other side of the story? Cohan never wanted to sell to Ellison and used the Oracle billionaire's presence in the process to ramp up the bids.

"It was an auction process, so who knows what really went on," Lacob said after being awarded the team. "We did what we felt was right. We've been in it all the way. I'm incredibly proud of the fact that we stayed out of the news. We were not under the radar with respect to Chris Cohan. We did our due diligence. I think we wanted it more than the other guys and I think we are more knowledgeable about basketball than all these others guys. And if I didn't think so we wouldn't have done this."

After 15 years of frustration and drama, the Golden State Warriors were finally under new ownership.

62 Joe Barry Carroll

In seven seasons with the Warriors, he averaged 20.4 points, 8.3 rebounds, and 1.7 blocks per game, the best numbers by a Warriors center since they traded Nate Thurmond to Chicago.

Yet Joe Barry Carroll is infamous in Warriors history. He is on the starting five of Golden State futility, one of the prime examples of the franchise's former haplessness and best known by long-suffering Warriors fans as Joe Barely Cares.

How did it get to this? How did a player of such obvious talent, and solid statistics, become such a villain? Truth is, Carroll never stood a chance against his expectations. His production was never going to meet his potential.

Strike One: He was a No. 1 overall pick. That status comes with expectations few players ever actually meet. And it just so happened the previous top pick in the NBA draft delivered right off the bat: Magic Johnson. The bar was clear. Carroll needed to be a savior. His baseline was being able to elevate the team to new heights.

Strike Two: The Warriors gave up quite a bit to get Carroll, getting fleeced by Celtics coach and general manager Red Auerbach. It would be different if the Warriors were simply awarded the No. 1 pick. That not panning out is bad enough but they would have lost nothing other than the opportunity to draft someone else. However, in order to get Carroll, the Warriors traded center Robert Parish and the third overall pick to Boston for the first and 13th selections. The Celtics ended up using the third pick to draft Kevin McHale, while the Warriors selected Carroll out of Purdue and Rickey Brown out of Mississippi State.

Parish was a seven-footer who seemed to be coming into his own as the replacement for Clifford Ray. In his third and fourth seasons with the Warriors, Parish averaged 17.1 points, 11.5 rebounds, and 2.2 blocks per game. He and McHale teamed with Larry Bird to win a championship in their first year together and they eventually won three titles together. Parish and McHale are now in the Hall of Fame.

The Warriors didn't make the playoffs with Carroll until 1987.

Strike Three: Carroll held out for more money. Twice.

It was not all his fault. Warriors owner Franklin Mieuli was perennially cash strapped. It cost him several players over the years and was the reason behind the trading of Parish because he was due a contract extension the Warriors could not afford and Carroll was a cheaper option.

After a solid start to his career, Carroll really broke out in his third season: 24.1 points, 8.7 rebounds, and 2.0 blocks. He shot 51.3 percent from the field while logging a career-high 37.8 minutes and playing like a centerpiece after the Warriors lost Bernard King in free agency.

Like Parish before him, Carroll was looking for a contract extension heading into his fourth year. He did not get it, played out his fourth season, and then held out again. In a move that is almost inconceivable now, Carroll missed the entire season, playing in Italy, after he did not get a deal from the Warriors.

Carroll came back a restricted free agent in 1985. He wanted to leave the Warriors and got the big offer he wanted from Milwaukee, who saw Carroll as the missing center to get them over the hump in the Eastern Conference. Shockingly, the Warriors matched the contract offer and Carroll became the highest-paid player in franchise history. Wilt Chamberlain, Rick Barry, and King all left at least partially because of the Warriors' money issues but Carroll got paid.

He was scorned for leaving to play in Italy and then for being the highest-paid player.

On top of that, Carroll was an introvert. He avoided the media as best he could and was not animated on the court, instead cerebral and stoic. Playing for a team that boasted Chamberlain and Thurmond in its lineage, it was also different that Carroll did not dominate physically like most of his seven-footer brethren. He had a post-up game that featured an array of moves instead of being an overpowering physical presence capable of dominating the boards and paint.

The combination of it all made it look as if he was not trying on the court.

In 1986–87, the Warriors had a new head coach in George Karl and some help around Carroll. With Sleepy Floyd at point guard, Chris Mullin on the wing, and a proven scorer in Purvis Short coming off the bench, Carroll had another good season. He even made his first and only All-Star Game as a reserve. The Warriors made the playoffs and Carroll had a game-high 24 points to go with eight rebounds and six blocks in a series-clinching Game 5 win at Utah. He even averaged 20 points on 47.6 percent shooting in the next round as the eventual-champion Lakers easily handled the Warriors.

In a turn that was sadly appropriate and fitting, Carroll's success that season did not matter. Despite his clutch playoff performance helping fuel the Warriors' first playoff series win in 10 years, his reputation in Oakland was irreparable. Don Nelson came on as an executive during that off-season and traded both Carroll and Floyd to Houston a month into the 1986–87 season for aging center Ralph Sampson.

Carroll is still among the Warriors' franchise leaders in scoring, rebounding, and blocks.

63 Bob Myers

On January 15, 1982, the New York Knicks visited Oakland to take on the Warriors. Bernard King scored 32 points and World B. Free had 29 as the Warriors pulled out a nail biter, while the Knicks had three players score at least 20 points: Maurice Lucas, Michael Ray Richardson, and Bill Cartwright.

In the crowd that day was an almost-seven-year-old boy from Danville experiencing his first NBA game. He became an instant basketball fan and the Warriors were his newest treasure.

To this day, Warriors general manager Bob Myers keeps that ticket in his wallet. His mother gave it to him when he got a job with his favorite team growing up. It was still there in Cleveland, protected from the champagne, as they celebrated the NBA championship.

"Growing up in this community and watching for 25 years makes you appreciate this success," Myers said. "I wasn't someone that grew up in another city, another team. This is all I know."

Myers took a unique path to becoming an historic figure in Warriors history as architect of a champion.

The Monte Vista High School graduate walked on at UCLA after a productive high school career. He played under Jim Harrick and alongside star Ed O'Bannon, winning the 1995 NCAA national championship.

At the end of Myers' college career, Harrick secured him an internship with super agent Arn Tellem in 1997. While Myers did not have "sports agent" on his list of desired careers, Tellem hired him a year later, so Myers took night classes at Loyola Law School while learning the ropes under Tellem.

He wound up being one of Tellem's best associates. Myers was good at recruiting players and negotiating contracts. By 2000, Myers was vice president of Tellem's agency and wound up with his own client base of 19 clients, including Brandon Roy, Brook Lopez, and Tyreke Evans.

Myers carved out his niche from contradicting the stereotypes of agents with honesty, humility, and hard work as his calling cards while he negotiated $575 million worth of deals during his 14 years as an agent. He would give it to the player straight, operate in good faith with opposing teams, and go the extra mile for his clients.

So when he left his practice and crossed over to the team side, he brought a reputation with him as someone easy to get along with and fair to deal with.

"One thing about Bob is that he's remarkably grounded," Tellem said. "He's the same person who grew up in the East Bay. The position of success hasn't changed him. He carries with him humility and grace that will serve him well. Those values he carries with him will be ever present."

Those same characteristics made Myers a quick study once he got to the Warriors. The team hired him as an assistant GM under Larry Riley so he could be groomed for the head job. During that time he was integral in two major moves by the Warriors.

After the 2011 lockout ended, Golden State made a play for Los Angeles Clippers restricted free agent center DeAndre Jordan. The newly agreed-to Collective Bargaining Agreement included an amnesty provision, the general manager equivalent of a "get out of jail free card" because it allowed each team one opportunity to cut a player without his remaining contract counting against either the salary cap or the luxury tax. In order to clear more space to make a lucrative offer to Jordan, the Warriors used their one-time amnesty to release troubled guard Charlie Bell, who had only one year and $4 million left on his contract. To add an additional $272,015 to Jordan's offer, the front office also cut second-year guard, local product, and fan favorite Jeremy Lin before the team's first post-lockout practice.

Even after Golden State took those painful steps to make it richer, the Clippers matched the Warriors' offer and retained Jordan. On top of that, the team had no other high-end targets to spend that newly created cap flexibility on, so they wasted their amnesty instead of saving it for either Andris Biedrins or David Lee years later. Adding insult to injury, Lin became a phenomenon with the New York Knicks that season as Linsanity helped lead the Knicks to the playoffs.

Myers redeemed himself three months later, even though very few knew it at the time. At that season's trade deadline, he shipped popular guard Monta Ellis to Milwaukee for center Andrew Bogut in a five-player deal.

Usually trading a small player for a big one is a good idea, as size is so coveted in the NBA. This particular move carried significantly more risk because Bogut was still recovering from a broken ankle, the third major injury of his career. Even so, it became a franchise-changing move. It gave the Warriors their elusive quality center and Bogut possessed an unusual combination of defensive prowess and passing skills. The deal also paved the way for Stephen Curry to become the star of the team. On and off the court, Ellis' presence made it harder for Curry to thrive as the veteran preferred the ball in his hands and his temperamental demeanor negatively impacted the chemistry of the locker room, which would change drastically under Curry. Additionally, the move depleted the Warriors' roster by trading their healthy leading scorer, along with backup big man Ekpe Udoh, for an injured center. Finishing the season with youngsters and players they found off the street allowed the Warriors to finish 23–43 and eventually retain their first-round draft pick after winning a coin flip.

At the end of that season, in April 2012, the Warriors demoted Riley and gave Myers the keys to the kingdom. It was faster than even CEO Joe Lacob expected but Myers delivered on their trust with a remarkable off-season that created a significant amount of the framework for the team's remarkable recent success.

He had an incredible draft, getting forward Harrison Barnes with the draft pick the team retained by falling so hard to end the season, center Festus Ezeli with the choice he acquired by taking on Richard Jefferson's onerous contract, and forward Draymond Green with their second-round selection. That July, he signed guard Jarrett Jack and Carl Landry, who proved to be key complementary pieces in the Warriors' playoff run the next season.

While those transactions continue to loom large, Myers made another immensely significant move that would set the Warriors up to become an elite NBA team the day the 2012–13 season began: signing Curry to a four-year, $44 million contract extension. At the time, both sides were taking a risk, since the Warriors were giving a long-term deal to a player coming off his second ankle surgery, while Curry was passing up free agency and the potential for a huge contract if he had a big fourth year.

Over the next five years, Curry's extension proved to be the best contract in the entire league, as he won two MVPs and one championship while making less than half as much as some of his peers. Having a star at about $15 million below market value also opened the door for Golden State to add significant talent using cap space and build a powerhouse.

The next off-season, Myers pulled off a minor miracle and acquired talented swingman Andre Iguodala while the team was in hot pursuit of center Dwight Howard. Without enough cap space to sign him outright, Myers pulled off a three-way deal with Utah and Denver involving expiring contracts and draft picks to get Iguodala in the fold at below his market value. The Warriors won 51 games and made their second consecutive playoff appearance.

With a talented team already in place, Myers had a different challenge. After the team replaced Mark Jackson with Steve Kerr, he signed guards Shaun Livingston and Kerr-favorite Leandro Barbosa to improve the team's guard rotation and negotiated a contract extension with Klay Thompson at less than his absolute maximum. A deeper Warriors team finished with the league's best record and Myers won the 2014–15 NBA Executive of the Year Award before the team won their first championship since the year Myers was born.

Faced with the challenge of retooling a champion, Myers re-signed Green for less than his maximum, traded team stalwart David Lee to the Boston Celtics without having to give up an asset to unload his significant contract, re-signed Barbosa, and brought in guard Ian Clark. He also faced a challenging decision with whether to give championship contributors and 2012 Draft picks Barnes and Ezeli contract extensions and the sides did not end up agreeing to new deals in either case. In the ensuing season, Golden State set an NBA record with 73 wins.

Years of reasonable contracts and elite cap management came to fruition in 2016 when the 73-win Warriors secured a meeting with 2013–14 MVP Kevin Durant. Thanks to Myers' work, Golden State was able to pitch the Oklahoma City star on joining an already-elite team that would not have to sacrifice any of their three All-Stars to fit him in. Once Durant shocked the basketball world by agreeing to join the juggernaut, the general manager had to make tough moves to clear the space, including letting both Barnes and Ezeli leave for new teams and trading Bogut to the Mavericks. But those sacrifices paid off with the league's best record for the third time and another Executive of the Year Award for Myers.

While the players on the court determine the outcome every time, Myers deserves an immense amount of credit for adding depth on reasonable contracts and drafting well, which helped the Warriors maintain enough flexibility to build and maintain a powerhouse.

64 Chris Webber

Losing Chris Webber stands as one of the largest failures and disappointments in Warriors history.

After years of trying to find a big man with the vast skill set required to thrive in Don Nelson's system, the opportunity presented itself in 1993. Despite finishing the season with the league's seventh-worst record, the Warriors jumped up to the third pick in the draft, which put them in range for the Michigan big man.

Webber represented the best of both worlds due to his unusual combination of skill and physical capability. At 6'9" and 263 pounds, with a 7'3" wingspan and impressive athleticism for his size, Webber could rebound and block shots well enough to serve Nelson's purposes but his offensive talents were what set him apart. He could dribble the ball well and saw the floor like a guard, with hands that smothered the ball, making him great at catching passes in traffic and finishing with authority. Importantly, Webber also loved to pass and could make shots all over the floor.

As a member of the iconic Fab Five at Michigan, Webber averaged 15.5 and 19.2 points per game during his two college seasons and actually made 33.8 percent from three during his sophomore season. He was the low-post player the Warriors were desperate for with the skills to play in their up-tempo style.

The fit was so natural, the Warriors giving up the third overall pick (which became Penny Hardaway) and three additional future first-round picks seemed like a reasonable price to get the elusive missing piece for a team that still had Chris Mullin and Tim Hardaway, along with rising star Latrell Sprewell.

Even before the season, there were signs of impending trouble. In an era without a scale for rookie contracts, high draft picks were commanding massive contracts before playing in their first NBA game. Originally, the Warriors and Webber agreed to a deal with seven guaranteed years, but Nelson objected vociferously since the rookie would wield so much power over him and the organization more broadly. The team then went back to Webber and they hammered out a 15-year, $74 million contract that also gave the first overall pick a fateful opt-out after his very first season.

In just his fourth game, Webber announced his presence loudly. On a fast break against the Suns, Webber took an outlet pass from Latrell Sprewell, circled the ball around his back and threw down a one-handed dunk over reigning league MVP Charles Barkley. That highlight wound up in a Nike commercial and helped fuel Webber's Rookie of the Year campaign.

The Warriors had a sensation, a player made for their open-court style.

Three months later, in a win over Denver, Webber snagged a rebound off Sprewell's missed jumper, took one dribble to gather himself, then turned and dunked on Nuggets seven-footer Dikembe Mutombo. The rookie scowled at Mutombo on his way back down court.

While it looked like the Warriors finally had their inside presence and a player who combined the necessary physicality with uncommon skill, the conflict between Webber and Nelson was reaching a boiling point.

The long story has layers of context to weed through. One of the oft-reported layers is that Nelson wanted Webber to play center while Webber, who played power forward at Michigan and loved to flex his perimeter skills, scoffed at the notion. That conflict came when Webber and Nelson met before the team drafted him first overall and potentially helped lead to Nelson's opposition to giving Webber seven guaranteed seasons and the subsequent fateful decision to give him the opt-out after one year.

In January 1994, Nelson had a film session with the team's guards that included him telling Avery Johnson, "You don't give it to him," in situations where Webber asked for the ball before the team initiated their offense.

While that meeting focused on other topics, word got back to Webber as teammate Jeff Grayer told him, "Coach says you're costing the team games."

A little less than two months later, the *San Jose Mercury News* reported that Webber was considering using his opt-out and Nelson followed up in an attempt to find out who leaked that information. When one of the questioned reporters broached the possibility that it came from Webber himself, Nelson responded, "Oh, my God… if that's true, I'm a dead man."

While the Warriors ended up winning 50 games and making the playoffs, after the season the reigning Rookie of the Year wanted to leave and unlike modern times, when teams have control over their drafted stars for at least their first four seasons, he had the ability to force his way out.

Webber opted out of his contract and sat out the start of the 1994–95 season in search of a new deal, which he reportedly wanted to include another out clause. The Warriors scoffed at giving him that much control again and perhaps that was part of the problem, too. Webber, who entered the NBA as a household name during his days at Michigan, began his professional career with so much power. Most young players have to work for years to accrue the control he wielded at just 21 years old.

In a last-ditch attempt to appease their fuming star, late in the preseason the Warriors traded Billy Owens for center Rony Seikaly to limit Webber's time playing center. It was too little, too late. In fact, Owens told the *New York Times* that when the trade happened, "Web told me he was not going to play there."

November 17, 1994, one year and one day after his dunk over Barkley, the Warriors announced they had traded Webber to the Washington Bullets.

"This is not a happy day for us," coach Don Nelson said at the press conference. "We were building a championship team and Chris Webber was a part of that, but circumstances didn't turn out that way."

While the Warriors received Tom Gugliotta and three first-round picks, two of which were their own from the trade to acquire Webber the previous off-season, they lost their future by trading the rare player capable of living up to the hype and responsibility of being a franchise savior.

Significantly, new owner Chris Cohan wanted Nelson to coach his team. On the day of the trade, Cohan said, "I want Don to stay. I was told over and over again that if Don stays, we've got a problem with Chris. The lines got drawn in the sand, and I didn't think it could be repaired."

It took the Warriors 13 years to make the playoffs again. Webber made five All-NBA teams and played in five All-Star games, averaging 21.2 points, 9.9 rebounds, and 4.3 assists per game in his 13 seasons away from Oakland.

In a surprising turn, Webber returned to the Warriors on January 26, 2008, saying, "This organization and city has always had a special place in my heart because it is where my dream of being an NBA player first came true." Coming back to Golden State meant playing for Nelson again, as Golden State tried to make their way back to the playoffs after the We Believe season. Unfortunately, persistent knee issues limited Webber to nine games and 126 total minutes, but the likely Hall of Famer started and ended his career with the Warriors.

65 Ellis for Bogut

Joe Lacob had enough. He was already considering a trade. But after he read Monta Ellis' comments, published after shootaround before a game at Sacramento, Lacob was ready to pull the trigger.

"I probably could go to Orlando or Chicago and get a championship," Ellis said. "But if they don't move me, what can I do? Hopefully—if they don't move me—they get somebody in here so we can win and I don't have to go through this every year."

It was March of 2012, the Warriors were spiraling toward a losing season, and Ellis was frustrated. He had grown increasingly unhappy with the franchise since it broke up the 2007 team that made the playoffs, featuring Baron Davis, Stephen Jackson, and Jason Richardson. Though the moves the team made vaulted him to the top of the totem pole, Ellis wanted the Warriors to give him some help.

Over the years, Ellis became less the quiet, humble kid from Jackson, Mississippi, and more a disgruntled star whose disposition impacted the locker room, yet he was still a talented player who was a draw for fans. What's more, his value was not incredibly high around the league. All of that made trading him a risk.

However, Ellis' latest comments got Lacob on board with the deal the Warriors had in the works even if it made his fiancé, Nicole Curran, stop talking to him for days.

Just before they played in Sacramento on March 13, 2012, Golden State pulled the trigger on the trade that would change the course of the franchise.

They sent Ellis and backup big men Ekpe Udoh and Kwame Brown to the Milwaukee Bucks in exchange for center Andrew Bogut and a returning Stephen Jackson, who was almost immediately moved to San Antonio for Richard Jefferson and a first-round draft pick that became Festus Ezeli.

Andrew Bogut, the first overall pick out of Utah in the same year Golden State selected Ellis 40th, was at his best a top-five center. The Australian was known for defense but also had plenty of offensive skill for a big man, even though he did not score. In 2009–10, Bogut made third-team All-NBA, a distinction Ellis never received.

Bogut was perfect for the Warriors since they desperately needed a good defender and rebounder who did not care much about scoring. They had enough offense and needed some toughness and Bogut made perfect sense.

The problem with this deal, on the surface, was that Bogut was injured. Not even two months earlier, he fractured his left ankle and was out indefinitely. After Golden State acquired him, Bogut had arthroscopic surgery to clean out debris from his ankle and that knocked him out for the season.

It was far from his first injury.

In April 2010, a nasty fall left Bogut with a dislocated right elbow, a fractured right hand, and a sprained wrist. It permanently changed his shooting as his right arm was never the same. A sprained foot in 2007 shut him down for the remainder of the season and issues limited him to fewer than half the games the following year.

The fan base was divided about this move. There was a contingent that saw Ellis, who had grown into an inefficient scorer who slacked on defense, as holding the Warriors back, particularly with the budding talent of backcourt partner Stephen Curry and second-year shooter Klay Thompson. Others thought it was crazy to trade the leading scorer and two key role players for a guy nobody was certain would ever be the same again.

Truth is, it was Bogut's propensity for injury that lowered his trade value enough for the Warriors to get him. Talented centers are so coveted in the NBA that teams rarely trade them and typically want a ton in return. Even though the Bucks had soured on Bogut's injuries (and grumpy personality), the Warriors still had to give up three players and take one of Milwaukee's undesirables in Stephen Jackson to make the deal palatable.

Bogut always contended his injuries were freak accidents and not a matter of him being injury prone. The Warriors bought his explanation and took the risk.

It did not seem to pay off as five games into the next season, Bogut had to be sidelined again. He said he rushed back too fast from the fractured ankle, fueled by the criticism he was injury prone, and started having back issues as well. He eventually returned to finish the season, and in the process he justified both the controversial trade and the long wait.

Bogut played 32 games that regular season, averaging 7.7 rebounds and 1.7 blocks in 24.6 minutes. He became the anchor of a Warriors defense that was suddenly good, thanks to having the size to battle inside with the big boys and the cerebral game to lead Mark Jackson's pack-the-paint and protect-the-rim approach.

In the playoffs, though he had reinjured his ankle, Bogut was a big factor in the Warriors' first round upset of Denver. He was the force to complement the Warriors' up-tempo, finesse style of play.

It was clear if he could just get and stay healthy, the Warriors finally has a center.

66 Mark Jackson

Stephen Curry was on a phone call, talking about all the drama surrounding his head coach, Mark Jackson. He was befuddled by the reality that the Warriors franchise had done a complete 180-degree turn from their woeful ways under Jackson, yet the most productive coach of his pro career was on the hot seat.

In the middle of his conversation, Curry got another call. It was Mark Jackson. And he had bad news.

"We finally created a winning environment," Curry said then. "We were headed in the right direction."

While the Mark Jackson era ended in turmoil, controversy, and drama, how it ended does not encapsulate the accomplishments of his three-year tenure.

When Jackson was hired in June 2011, he promised at his introductory press conference that "things be a-changing," and they certainly did.

Owner Joe Lacob fired Jackson after a 51-win season where they nearly upset the higher-seeded Los Angeles Clippers despite not having a healthy center for the series. Jackson led the Warriors to consecutive playoff appearances for the first time since Don Nelson in the 1990s and his nine playoff wins in three seasons were the most by a Warriors coach in that same timeframe since Al Attles in the mid-70s.

It was far more than most expected when the Warriors hired Jackson out of the broadcast booth. After all, the 17-year NBA vet, who totaled the fourth-most assists in NBA history, had zero coaching experience when he was hired. None as a head coach or even as an assistant at any level.

Jackson had interviewed for coaching positions multiple times before while becoming a fixture during big NBA games on ESPN and ABC, but he convinced the Warriors he was ready despite his inexperience.

"I guarantee you he is going to be great for us," Warriors CEO Joe Lacob said at Jackson's introductory press conference.

The dividends did not pay off right away, as the Warriors went 23–43 in Jackson's first year, but evidence of change came almost immediately. He started by publicly dismissing any ties to previous Warriors disappointments, created the team slogan "Just Us" and built the camaraderie exemplified by a lively bench that got excited about defense and hustle plays.

Jackson also brought his faith to the team, which was predominantly comprised of Christians, including star guard Stephen Curry. He got rid of music in the locker room, usually profane hip-hop, attended pregame chapel with many of the players, and served as an unofficial life coach for several of them as well.

Mark Jackson talks to David Lee and Klay Thompson in a game against the Memphis Grizzlies. (AP Photo/Danny Johnston)

His unique methods helped create unique chemistry. The Warriors went a long way toward filling the holes on their roster just by being bonded in a way most coaches dream about. It made guard Jarrett Jack not want to leave and inspired swingman Andre Iguodala, who would end up being the 2015 NBA Finals MVP, to consider joining the Warriors.

Jackson, who was the head pastor at a Southern California church he started, was also a noted motivator. Used to delivering sermons, he milked that public speaking skill—and decades of practice as a trash talker—to coax confidence into many of his players.

Stephen Curry flourished under Jackson and became an All-Star. Klay Thompson became one of the best shooting guards in the NBA. Rookies Harrison Barnes, Draymond Green, and Festus

Ezeli grew up fast enough to contribute in the 2013 playoffs, which was where Jackson shined.

The Warriors made the playoffs as the No. 6 seed and upset the third-seeded Denver Nuggets in the first round as Jackson out-dueled George Karl. All-Star forward David Lee tore his right hip flexor in Game 1 and Jackson threw a curveball by bringing in a third guard, Jarrett Jack, and sliding starting small forward Barnes up a position to power forward. Karl did not have a counter.

In the next round, the Warriors gave eventual Western Conference champions San Antonio all they wanted. Curry and center Andrew Bogut were playing through ankle injuries, yet the Warriors pushed the Spurs to six games and came devastatingly close to winning both of the first two in San Antonio. Jackson employed the strategy of not double-teaming Hall of Fame–bound Tim Duncan and putting shooting guard Thompson on the Spurs' speedy point guard Tony Parker, and it nearly worked.

The next season they won 51 games, the franchise's most in 22 years.

Jackson's emphasis on defense played a major role in shaping the Warriors' success both under him and after his departure. In Keith Smart's season as coach, Golden State finished the year 26th in defense. After one season of adjustment and talent turnover, the team improved to 14th Jackson's second year and a remarkable fourth his third season. While some of that can and should be attributed to additions like Andrew Bogut and Iguodala in 2013, Jackson and his assistants worked to improve both Thompson's and Green's skills as defenders, which helped them become pivotal pieces in the years to come.

In the midst of the Donald Sterling scandal at the start of the 2014 playoffs, with the nation tuned into the NBA and the Los Angeles Clippers, the Warriors nearly pulled off another first-round upset. Despite losing centers Andrew Bogut and Festus Ezeli to injury, the Warriors pushed the Clippers to the brink, losing a nail-biter in Game 7.

It was clear the Warriors were on their way to greater success, but behind the scenes, Jackson's tenure was falling apart.

On March 22 of that season, Golden State lost to the Spurs at Oracle and Jackson became increasingly frustrated with assistant coach Brian Scalabrine. In a sign of tension, Scalabrine had joined Jackson's staff that season but was chosen by the front office rather than Jackson. After a tense meeting where the head coach forced the other people in the room to take sides, he effectively blackballed Scalabrine, but did not have the authority to fire him, so they reassigned him to their Developmental League affiliate in Santa Cruz. Interestingly, Scalabrine still appeared on the Warriors' media notes as an assistant during the playoff series against the Clippers a month later, despite his continued absence from the sidelines, another reflection of the tension between Jackson and the front office.

The feeling of uncertainty actually grew from there when the team fired assistant coach Darren Erman two weeks later for a "violation of company policy." Jackson's No. 2 assistant had been with the team since 2011, but had been taping the team's coaches and players without their knowledge or consent.

Two days after falling to the Clippers in Game 7, ownership decided to fire Jackson. While his tenure as head coach only lasted three seasons, Jackson produced a lasting impact on a team that would became a dominant force in the seasons that followed. One year and six weeks after that Game 7 loss to the Clippers, Jackson watched the Warriors win the 2015 NBA championship from the ABC announcers' booth just off the court.

67 David Lee

In 2004, the Warriors spent lavishly to entice Derek Fisher to leave the Lakers. In 2008, after Baron Davis spurned them for the Clippers and both Gilbert Arenas and Elton Brand rejected lucrative offers, Golden State's big free agent splash was former Clipper Corey Maggette.

Two years later, the Warriors possessed a massive amount of salary cap space yet again and it looked like the top free agents would be taking their talents elsewhere. That landscape made the team signing David Lee even more surprising.

Lee transformed from unheralded late-first-round pick at the end of the bench to star over his five seasons with the New York Knicks. After only starting 55 games in his first three NBA seasons, Lee made the 2010 All-Star team and averaged 20 points and 10 rebounds per night in 2009–10.

Even with that profile, Lee's free agency stayed out of the limelight since superstars LeBron James, Dwyane Wade, Chris Bosh, and Amar'e Stoudemire were all on the open market.

While Lee paled in comparison to those massive figures in the sport, he had a significant profile for the Warriors. After all, he torched them for an average of 27 points and 14 rebounds in two games the season before, including a triple-double in his only appearance at Oracle.

With the stars out of reach, the Warriors went after Lee and signed him to a five-year, $80 million contract. It was the largest deal the Warriors signed since giving Antawn Jamison the maximum, twice as much as Baron Davis wanted two years before which they refused to pay, and more than fan favorites Jason Richardson and Monta Ellis. Many were concerned because Lee's teams had never won. While part of that fell on the shoulders of the dysfunctional Knicks, shelling out significant money to a player whose best team went 33–49 raised legitimate questions. On top of that, Lee had a reputation for being a stat-stuffer who put up big numbers on losses, exemplified by his aforementioned triple-double at Oracle coming in an 11-point defeat.

Over time, Lee proved to be valuable for the Warriors, especially compared with the disastrous big contracts they had doled out in prior off-seasons.

Lee instantly provided reliable production, averaging 16.5 points and 9.8 rebounds his first season in Oakland. While that was not nearly enough to elevate the Warriors to contender status, he played a role in stabilizing a franchise rife with drama.

Importantly, the low-maintenance star was a good ambassador for a franchise in the midst of change. Having cut his teeth in New York, Lee was good with the media and the perfect player to interact with sponsors and the community. He was likable and, after years of Baron Davis, Stephen Jackson, and Monta Ellis, stars known for being problematic in matters off the court, his amenability mattered. It endeared him to ownership, connected him with fans and built a friendship with future superstar Stephen Curry.

For a while, those intangibles made his poor defense tolerable.

The following season, Lee endeared himself even more by gutting out injuries to finish the season. In March, Curry's ankle injuries knocked him out for the season and the Warriors traded for injured center Andrew Bogut, giving up three players, including former centerpiece Ellis. They were left with scraps from the end of the bench and the NBA Development League and Lee. With aching knees, he kept playing when most veterans would have shut it down, which helped provide an example as new coach Mark Jackson worked to change the culture of the franchise, emphasizing togetherness and sacrifice. Despite those limitations, Lee finished the season averaging 20.1 points and 9.6 rebounds before the team sat him out the final stretch of games.

With Ellis gone and the reigns now belonging to Curry, Lee flourished as a leader in the 2011–12 season. His bond with Curry allowed them to work together in harmonizing a once-fractured locker room. Lee would organize teambuilding events and was aggressively enthusiastic celebrating teammates' success.

On the court, he thrived in a 1-2 punch with Curry, averaging 18.5 points, 11.2 rebounds, and 3.5 assists. That season, he became the Warriors' first All-Star since Latrell Sprewell in 1997 and helped put the Warriors in the playoffs for the first time in six years.

However, in the third quarter of his first career playoff game, on a dive to the basket, Lee suffered an injury to his hip that was supposed to end his season.

Shockingly, in Game 6 of that same round, with a torn hip flexor leaving him with no strength or explosiveness in his right leg, Lee made an emotional return to action. The sixth-seeded Warriors had a chance to finish off the third-seeded Denver Nuggets and an injured Lee gave the Warriors an inspirational minute and 27 seconds.

Oracle roared when he got up and walked to the scorer's table, cheered as his name was announced when he checked in, and exploded when he grabbed a rebound.

It was not exactly a Willis Reed moment for the former Knick, but for Lee it was validation for his role in getting the team to that level. He helped raise the standard for Warriors basketball.

Eventually, the rapid progression of that standard would make Lee expendable. He regained his starting spot the next season and produced stats largely in line with his prior seasons as the Warriors put up a 51–31 record. In Lee's first full playoff series as a starter, he averaged 13.9 points and 9.1 rebounds in a seven-game loss to the Clippers.

The next season, Lee injured his left hamstring in the team's final preseason game and missed all but one of the first 25 games of that season. In that time, third-year forward Draymond Green had thrived in Lee's place and the former All-Star willingly accepted a place as a contributor off the bench, paralleling both Andre Iguodala that year and the Warriors' combination of Jeff Mullins and Bill Bridges 40 years earlier. Lee stayed in a reserve role all season but ended up helping the team rediscover the value of high pick-and-rolls late in Game 3 of the NBA Finals. Three games later, Lee reveled in the culmination of the franchise's transformation when they won the championship.

That Game 6 in Cleveland ended up being Lee's last game as a Warrior. The team traded him to the Boston Celtics, who offered a more reliable chance at playing time and he finished the 2015–16 season as a member of the Dallas Mavericks before joining the San Antonio Spurs the following year.

Even though Lee's star fell during his time with the Warriors, he made a significant mark on franchise history as a player who helped the franchise transition from cellar-dweller to powerhouse.

68 Baron on Kirilenko

At each Warriors home game, they choose a Season Ticket Holder of the Game and ask them a few questions during a game stoppage, including their favorite moment. Even after a second championship and all of the memories of recent seasons, those fans choose a single play remarkably frequently: Baron Davis' dunk on Andrei Kirilenko.

It makes a ton of sense. The dunk itself is an amazing highlight: a point guard going over and through a big forward. It took on an even larger footprint because the local television broadcast did not immediately go to commercial during the subsequent stoppage, allowing viewers to take in the Oracle crowd going absolutely insane and play-by-play announcer Bob Fitzgerald effusively trying to process what he just saw.

The broad context helps too, as Kirilenko had built a reputation as one of the league's best defenders, including a place on the NBA's All-Defensive first team the previous season after being the league's block leader in 2004–05. The Russian had also played a massive part in the series to that point with 16 blocks in just three games.

However, the reason outside the highlight itself that the Davis over Kirilenko dunk resonates with fans is the emotion and situation behind it. Davis helped lead the Warriors back to the playoffs after 12 seasons of mostly horrendous basketball and then played a key role in orchestrating one of the biggest playoff upsets in league history over the Dallas Mavericks. His dunk was also the capper on the team's first game back at Oracle Arena since eliminating the Mavericks and it put them up by 22. That win kept the Warriors undefeated at Oracle during the playoffs and allowed them to stay in the series after the Jazz won their two home games to start it out.

While the dunk itself and the context surrounding it explain its appeal, one of the most interesting elements of its continued resonance is what followed. Two nights later, Utah rode a 40–23 fourth quarter to a 14-point win and closed out the series in Salt Lake City in Game 5, so Davis' dunk punctuated the Warriors' only win in a 4–1 series. The following year's team won six more games but finished with the most wins of any NBA team to ever miss the postseason. After that, Davis left to play with the Clippers and the Warriors spent another five years out of the playoffs.

Davis' dunk on Andrei Kirilenko is a spectacular highlight deserving of its place in the heart of Warriors fans while its standing as the franchise's high water mark for more than a decade has allowed it to maintain and even expand its resonance over time.

69 Monta's Moped

Monta Ellis, donning a baggy white t-shirt and a white, fitted baseball cap, cruised around the Warriors practice facility. Gripping the opposite ends of a handlebar, pushing with his right leg, Ellis smiled as he zig-zagged across the hardwood, from teammate to teammate, chatting and laughing.

He could not play with them because his left ankle was confined to a boot. While Ellis could not practice and was stuck on a scooter designed to keep his left foot off the ground, the Warriors' young guard was in good spirits. Unlike many fans and media members, he was absolutely certain he would be back.

"Never worried," Ellis said in December 2008. "At all.… [I'll be] the same player I was before I left, or even stronger."

While Ellis turned out to be correct when his ankle healed and he became the star player he was always expected to be, the saga would permanently impact his tenure with the Warriors. That drama planted the seeds that would eventually lead to him being traded three and a half years later.

It all began on July 24, 2008, when the Warriors announced they had signed Ellis to a six-year, $66 million contract that solidified his place as part of the franchise's core moving forward.

The Warriors had drafted Ellis in the second round of the 2005 NBA Draft, 40th overall. After spending the first half of his rookie season mostly on the bench, he blossomed into a key role player. In the short term, he became a key figure off the bench while the Warriors had stars like Baron Davis and Jason Richardson, including winning the league's Most Improved Player Award his sophomore season before starting the first five games of the team's stunning upset of the Dallas Mavericks. After 14 months of turmoil and turnover, Ellis was in line to replace his former backcourt mates as the team's frontline star, which explains why they paid him $11 million per year.

August 21 happened while Ellis and the team were still in the afterglow of his new contract. In his hometown of Jackson, Mississippi, Ellis injured his left ankle badly enough to require surgery. He informed the Warriors about getting hurt and told general manager Chris Mullin he sustained the injury playing basketball.

The Warriors were not convinced and sent someone from the organization to check, who confirmed Ellis' injuries were not consistent with playing basketball.

Ellis tore his deltoid ligament, which runs on the inside of the ankle and is thicker and stronger, not designed for movement. Tearing the deltoid ligament requires incredible force, the kind of force that is extremely rare on a basketball court. Instead, Ellis' injury was consistent with motorcycle injuries. Plus, he had scrapes on his leg.

Eventually, Ellis confessed that he sustained the injury riding a moped and said it was just a quick, random spin on a friend's moped. He was just unfortunate and fell off, getting hurt in the process. However, riding mopeds and vehicles like it violated the NBA's Uniform Player Contract, which prohibited players from participating in specific, named activities that pose a higher risk of injury.

Ellis had surgery on August 27 and was scheduled to be out at least three months, but on October 11, team president Robert Rowell dropped a bomb.

Before a preseason game, Rowell announced the Warriors were suspending Ellis for 30 games. Behind the scenes, top brass clashed because Mullin thought Ellis had suffered enough and the incident provided an opportunity to support the 22-year-old, while Rowell disagreed, overruled Mullin, and punished Ellis.

The 30-game suspension amounted to a $3 million fine, since Ellis was missing those games anyway. Rowell also made it clear the team was reserving the right to terminate the newly signed contract Ellis violated. They wanted to make sure he could play again before committing to pay $66 million when there was a risk he would never be the same.

Ellis was not happy with the team's stance. While he understood being suspended, he and his camp wanted the team to make a decision on whether or not they would terminate the contract instead of holding it over his head for months. The young guard took it as a sign the franchise did not believe in him and was fine getting his contract voided and earning a new one with another team.

In November, Ellis had surgery to remove the screws from his ankle and three weeks later he was back with his teammates in practice. In early January, he was approved for strenuous activity. A week later, Ellis had his first full practice, afterward launching this now-legendary response to rumors he wanted out of Golden State.

"Listen, whatever it is about me leaving, wanting to go, I don't want to play for Nellie—that never came from my mouth," Ellis told a group of reporters he gathered together for an impromptu press conference. "I don't know where they got that from, but I'm here for the next six years. I'm a Warriors. I'm going to always be a Warriors. Whoever put that out there did it because they wanted a story. I'm making it known right now that I'm a Warriors."

Ellis returned to action on January 23 against Cleveland, scoring 20 points in 34 minutes as the Warriors lost on a buzzer-beater from LeBron James. He played 25 games that season and scored a career-high 42 points in a win over Sacramento on April

1. After proving his ankle was no longer an issue, Ellis shut it down for the rest of the season. His statement was made.

Two weeks later, the Warriors made their statement: they were relinquishing their right to void the contract. Ellis, as he declared, would stay a Warriors.

70 The Gilbert Arenas Provision

The Warriors had a long history of misfiring in the NBA draft. No matter where they were selecting, somehow it went wrong. They missed out on superstars; passed on Hall of Famers like Larry Bird, Kobe Bryant, Kevin Garnett, and Steve Nash; and squandered picks with duds that fizzled out quickly, including Chris Washburn, Russell Cross, and Todd Fuller. Even when they did make the right pick, that player often wound up flourishing elsewhere eventually, including Robert Parish, Mitch Richmond, and Chris Webber.

Great franchises build through the draft, which was a big part of the reason why the Warriors were anything but a good franchise for such a long time. After all that misfortune, it appeared the franchise's luck was about to change.

The Warriors had a great draft in 2001 following the worst season since the franchise moved to the West Coast. At number five, they selected Jason Richardson, an elite athlete out of Michigan State. Golden State also added Troy Murphy from Notre Dame, a rebounding big man with a nice outside shot.

While both Richardson and Murphy ended up starting for the Warriors, the real find came in the second round with the 30th overall pick. After an appearance in the Final Four in his sophomore year, guard Gilbert Arenas turned pro at age 19 and Golden State took a flyer on the kid who many thought would be a first-round pick.

His talent was obvious immediately, as the 6'3" Arenas had great size and athleticism for a point guard but it did not become clear what they had until coach Eric Musselman made him the starting point guard. Up to that juncture, the Warriors had been playing Larry Hughes, a 6'5" athletic shooting guard who could handle the ball, at point, but Hughes was not a natural primary distributor and his below-average shooting made him easier to defend.

On March 1, Arenas took over as the starting point guard and added a dimension to their offense as a great shooter with range and a superior passer to Hughes. From that point forward, Arenas averaged 17.9 points, 4.9 assists, and 3.6 rebounds per game in 32.1 minutes and it was clear the Warriors had unearthed a gem in the draft. Imagine that.

In a significant development, Arenas jelled with Richardson to create a young, potent guard combination. The Warriors had legitimate promise in their backcourt, along with two productive forwards in Antawn Jamison and Murphy, to form a real core.

That carried on through the next season, as the Warriors jumped from 21 wins to 38. While they missed the playoffs, the season was an electrifying statement of the Warriors' pending success.

Arenas averaged 18.3 points, 6.3 assists, and 4.7 rebounds per game as the full-time starter. Both he and Richardson shone in the Rookie Challenge during NBA All-Star Weekend in Washington and Arenas looked destined to be a star. At the end of that season, the league honored the second-year guard with the 2003 NBA Most Improved Player Award.

In then-typical Warriors fashion, the good times ended in abrupt and brutal fashion. This time, it happened in a manner that epitomized the Warriors' run of poor management and horrendous luck.

Back in August 1999, the team gave center Erick Dampier a seven-year, $48 million contract extension, then signed forward Danny Fortson to a seven-year, $38 million contract a year later. Two months after drafting Arenas, Richardson, and Murphy in 2001, they agreed to a maximum contract extension with Antawn Jamison for six years and $86 million. Those contracts combined for a massive financial outlay for their frontcourt.

That spending also created a major problem because when it came time to pay Arenas, the Warriors did not have any salary cap space.

Arenas signed a two-year contract with the Warriors after they drafted him, then very common for a second-round pick. However, Arenas became an anomaly that the system was not prepared for because he emerged so quickly. At the time, the league's Collective Bargaining Agreement required a player to have three years of experience on that team or contract before the team could use an exception known as "Larry Bird rights" to re-sign that player even if they did not have enough room under the salary cap.

Since Arenas had only been in the NBA and on the Warriors for two years, the most the Warriors could offer him was their mid-level exception with a starting salary near $4.9 million. While Arenas was a restricted free agent and that process ostensibly gave Golden State the ability to match an offer sheet he signed with another team, the Washington Wizards offered a six-year, $60 million contract that the league's rules did not allow them to offer or match because of their lack of salary cap space and Bird rights.

Even with that major hurdle, the Warriors still had hope. If they could somehow convince Arenas to spurn the six-year offer from Washington and sign a one-year deal with the Warriors, Golden State could give Arenas the big contract the following summer.

Arenas, who loved the Bay Area and had bonded with his teammates, wanted to stay with the Warriors and agreed to that plan but wanted owner Chris Cohan to give him some assurances the Warriors would give him a big contract the following year. Cohan declined, so Arenas signed with Washington.

While a formalized agreement of that nature is not allowed in the NBA, Arenas exposed the discussion in a radio interview. "I would be a Golden State Warrior," Arenas told the Bay Area's KNBR radio. "That's all he had to do was shake my hand and let me know…. I was not planning to go anywhere."

In 2005, the league and players agreed to a new Collective Bargaining Agreement that included a new rule preventing other teams from making offers to second-year players worth more than the non-taxpayer mid-level exception that their prior team could not match. While Arenas' name does not appear in the document, the change is commonly referred to as the Gilbert Arenas provision and exists to this day.

While it provides little consolation considering Arenas made three All-NBA teams and three All-Star games as a member of the Wizards, the Warriors' futility actually made a bit of NBA history.

71 Splash Brothers

Mark Jackson took the podium in Denver. His Warriors had just won Game 2 of their 2013 first-round series against the Nuggets. It was a blistering offensive performance by the Warriors where they scored 131 points and shot 64.6 percent, including 14-for-25 from three in the high altitude of Denver's home court.

It was the biggest win of Jackson's tenure and the loudest announcement that the Warriors were no longer an NBA pushover. Then Jackson made a louder statement.

"In my opinion," Jackson said, "they're the greatest shooting backcourt in the history of the game."

A media firestorm ensued. Water coolers across the nation debated whether the Warriors' young backcourt deserved such an honor.

Curry had just broken Ray Allen's NBA record for most three-pointers in a season with 272 while Thompson made a career-high 211 in his first full season as a starter, giving them the most three-pointers by teammates in league history.

Better than Gail Goodrich and Jerry West? Than John Stockton and Jeff Hornacek? That was considered lofty praise for players who were still wet behind the ears.

Many called Jackson crazy. So much so, he had to explain further days later.

"I've been listening and watching to all the reactions," Jackson said later. "You have to understand, I'm not comparing them as a tandem to the greats. But I am saying as a tandem shooting the basketball, to me it's not even a debate. These two guys, when you're talking about putting all-time greats in a room, they're going to go in the room and they very well can come out. You can't say that about any other tandem that's played. It's who they are. They were born to shoot the basketball. There's no other two players in a backcourt together that were born to shoot the basketball."

It did not take long for Jackson's once lavish, outlandish praise to become accepted orthodoxy. Curry and Thompson even have a universally acknowledged nickname: Splash Brothers.

The moniker was thought up by then-Warriors.com writer Brian Witt, who tweeted it out at halftime during a Warriors home game against Charlotte on December 21, 2012. It was perfect because both guards frequently made the nets splash, raining three-pointers on opponents, and it had an instant ring in the Bay Area, where two decades earlier Jose Canseco and Mark McGwire became known as the Bash Brothers due to their massive home runs in the next-door Oakland Coliseum.

Curry and Thompson went on to combine for 67 three-pointers in 12 games that same postseason Jackson touted them as the greatest but that was just the beginning.

Over the next two regular seasons, they combined for 1,009 three-pointers. In 2014–15, Curry again set a new mark for three-pointers in a season (286) and the Splash Brothers started the 2015 All-Star Game together since Curry was the leading vote-getter and Thompson replaced injured starter Kobe Bryant.

Curry and Thompson celebrate after wining the final World Basketball match against Serbia at the Palacio de los Deportes stadium in Madrid, Spain, on Sunday, September 14, 2014. (AP Photo/Daniel Ochoa de Olza)

That same year, Curry made 98 threes in the playoffs and Thompson made 57, combining for more than 13 of the other 15 teams made in that postseason. In 2016, Curry again broke his own record with an incomprehensible 402 three-pointers while Thompson achieved his own career high with 276, more than any player other than his teammate had ever made in an NBA season.

The two eliminated any doubt they are the best shooting backcourt ever long ago but are now entering the discussion for best backcourt ever. Since the two are still in their prime, they have years to make their case.

While they have more time to make that case, the Splash Brothers have already won a championship, started in an All-Star game, and won Olympic gold medals together. They power an electric offense that is revolutionizing the NBA and help lead what is becoming one of the best runs of any team in league history.

The Splash Brothers validated and vindicated their coach's praise but still have plenty of work to do together.

72 Bernard King

During their worst years, the only way the Warriors could get elite talent was by overpaying or by accepting top talents with excessive baggage. It was part of Golden State's tradition, trying to coax the best out of troubled greats.

At the top of that list is Bernard King.

King was and is one of the best natural scorers in NBA history, but character issues brought him to the Warriors, where he, in a sense, rehabilitated himself.

Born and raised in Brooklyn, King was a prodigy at the University of Tennessee, averaging 25.8 points his junior season before declaring himself eligible for the 1977 Draft. However, he was also a controversial figure, getting arrested twice while playing for the Vols for smoking marijuana and drunk driving. Despite his run-ins with the law, the Nets drafted King seventh overall in 1977. He was arrested twice before the season began, the first exactly a month after he was drafted when he allegedly broke into the University of Tennessee and stole a television from the athletic department. Five days later, King was arrested again for marijuana possession and resisting arrest.

Even with all that dragging King down behind the scenes, he was truly special once he took the court. Even though they moved to New Jersey before the season began, the Nets had a local legend on their roster. King lived up to the hype off the bat, averaging 24.2 points and 9.5 rebounds as a rookie, which both led the Nets.

Two months into his second season, King was arrested again. In December 1978, police reportedly found him passed out in his Corvette with a small amount of cocaine. He escaped with probation instead of jail time but eventually the Nets grew weary of King's issues and traded him to Utah for big man Rich Kelley. King's stint with the Jazz, who had recently moved from New Orleans, lasted 19 games. The 23-year-old was arrested again on New Year's Day of 1980 and was suspended indefinitely after a woman accused him of forcing her to have repeated sex with him. King pleaded no contest to one count and went to a treatment center for substance abuse. In September 1980, he was traded to the Warriors.

It was a steal for Golden State, who gave up only reserve big man Wayne Cooper and a second-round pick. King returned to form with the Warriors and put together a two-year stretch that launched him into the NBA stratosphere.

King was a right-handed player who loved the left side of the floor, often dribbling left and pulling up. At 6'7", he could get his shot off over most small forwards and he was quick enough to get to his spots. King thrived with a defender on his hip, like he needed to feel the defense, and would spin off them and pull up, lean into them to set up the fadeaway, or dip his right shoulder to force his way to the rim.

He was rolling by the second half of the season and was named NBA Player of the Month in January after averaging 27.4 points in 13 games. With King, World B. Free, Joe Barry Carroll, and Purvis Short, the Warriors were in the thick of the playoff hunt after winning just 24 games the year before. They lost nine of their last 12 games to miss the playoffs but were headed in the right direction. King was named NBA Comeback Player of the Year.

The next season, King elevated his profile even more. He upped his scoring average from 21.9 to 23.2, made the 1982 All-Star Game, and became Player of the Month again in December of 1981, which included a 45-point game in a win over Phoenix.

The Warriors were sitting pretty for a shot at the playoffs but they lost their last two games of the season, at the Lakers and Seattle, and missed the postseason by a single game. King had just eighteen as the Warriors blew a big lead.

"It came down to the last game of the season," King said in an interview with Warriors.com. "I think we were up by 18 or 20 points and somehow we blew the lead and lost the game and missed out on the playoffs. We wound up with a record of 45–37 and that's typically good enough to get into the playoffs but we were in such a powerful conference. In spite of that record, we missed out and I became a free agent…. I had honestly thought that I would end my career in Golden State. I wanted to remain there. I loved the community, I loved playing for Al Attles, and all of my teammates were great guys to play with. I thought our future was bright and that we could do some really dominant things in the league."

Eventually King, now in high demand, signed a lucrative offer sheet with the New York Knicks, his hometown team. The

Warriors had announced they would match the offer, which was surprising since owner Franklin Mieuli did not have the money to pay King. However, the Warriors ended up trading King to the Knicks instead of losing him for nothing.

King went on to become an all-time great with the Knicks. He led them to the playoffs immediately, and then the 1983–84 playoffs happened. King topped 40 points in four straight games, including 46 in back-to-back games, as the Knicks beat the Pistons in the first round. He had 44 in the do-or-die Game 5 clincher, outdueling Isiah Thomas in Detroit. The next round, the Knicks took Larry Bird's Celtics to seven games. King topped 40 twice, including 44 points on 16-of-25 shooting to stave off elimination in Game 6, besting Bird's 35. The Knicks were routed in Boston in Game 7, as Bird outscored King 39–24, and the Celtics went on to win the title.

Even without a title, that performance had already solidified King's status in New York. He followed that postseason by leading the NBA in scoring in 1984–85 with 32.9 points per game, including a 60-point performance on Christmas Day against New Jersey. Unfortunately, the Knicks, who lost center Bill Cartwright to a broken foot and Ray Williams to Boston in free agency, returned to the cellar of the Atlantic Division in the East. On March 23, 1985, the Knicks lost King, too. He suffered a devastating knee injury, tearing his ACL and knee cartilage and fracturing his leg. At the time, players did not come back from such injuries. He missed the entire 1985–86 season and did not return to action until April 1987, more than two years after the injury. Concerned, maybe even convinced King would never be the same, the Knicks released him.

King signed with the Washington Bullets and proved the Knicks wrong. Over his four seasons in Washington, he averaged 22 points on 48.3 percent shooting, returned to the playoffs once more and made the All-Star Game in his final season as a starter.

King closed his career on the New Jersey Nets' bench, having survived 14 seasons marked with brilliance and drama.

In 2013, King was enshrined in the Naismith Memorial Basketball Hall of Fame. His road to basketball's highest honor began in earnest with the Warriors.

73 Jamison's 51s

While the 2000–01 Warriors season soured quickly, third-year forward Antawn Jamison was showing even more of the promise that inspired the team to use the No. 4 overall pick on him in the unpopular trade involving Vince Carter. In the first 17 games of the season, Jamison averaged 20.6 points and 7.6 rebounds per game without missing any, which was encouraging after he was sidelined for the final two months of the 1999–2000 season due to a knee injury.

Jamison took that momentum to Seattle, where the Warriors faced the SuperSonics, who had fired coach Paul Westphal the week before. The Golden State forward started early, scoring 31 points in the first half and passing his previous career high of 37 before the end of the third quarter. Even with that outburst, the Warriors still trailed by nine heading into the fourth. Jamison ended the game with a remarkable 51 points on 23-for-36 shooting and even made two three-pointers. After the game, Jamison said, "It was one of those nights I was feeling it."

Sonics forward Jelani McCoy described Jamison's performance by remarking, "It seemed like there was two of him out there." Even with Jamison's 51 points and 14 rebounds, the struggling Warriors lost by 16.

The Warriors' next game was back at The Arena in Oakland against the reigning NBA champion Lakers and scoring leader Kobe Bryant, who had it rolling. Fresh off his first championship, Bryant was coming into his own as a dominant player in the league and stepping out of the shadow of Shaquille O'Neal. He opened the 2000–01 season like he was bent on proving he was the most dominant player in the world, including scoring at least 30 points in five straight games in November. Bryant started December by dropping a new career-high 43 in a showdown against Tim Duncan and surpassing a Spurs team that would finish with the best record in the West, outshining Dirk Nowitzki by scoring 38 against Dallas and then tallying 36 in a duel with Allen Iverson in a win over the best team in the East. Even with Bryant's rapidly expanding profile and the two teams' very different paths, any Lakers-Warriors game in Oakland was a big deal and Jamison's 51 in Seattle gave the home fans more hope.

Jamison and Bryant delivered, each producing multiple double-digit scoring quarters as the teams battled throughout. The Warriors took an early lead but the Lakers exploded with a huge 35–19 quarter where Bryant nearly outscored the home team with 17 of his own. Golden State battled back with scoring from Jamison, Larry Hughes, and Vonteego Cummings, with a Cummings free throw off a flagrant foul by Shaquille O'Neal tying the game at 107 with 1:33 remaining.

Amazingly, neither team scored for the rest of regulation, as Bryant missed three shots, including a potential game-winning three at the buzzer. Jamison ended the fourth with 43 points and Bryant had 39. At one point, O'Neal yelled, "Somebody guard his ass!" in an attempt to get extra manpower on Jamison.

After the fact, Jamison said, "To hear someone like Shaq say that, that really means something."

Overtime became a contest between the two scorers, including an almost two-minute stretch in the final minutes where they took every shot for their respective teams. However, Bryant was shouldering the load trying to make a comeback because the Warriors started out the overtime on an 11–5 run. With the game tied and a minute to go, Jamison made a 20-footer to give him 51 points and the Warriors a lead. After a Bryant turnover, Hughes made two free throws to build a four-point lead they never relinquished, though Bryant had the chance at a game-tying three as time expired.

The Warriors picked up a nice win over the reigning and eventual champions and both Jamison and Bryant ended with 51 points, becoming the first opponents to score 50 or more in the same game since the Warriors' Wilt Chamberlain and the Lakers' Elgin Baylor almost exactly 38 years before. Jamison's back-to-back games with 50 or more points put him in exclusive company, as only seven other players in league history have ever accomplished that feat, a list that includes former Warriors Rick Barry, Wilt Chamberlain, and Bernard King, along with his dueling partner in the game, Kobe Bryant. His final line was 51 points on 21-for-29 shooting (2-for-5 from three), with 13 rebounds and five assists, while Bryant finished with 51 points on 18-for-35 shooting (2-for-7 from three), eight assists, and seven rebounds.

After the game, Jamison said, "I never imagined me doing this.... I think this is going to open a lot of people's eyes." His history-making performance certainly accomplished that.

74 Strength in Numbers

General manager Bob Myers was in a quiet corner, tucked in the bowels of Quicken Loans Arena, where the chaos and ecstasy did not dominate his hearing. While everyone celebrated with family and friends, he stole a moment behind the scenes to exhale. His suit jacket was gone. His white button-up shirt was open and damp.

The playoff run had been an intense affair for the architect of these 2015 NBA champions. He needed a moment to soak it all in, to reflect on how it all happened. He struggled to even explain it. After listing off the things that broke right for the Warriors, he paused, and just stood there staring at the ground, in a trance as he twisted his lip with his fingers.

Suddenly, his eyes widened. His voice escalated to a mild shout. He'd snapped out of it.

"And Andre Iguodala wins Finals MVP!" Myers said. "Perfect ending. Perfect. Hollywood couldn't make this stuff up. I couldn't be happier for him. That's our team right there. That sums us up."

While some associate "Strength in Numbers" with the shirts given out during the Warriors' 2015 playoff run, the phrase had more meaning to the team and their coach. Between Game 1 and Game 2 of the 2015 NBA Finals, coach Steve Kerr explained that in "the first meeting of the season the night before training camp, we had a team dinner, and that was a big theme was strength in numbers. We're going to try to use our depth throughout the regular season and in the playoffs, and that's been a big part of our team."

That started higher up the totem pole with both Iguodala and David Lee accepting bench roles after being longtime starters, but it ran through the entire team. The front office built a talented, versatile bench Kerr deployed confidently throughout the season and even in the Finals. Strength in Numbers also combined with a cohesive "Next Man Up" mentality where the coaching staff encouraged players all the way down the roster to be ready in case they were needed. While injuries are the most common impetus for a team using their bench depth, Kerr and his staff also worked

Stephen Curry holds the championship trophy and Andre Iguodala holds the MVP trophy as they celebrate winning the 2015 NBA Finals.
(AP Photo/Paul Sancya)

to try out players in circumstances and matchups that gave them a better chance to succeed, keeping the team more engaged.

Those fundamental concepts produced significant effects during Kerr's first season as head coach. Iguodala and Lee's sacrifices helped set the tone, but Strength in Numbers required the right personnel and buy-in from the roster. Guards Shaun Livingston and Leandro Barbosa both joined the team for that inaugural season and then played integral roles when Stephen Curry and Klay Thompson needed rest, while 2013 signing Marreese Speights and 2012 first-round pick Festus Ezeli provided needed minutes at center. While younger role players Justin Holiday and James Michael McAdoo were not major factors in that playoff push, each had multiple 20-plus minute games in the regular season and Holiday started four games that March.

Relying more heavily on the bench that first season ended up helping in another key way when the Warriors made a surprisingly deep playoff run. Even though Stephen Curry, Klay Thompson, and Draymond Green each missed five or fewer games in the regular season, no one on the team played more than 32.7 minutes per game. While partially helped by blowing out opponents early enough that their stars did not need to play as many fourth quarters, the Warriors entered the postseason with a younger, more rested core. That dynamic allowed all of their key players to meaningfully ramp up their workload in the playoffs without some of the cumulative wear and tear that challenge the best teams during a long postseason run. Remarkably, the best representation of that dynamic that season was Iguodala, who averaged 26.9 minutes per game in the regular season before ramping it up to 37.1 in the NBA Finals when he returned to the starting lineup and won Finals MVP.

A year later, Golden State again relied on depth throughout the regular season, with big performances by Ezeli, Barbosa, and Brandon Rush contributing to their historic 73-win season. It also extended to the coaching staff, as Kerr had to take an extended leave of absence due to complications from off-season back surgeries. Luke Walton took over as interim head coach and the team responded with a league-record 24 wins to start the season and a 39-4 mark before Kerr's return to the sideline. Livingston, Barbosa, and 2015 signing Ian Clark all had to step up after Curry sprained his MCL during the Houston series while his four-game absence and subsequent recovery forced Thompson and Green to take on more of the playmaking and scoring burden during the MVP's absence. Curry's injury illuminated the depth of an already historic team as they went 4–1 against the Rockets and Trail Blazers.

After finishing off Portland with Curry and then outlasting the Oklahoma City Thunder in a seven-game Western Conference Finals, the Warriors' mantra faced another challenge when Andrew Bogut injured his left knee in Game 5 of the 2016 NBA Finals. Even though the team had won the championship behind the "Death Lineup" with Draymond Green at center the year before, Kerr turned to Strength in Numbers, trying out Ezeli, McAdoo, Speights, and former Cavalier Anderson Varejão during the last three games, including fateful minutes for Ezeli and Varejão in the second half of Game 7.

While that reliance on bench players made life more difficult on the Warriors during those pivotal contests, Strength in Numbers continued to play a major role in the team's overwhelming success. The next season, Golden State won 67 games despite not having a single player among the league's top 25 in minutes per game. Holdovers including Livingston and Clark combined with an entirely new center rotation of Zaza Pachulia, David West, and JaVale McGee and second-round pick Patrick McCaw as the front office overhauled the bench after clearing enough salary cap space to sign Kevin Durant.

Relying on three different centers allowed each to stay fresh and McGee revitalized his career after making the team in training camp on a non-guaranteed contract. Guards McCaw and Clark represented the Strength in Numbers ethos at different points during the season, with Clark replacing Barbosa and scoring more than 20 points four separate times, then posting five double-digit games in the playoffs. With a chance to secure the championship in Game 5 of the 2017 NBA Finals, Kerr changed his rotation, turning to Iguodala and McCaw instead of McGee and Clark, again relying on a deep bench. The two responded with strong games and Golden State won their second title in three seasons.

Part of the reason Kerr's mentality worked so well was that it kept players energized and active even when they were not on the court. Incidentally, Speights summarized the benefits of this well after leaving the team. Comparing the Clippers to the Warriors, he said, "Guys just got to sacrifice, do some things other than scoring, do some other things than your personal goals" like his teammates had when he was in Oakland. Similarly, the coaching staff used the connected "Next Man Up" concept when they needed to replace Kerr on the sideline in both 2015–16 with Luke Walton and 2016–17 with Mike Brown.

Fully deployed as both mantra and philosophy, Strength in Numbers also attracted free agents even though the team did not have much money or high-profile playing time to offer. West and Pachulia both took lower salaries to play on the Warriors in both 2016–17 and 2017–18, while the team was also able to add Nick Young and Omri Casspi on low-cost, one-year contracts in July 2017.

While circumstances may have inspired Coach Kerr's focus on Strength in Numbers, his enthusiastic support of the concept helped shape the most successful run in franchise history.

75 Jim Barnett

Jim Barnett has become an institution for Warriors fans with 32 years as the team's analyst for television broadcasts.

After starring at the University of Oregon, the Boston Celtics took Barnett in the first round of the 1966 NBA Draft and he quickly built a reputation as a fierce competitor without fear of driving in the paint against bigger players. After one season with the Celtics, three with the San Diego Rockets, and one with the Portland Trail Blazers, he joined the Warriors after they traded three future draft picks for him. Coach Al Attles had battled Barnett as a player and saw a place on the team for the man nicknamed "Crazy Horse."

Barnett immediately fit in as a key piece of the Golden State guard rotation, averaging 27 minutes and 12 points per game in each of his first two seasons with the team. His best playoff performance came against the loaded Milwaukee Bucks in 1972, when he averaged 21.6 points per game in the series and scored 30 in the Warriors' Game 1 win.

The New Orleans Jazz selected Barnett in the 1974 Expansion Draft, ending his time with Golden State, but he played another three seasons for the Jazz, Knicks, and 76ers before retiring in 1977. Playing for six different franchises over 11 NBA seasons allowed Barnett to amass a wealth of knowledge and perspective that proved invaluable in his next career.

Barnett returned to the Warriors organization as a broadcaster for the 1985–86 season and has stayed in that courtside seat ever since, calling games for a remarkable 32-season stretch for the franchise. His insight proved vital in the darker days, like their 19-win 1997–98 campaign, but he shined when the Warriors played their best, including during Run TMC, We Believe, and the franchise's amazing current run. His intense passion for the game and its history allows Barnett to serve as a connection to franchise and league history for both lifelong and more recent fans.

Before the 2013–14 season, the Warriors intended to find a younger color analyst to pair with longtime play-by-play announcer Bob Fitzgerald and the sides announced a "mutual agreement" that 2013–14 would be Barnett's last season broadcasting the team. After an intense show of support from fans, Barnett announced that he would come back for 2014–15, telling the *Bay Area News Group* he would stay "as long as I'm able to do it and do a good, credible job, and as long as people want me." As luck would have it, that return allowed Barnett to be a part of Golden State's 2015 championship run after missing their prior title by one season exactly 40 years before.

76 Alex Hannum

Alex Hannum has a unique place in both Warriors history and Bay Area basketball history, a wonderful reflection of his unusual career.

He focused on both defense and conditioning and that often led to him challenging players, including Wilt Chamberlain for two different franchises. Future Hall of Fame coach Pat Riley played for Hannum in 1969–70 and told a story of when Hannum told that team to run the steps of the San Diego Sports Arena but did not tell them where or when to stop. After three hours, Hannum ended the conditioning by calling the trainer from home.

Hannum made a transition that is actually impossible in the current NBA: player to player/coach to coach. He bounced around the league for seven and a half seasons then signed with the St. Louis Hawks mid-season and became their player/coach. The next season, he retired from playing and coached those same Hawks to the NBA championship, beating the vaunted Celtics in six games.

After a few seasons with the Syracuse Nationals, Hannum signed on with the Warriors to coach their second season in San Francisco. That season, the Warriors jumped from 31 to 48 wins, finishing first in the Western Division and making the NBA Finals after defeating the Hawks in seven games. They ended up falling to the Celtics in the first Russell vs. Chamberlain NBA Finals, but Hannum's credit for the turnaround came in his first Coach of the Year Award.

Unfortunately, that rosy start did not continue, even though the team had a young Wilt Chamberlain, Nate Thurmond, Tom Meshery, and Al Attles. Despite that amazing collection of young talent, the Warriors disappointed early in the 1964–65 season and it turned even more dramatically at the All-Star break. As Hannum later wrote for *Sports Illustrated*, owner Frank Mieuli was ready to move on from Wilt Chamberlain and told Hannum, "He'll be traded before I go home," which ended up happening, as Wilt was sent back to Philadelphia for Paul Neumann, Connie Dierking, Lee Shaffer, and cash.

Both the decision to trade Chamberlain and the return greatly disappointed Hannum and the Warriors finished the season at a devastating 17–63, last in the entire NBA by 14 games. That futility opened the door for the team to draft Rick Barry with the second overall pick and provided Hannum the opportunity to help guide the development of another future Hall of Famer. However, Barry's rookie year was Hannum's final season with the Warriors and he coached his final game for the franchise at just 42 years old.

Hannum then jumped from Wilt Chamberlain's old team to his new one, coaching him again for the 76ers about 18 months after the trade. That first year, Chamberlain, Hannum, and the 76ers won the NBA championship, beating Russell and Auerbach's Celtics in the

Eastern Division Finals and then the Warriors in the Finals. That made Hannum the first coach in league history to win championships with different teams, a feat that has only been matched by Phil Jackson and Hannum's former player Pat Riley. Plus, those titles in 1958 and 1967 were the only two times in Bill Russell's playing career that his team did not win the NBA championship.

Amazingly, Hannum only spent one more season with the 76ers then left for another fascinating destination. He returned to the Bay Area but with the ABA's Oakland Oaks instead of the Warriors. After sitting out a year, that was also former rookie Rick Barry's first season in the ABA. Hannum, Barry, and a fascinating Oaks team that also featured future head coaches Larry Brown and Doug Moe dominated the league, winning 60 regular season games and the league championship, despite Barry missing the second half of the season due to a knee injury, meaning the Oaks won a league title before the San Francisco Warriors in only their second year of existence. Hannum won his second Coach of the Year Award and that championship also made him the first coach to ever win titles in both the NBA and ABA (later joined by Bill Sharman, who replaced Hannum and coached the Warriors in that 1967 NBA Finals the 76ers won). Interestingly, all three of Hannum's championships came in his first full season coaching that franchise.

After that triumph, Hannum changed teams again and worked for both the San Diego Rockets (NBA) and Denver Rockets (ABA) before retiring in 1974. He was enshrined in the Naismith Memorial Basketball Hall of Fame in 1998 and coached 13 Hall of Fame players in his 16 seasons.

77 Chris Mullin's Jersey Retirement Ceremony

Joe Lacob just stood there, helpless, dead center on the court of a darkened Oracle Arena, the spotlight highlighting his discomfort. He tried to wait it out, then talk through it. He did his best to hide the anger and hurt.

But the boos were just too loud.

Loud enough for Chris Mullin, the former star player whose jersey retirement ceremony was being interrupted, to leave his seat and come stand with Lacob. Mullin hoped his status as a Warriors legend would shield the new owner, not even two years into his reign. Cheers followed Mullin to center court as he put his arm around Lacob and addressed the crowd.

"Change is inevitable," Mullin assured the angry crowd. "It's going to work out just fine.... This thing is going the right way."

It seemed to work. Mullin drew an ovation from the crowd. The tide in the arena had changed. As he'd done so many times during his playing career, Mullin made Warriors fans feel better.

Then Lacob grabbed the mic again and the boos returned. Rick Barry, another Warriors legend, had seen enough.

"C'mon people!" Barry said after grabbing a microphone and stepping into the spotlight. "You fans are the greatest fans in the world.... Show a little bit of class. This is a man that I've spent some time talking to. He is going to change this franchise. This is crazy. Seriously. C'mon. You are doing yourself a disservice."

While it was not that long ago, the Warriors were in a dramatically different place on March 19, 2012. The new ownership group had been working diligently to reconnect with the franchise's history and retiring the jersey of an all-time great fit in well with that effort, particularly since Mullin was months away from being enshrined in the Naismith Memorial Basketball Hall of Fame.

However, the ceremony came at exactly the wrong time. Lacob had guaranteed a playoff appearance to season ticket holders in March of 2011 and the lockout-shortened season started with optimism due to their young talent, but it'd gone off the rails. Beyond trading fan favorite Monta Ellis to Milwaukee for injured center Andrew Bogut a week before, the team had also recently shut down Stephen Curry due to his ankle issues and an incentive to lose to retain their first-round draft pick which was top-seven protected that year. (It ended up taking a 5–19 finish and winning a coin flip to keep the pick that became Harrison Barnes.) To make matters worse, the skeleton crew still on the court had only scored 35 points in the first half against a Minnesota team that had lost by 16 points in Sacramento the night before and finished the season 26–40.

The frustration of a fifth straight season without a playoff berth after big promises burst to the forefront and created a startling return to the national sports world for the first time since the We Believe season. Many, including Rick Barry, saw the outpouring of emotion as classless or uncalled for, but it also showed the boundless passion and justified frustration of a long-tortured fan base.

It took a few years, but the incident has also taken on a new legacy after the team's recent success. Mullin and Barry's pleas for patience turned out to be correct as the Warriors have made the playoffs every single season since 2011–12 and won the championship exactly four years and three months after the ceremony. What started as a genuine display of frustration for decades of futility and disappointment has turned into the grand finale of a dark time for the franchise.

78 The Defenders

In the 37 seasons following their 1974–75 NBA championship, the Warriors had six campaigns where they allowed fewer than 105 points per 100 possessions. Four of those were by teams coached by Al Attles in the years following that championship.

Of the 15 coaches who followed Attles, only three had managed to produce a defense even slightly better than league average: Don Nelson in 1988–89 and again in 1993–94, Mike Montgomery in 2005–06, and P.J. Carlesimo in the strike-shortened 1998–99 season.

For the longest time, the Warriors and defense were like kids and vegetables. They were known around the league for being a high-scoring team that was exciting to watch and sometimes dangerous to play but Golden State was never taken seriously because they did not play defense.

And, as the saying goes: offense wins games, defense wins championships.

All that began to change, starting with the hiring of Mark Jackson, the longtime NBA point guard and popular broadcaster. The 17-year NBA veteran point guard made his name in the rough-and-tumble Eastern Conference with the Pacers and Knicks.

"They will be held accountable and there will be a price to pay," Jackson said of his defensive philosophy when the Warriors hired him in June 2011. "I've come to the mindset that the only way to win in this league and win big is defensively. So we will be committed on the defensive side of the ball."

It sounded remarkably similar to what past new coaches had said since so many promised defense and pledged to change the culture of fun-and-gun so they could turn the Warriors into legit contenders. However, under Jackson, that actually changed. Young players like Klay Thompson, drafted shortly after Jackson was hired, grew defensively under his watch.

That said, it was more than just Jackson. The front office made some critical moves to give the team a chance on the defensive end, the biggest coming when they traded star guard Monta Ellis for Milwaukee center Andrew Bogut. That move showed how desperate general manager Bob Myers was to field a formidable team on both ends of the court. Ellis was regarded as the Warriors' best player and their star but the Warriors gave him up for Bogut, who was out for the season with a broken ankle.

It was a high-risk, high-reward gamble for the Warriors.

If Bogut—who had previously suffered a broken elbow and back injuries—was as injury prone as many thought, they might have given up their best player for nothing. However, if he got healthy and became the player drafted first overall in the 2005 NBA Draft, the Warriors would finally be getting the center they'd long coveted. When able to play, Bogut was a top-notch defensive center who would immediately improve the Warriors' credibility on that end.

"He will add an element of toughness to our team and will provide us with scoring, rebounding, and a defensive presence in the middle," then–general manager Larry Riley said. "We've lacked those elements in recent years and think that Andrew's addition will be a key factor in the growth of our team."

Bogut turned out to be exactly what the Warriors expected. Despite missing most of the 2012–13 season with the same ankle issues that kept him out after the trade, the center showed his worth in the playoffs.

On a hurting ankle, Bogut averaged 10.9 rebounds and 1.5 blocks in 27.3 minutes. He was the anchor in the middle as the Warriors upset the third-seeded Denver Nuggets in the first round and hung tough against the second-seeded San Antonio Spurs in a surprisingly competitive six-game series.

It was not so noticeable at the time but another critical move ended up emerging in the same postseason. With the 35th pick in the 2012 Draft, Golden State selected Draymond Green. Nobody knew it at the time, but the overweight and undersized forward out of Michigan State would be the elite defender who would take the Warriors to another level. He showed signs of it during the playoffs his rookie year, helping fill in off the bench for injured All-Star forward David Lee.

That summer, the next critical move came when the Warriors signed free agent Andre Iguodala away from the same Denver team they had just beaten in the playoffs. Iguodala, in his last days as a frontline NBA scorer, was still a savvy veteran who gave the Warriors a third elite defender.

This new emphasis on defense coupled with having players who were capable on that end of the court turned the Warriors into one of the best defensive teams in the league. In 2013–14, the Warriors won 51 games and finished with the third-stingiest defense.

In the playoffs, despite Bogut being injured, the Warriors nearly upset the Los Angeles Clippers in the first round. They pushed the favored Clippers to a win-or-go-home seventh game and a big part of it was the defense Green played on All-Star Blake Griffin while Iguodala guarded sharpshooter J.J. Redick.

The Warriors lost the series but the foundation was set. On top of that, Thompson and forward Harrison Barnes were steadily improving on defense. The Warriors went into the next season as a legitimate top-notch defensive team, which had not happened since Attles roamed the sideline in a leisure jacket.

Those developments culminated in a phenomenal defense the following year. The Warriors finished the 2014–15 season with the highest-rated defense (98.2 points allowed per 100 possessions) and a strong sixth in opponents' field goal percentage. In the playoffs, they got even stingier, allowing just 95.5 points per game. The Warriors have allowed fewer than 100 points per game five times since the franchise moved west from Philadelphia, with two of them coming after hiring Mark Jackson and reformulating the team.

That rapid progression was a big part of how the Warriors surprised so many when they won the 2015 championship. After all, the franchise had a well-earned reputation as an offensive team that buffeted at the three-point line. While many pundits like Charles Barkley consistently denigrated the Warriors as a jump-shooting team, few noticed they had become the best defense in the NBA.

The Philadelphia Warriors

The Warriors' move to San Francisco seems almost inconceivable now, looking back, when you consider how strong the Philadelphia Warriors were at that time, and how impressive their history had been.

In their final season in Philadelphia, the Warriors finished 49–31, the third-best record in the entire NBA behind the Celtics and Lakers, and fell to Bill Russell's Celtics by two points in Game 7 of the Eastern Conference Finals in the Boston Garden. What's more, that was not some high-water mark for the franchise—they were over .500 in six of their final seven seasons in the City of Brotherly Love and won the 1956 NBA championship behind strong performances from Hall of Famers Paul Arizin, Neil Johnston, and Tom Gola.

Even more astonishingly, the Warriors moved despite possessing a young superstar. Wilt Chamberlain joined the team three seasons after their 1956 championship, following a season with the Harlem Globetrotters. Chamberlain blew past lofty expectations, winning both Rookie of the Year and Most Valuable Player in his first NBA season, while also leading the league in scoring. His prominence only grew from there, increasing his scoring average to 38.4 points per game in 1960–61 and then setting the still-standing NBA record of 100 points in a game just 32 days before the Warriors' final game in Philadelphia.

Founded in 1946 as a part of the Basketball Association of America, the Warriors were a part of the transition to the NBA three years later, but their victory over the Chicago Stags in 1947 to conclude their inaugural season is considered the first NBA championship. Early star forward Joe Fulks helped bring the jump shot to the NBA and set the BAA/NBA single-game scoring record of 63 in 1949, which stood for 10 years. He was joined by Paul Arizin and Andy Phillip in 1950, then Neil Johnston one season later. A short lull in the early '50s partially caused by Arizin serving in the Korean War led straight into that 1956 championship and that run largely continued through the team's final season in Philadelphia.

Incidentally, the move itself ensured that some of the team's history stayed in Philadelphia, as Arizin retired from the NBA at 34 years old in favor of a more lucrative job at IBM and played three seasons for the nearby Camden Bullets, who were a part of the Eastern Basketball League. Gola made the move to San Francisco but only played 21 games before asking for a trade back to the East Coast.

In just 16 years of existence, the Philadelphia Warriors were graced with seven Hall of Fame players and made the playoffs 12 times.

80 Attend Lakers at Warriors

For years, the Lakers' biannual appearances at Oracle were surreal experiences. Due to their seemingly perpetual success and wide reach, the typically hyper-partisan Warriors crowd would become decidedly mixed, and in some cases closer to 50/50.

Part of what made those games so fun was that the remaining Warriors loyalists upped their intensity because of their frustration that rival fans had taken such a large part of the building and were able to sustain cheers for their favorites, especially Kobe Bryant during a vast majority of his 20-season career. Hearing "Let's Go Lakers" chants at Oracle certainly galvanized Golden State's most ardent supporters.

Beyond the rivalry and often personal animosity between fans of the two teams, it also helped that they played some memorable games at Oracle, even during down times for the Warriors, including:

- Sleepy Floyd's 51-point explosion in the 1987 playoffs
- Antawn Jamison and Bryant's dueling 51s in December 2000
- Run TMC beating the 58-win Lakers in the final week of the 1990–91 regular season, the same year they faced off in the second round of the playoffs
- Purvis Short dropping 43 points on 29 shots to beat Magic, Kareem, Worthy, and the 1983–84 team that made the NBA Finals
- Klay Thompson scoring a then-career-high 41 after signing his contract extension in 2014.

Those are just a few of the positive ones on the Warriors' side of the ledger, even during some strong stretches for the Lakers.

Those dynamics have changed in recent years, as the Warriors became a powerhouse at the same time the Lakers hit their roughest patch in recent memory. That has certainly changed the dynamic between the fan bases both broadly and in the building during games but they are still a distinct experience.

While it might be fun to wait until the Lakers are more competitive in a few years to experience one of these contests with added competitiveness, drama, and a feistier set of visiting fans, those games will only occur at Oracle Arena through the 2018–19 season if the Chase Center construction continues to stay on schedule. The chance to see these longtime foes face off in the building that housed so many matchups, including four playoff series, could hold greater significance for longtime fans.

81 Šarūnas Marčiulionis

Šarūnas Marčiulionis became a fan favorite in the early 1990s as a part of the Run TMC–era Warriors.

He joined the team after a tumultuous few years that began when he connected with Donnie Nelson, the son of then-Warriors coach Don Nelson. Golden State actually used a sixth-round pick on Marčiulionis in 1987, but the league ruled him ineligible for the draft process due to his age after the Hawks (who wanted Marčiulionis for themselves) tipped them off. The next year, he was a part of the USSR's gold medal–winning Olympic basketball team that featured four players from his home town in Lithuania, but ended up having to wait when the Soviet Union refused to allow him to leave to play in the NBA. After another two years, Marčiulionis finally joined the Warriors and played four seasons for the team.

As he described it, "my role was to come off the bench and bring great energy" as a part of Nellie Ball. Marčiulionis' combination of high motor and intelligence made him a perfect fit. Beyond providing energy, he was also a very productive offensive player, scoring 30 or more points six different times in a Warriors uniform, despite only starting a total of 26 games in those four seasons.

Marčiulionis' best season for the Warriors came in 1991–92. He averaged 18.9 points and 3.4 assists per game while coming off the bench and then increased those to 21.3 points and 5.0 assists per game in Golden State's playoff series against the Seattle SuperSonics. He finished second in Sixth Man of the Year voting behind Seattle swingman Detlef Schrempf, but looked to have many more years of productive basketball ahead of him at just 27 years old.

The summer following that 1991–92 season, Marčiulionis played an instrumental role in building and then playing for the Lithuanian national basketball team after they declared their independence from the Soviet Union in 1990. Through Donnie Nelson, Marčiulionis met with Jerry Garcia and Peter Weir of the Grateful Dead and the Lithuanian team's distinctive tie-dyed shirts came out of that meeting. Despite losing to the Russian team during group play in the Olympics, Marčiulionis and Lithuania battled their way into the semifinals and ended up defeating the same Russian squad 82–78 to win the bronze medal. While the first Dream Team made most of the headlines in the United States, Lithuania's team was an emotional favorite around the world. Arvydas Sabonis, Marčiulionis' teammate in both 1988 and 1992, said, "The medal in Seoul was gold, but this bronze is our soul."

Unfortunately, Marčiulionis was unable to convert that remarkable achievement into more NBA success as he battled leg and ankle injuries, including the one he battled through during the 1992 Olympics, playing only 30 games in the next two seasons. Golden State traded him to Seattle after the 1993–94 season and he played his last NBA game on December 3, 1996 as a member of the Denver Nuggets.

Marčiulionis was inducted into the Naismith Memorial Basketball Hall of Fame in 2014, presented by former teammate Chris Mullin.

82 Kevin Durant

It might seem strange to devote a chapter of a book about a franchise with 55 years in the Bay Area to a player who has only been on the team for one season, but Kevin Durant justifies that decision.

Durant made the rapid progression from elite prospect to star, becoming the first college freshman ever to win the Naismith College Player of the Year. The Seattle SuperSonics chose him with the second pick in the 2007 NBA Draft and he won the NBA Rookie of the Year before leading the league in scoring four times, including three of his first five seasons. After helping power his young Oklahoma City team to the 2012 NBA Finals, the Thunder traded away teammate James Harden and a year later Durant had his best season as a pro, scoring 32 points per game and winning the 2013–14 Most Valuable Player Award. After missing most of the following season with a fractured foot and then losing in the 2016 Western Conference Finals to the Warriors in devastating fashion, one of the league's brightest stars had his first chance to choose his professional team.

The Warriors were one of six teams Durant chose to meet with in person and they brought a large contingent, including Joe Lacob, Steve Kerr, Bob Myers, Stephen Curry, Draymond Green, Klay Thompson, and Andre Iguodala. While the team intended to wow Durant with a virtual reality presentation, the goggles malfunctioned, but that led to an open conversation between Durant and the Warriors' players. His prospective teammates pitched their "culture, dynasty, and style of play," while assuring the star that his presence would add to their collective success. Three days later, Durant shocked the basketball world by announcing he would sign with the Warriors.

Unsurprisingly, it took time for the team and Durant to adjust to each other. While playing in a system with more player and ball movement was part of what drew Durant to the Warriors, it was a significant change from his nine seasons with the same franchise. Even so, Durant and his teammates were able to be productive during that time and 2016–17 was the former MVP's most efficient season to date. He also embraced a larger defensive role in the regular season, which the Warriors needed without Bogut, Barnes, and Ezeli on the roster. Amazingly, Golden State scored more effectively with Durant on the floor that regular season than either of Curry's MVP years. Four months into the regular season, the incorporation process was moving along well, but then Zaza Pachulia fell into Durant's leg, causing a Grade 2 sprain of the medial collateral ligament in his left knee. That injury kept Durant out until April 8, a 19-game absence.

Durant faced another setback almost immediately, straining his left calf in the Warriors' first playoff game. He returned for Game 4, then had more time to recover for the second-round series against the Jazz. There, he carried them to a Game 3 win with 38 points on a night where Curry and Thompson combined to shoot 3-for-15 from three. Durant was instrumental in the Warriors' second-half comeback in Game 1 against the Spurs, with 12 points on just six shots in the fourth quarter, including the shot that gave Golden State their first lead of the half with just 4:09 remaining. Needing two wins to secure a place in the NBA Finals, Durant took control in San Antonio, averaging 31 points and 11 rebounds in two double-digit victories.

Five years after falling to LeBron James and the Heat in the Finals as a member of the Thunder, Durant finally had his second chance. In Game 1, he took advantage of some defensive lapses by the Cavaliers to score 23 first-half points on the way to 38 and a dominant 113–91 victory. Cleveland improved in Game 2, but Durant posted one of the best playoff games of his career, with 33 points, 13 rebounds, six assists, five blocks, and three steals in another blowout win.

While the Warriors had won both of the first two games at home the year before, having Durant fundamentally changed the Finals from the opening tip. Durant guarded James the majority

Kevin Durant celebrates with his mother, Wanda Durant, as he is named the NBA Finals Most Valuable Player. (AP Photo/Marcio Jose Sanchez)

of the time, and his performance allowed his teammates to focus more on help defense and rebounding. His presence also forced James to spend more energy on the defensive end, which may have contributed to dramatically decreased production and effectiveness in second halves throughout the Finals.

As the series turned to Cleveland, the Warriors had to weather an early storm that eventually became a five-point lead to start the fourth quarter. Durant poured in 14 points and helped key a huge late comeback. He punctuated that run with the definitive play of the series when he grabbed the rebound off a Kyle Korver miss then pulled up from three on James, despite only trailing by two points with 45 seconds remaining. The Warriors fell in Game 4, but Durant still contributed despite a poor shooting night by making 15-of-16 free throws.

Durant returned to form in Game 5 with 39 points on 14-for-20 shooting (5-for-8 from three) as the Warriors outlasted the Cavs to win the championship with Durant dribbling out the final seconds of the clock. A season spent as a villain around the league ended with vindication as he won the Finals MVP unanimously, averaging 35.2 points, 8.2 rebounds, and 5.4 assists for the series, while becoming only the sixth player in league history to score 30 or more points in every game of a Finals series.

After the season, Durant had a choice to make beyond which team to play for in 2017–18. Taking a few million dollars less than his maximum would allow the team to retain Iguodala and Livingston without complication and he ended up going even further, reducing his salary by another $6.8 million to open up more money for his teammates.

While no one knows exactly what the future holds, Durant has transformed the Warriors franchise and set the table for a truly remarkable run.

83 The 2012–13 Season

After a disappointing 2011–12 season that started with a playoff guarantee and ended with the team shelving Stephen Curry and David Lee in an effort to retain their draft pick, fans and the organization needed a lift.

That boost started with the 2012 Draft, where, after keeping their pick, the Warriors drafted forward Harrison Barnes seventh overall and also chose center Festus Ezeli with the last pick of the first round and forward Draymond Green 35th. All three of them had places in the rotation by the end of their rookie year. While trading Monta Ellis for injured center Andrew Bogut helped turn the 2011–12 season, Bogut never actually played, due to his injury. In the 2012–13 season, however, he played Opening Night. On top of that trio, they traded Dorell Wright for veteran backup point guard Jarrett Jack and gave more playing time to guard Kent Bazemore.

The revamped Warriors started out the season strong, as the new additions combined with a continued focus from the coaching staff helped fuel a massive improvement on the defensive end. After four straight seasons with a bottom-five defense, Golden State ended the season 14th while maintaining a potent offense, even without Ellis. They were a surprising 30–22 at the All-Star break and Lee became the first Warrior to make an All-Star team since Latrell Sprewell in 1997. While a year later than previously promised, the team ended the regular season 47–35 with the No. 6 seed in the Western Conference.

Finishing sixth lined the Warriors up with the dangerous Denver Nuggets. Incidentally, the Nuggets were coached by the last man other than Don Nelson to lead the Warriors to the playoffs: George Karl. While the Nuggets were justified favorites, Golden State showed their capability by taking the league's best home team to the brink in Game 1 as it took an Andre Miller layup with seconds left to secure a victory. In the fourth quarter of Game 1, David Lee went down with an injury that turned out to be a torn hip flexor. Without a clear replacement in the frontcourt, coach Mark Jackson turned to Jarrett Jack. Going small worked beautifully against the Nuggets as the Warriors won Game 2 comfortably.

The first playoff game at Oracle Arena since We Believe was a raucous atmosphere. Denver kept it close until the final whistle, but two turnovers in the final minute helped the Warriors hold a narrow lead. Curry continued his hot shooting in Game 4 and the Warriors took a shocking 3–1 advantage. After a comeback fell short in Denver, they got a big boost when Lee returned to come off the bench briefly in Game 6. After a dominant 33–20 third quarter and some late drama, the first Warriors playoff team in six years followed the We Believe model with a six-game first-round upset. Stephen Curry starred in the series, averaging 24.3 points and 9.3 assists per game and outplaying counterpart Ty Lawson.

Downing Denver was a massive sign of progress for the franchise, but they had a chance to make an even larger one against the perennial powerhouse San Antonio Spurs. The Spurs were coached by former Warriors assistant Gregg Popovich, who worked under Don Nelson for two seasons before becoming San Antonio's general manager in 1994. The Warriors astonishingly held a 104–88 lead on the road with four minutes to go in Game 1 but collapsed down the stretch and the Spurs forced overtime. Golden State actually led in both the first and second extra periods, but San Antonio eventually prevailed 129–127 in double overtime.

While a debilitating loss like that could sink a series, the young Warriors bounced back behind Klay Thompson's 34 points and still secured a split. San Antonio regained control as stars Tony

Parker and Tim Duncan were too much to handle in Game 3, but the Warriors again recovered and won Game 4 in overtime after a fourth quarter comeback. Unfortunately, that was their last high point in the series as the Spurs used a huge second half to win Game 5 and then stifled Golden State for the final four minutes to close out Game 6 and the series.

Even though it ended with some disappointment, the Warriors demonstrated their potential by upsetting the Nuggets and challenging the eventual Western Conference champions in a performance that helped set the table for the success to come.

84 Get Championship Gear

NBA championships require winning four best-of-seven series and deserve to be celebrated and commemorated regardless of how frequently they come.

Even though the Warriors' recent run of success has changed both the expectations and resonance of titles, fans would be wise to secure a keepsake to remember each of those seasons and how it made them feel. Despite being just two years apart, the 2015 and 2017 championships carry vastly different legacies that are worth appreciating.

The 2015 championship stands out because it was so out of the blue and that team was particularly memorable. While hindsight has changed the way we think and see it, that season was shockingly dominating and filled with captivating moments for a franchise that struggled for such a long time and relished short, eventually painful bursts of success. The 2015 championship also vaulted the

Warriors to a totally new level of popularity, so at some point in the future these mementos will serve as proof of participation.

2017 was less surprising and more dominant, particularly in the playoffs, but also carried the weight of the 2016 Finals collapse. In many ways, Golden State's second championship in three years encompassed both the historic 73–9 regular season the year before and Kevin Durant's first year with the team.

Unsurprisingly, there are a multitude of options, so one way to handle championships for a team in consistent contention is to focus on what made that title special. Beyond being the first one for almost the entire team, 2015 stands out because they entered the season without the hype that permeated every team after. A "Strength in Numbers" shirt could serve as an appropriate remembrance of that special team, though the bobblehead with Klay Thompson and his dog Rocco was a fan favorite too. Two years later, Durant, David West, Zaza Pachulia, JaVale McGee, and Patrick McCaw were significant new pieces. The highlight from a championship season does not even have to relate to the playoff run, as Thompson's 60-point night and Curry breaking the NBA record with 13 three-pointers were both standout moments from the 2016–17 season.

Another way to pick up interesting trinkets is through going to games the season after a championship. For example, a small group of fans have replica championship rings the Warriors gave out on November 4, 2015, and the same is true for the miniature replicas of the Larry O'Brien Trophy given out on November 20, 2015.

Someday, fans who experienced these title runs will tell their grandkids about these teams. The reasoning will change from person to person, for a specific game or moment or the larger significance of that season marking the start of the Warriors becoming an elite franchise or because they were such a change after a long run of mediocrity. Either way, that fervent joy is sure to be passed down a generation, just as disappointment was for so long.

With that in mind, it should be every fan's quest to make sure they have something to serve as a reminder of those truly remarkable seasons.

85 Chris Mullin the GM

The Warriors had successfully clawed their way back to mediocre as young head coach Eric Musselman led the Warriors to 75 wins over two seasons. For reference, the franchise had totaled 78 wins in the previous four seasons, so even finishing close to .500 in consecutive years signified real progress.

Even as they improved on the court, the Warriors were still battling for relevance and paying the price from some crippling moves, the most damaging of which was doling out huge contracts that left their salary cap in such a mess they could not keep burgeoning star Gilbert Arenas.

The franchise needed new leadership. With that in mind, they tabbed a Warriors luminary to guide them. After becoming a special assistant when he retired in 2001, the team promoted former star Chris Mullin to the head basketball honcho in April 2004. The Bay Area was excited about his return to the franchise and subsequent elevation in the hierarchy.

As Clippers fans of the time were well aware due to Elgin Baylor's struggles with that troubled franchise, Mullin's past as a great scorer did not guarantee success as a general manager. While that became evident through Mullin's tenure, he brought credibility to their front office, and the move established a role for someone who cared about the franchise. Mullin also had a good understanding of the modern NBA player, having retired just a few years earlier.

While his early moves exposed his inexperience, Mullin eventually came into his own as a solid general manager.

One of his first major decisions proved to be a misstep. He replaced Musselman with Mike Montgomery, the longtime head coach at nearby Stanford University. The NBA's history is lined with failed college-to-pro coaches because it is an entirely different world from college basketball. Oftentimes, college coaches have a hard time going from dictator of amateurs to a manager of egos and personality as one of the lower-paid people in the locker room. Montgomery, whose basketball mind was undisputed, struggled making that adjustment and was out after two 34–48 seasons.

Mullin's first draft pick was big man Andris Biedrins, an 18-year-old out of Latvia. After two years on the bench, Biedrins looked like a serviceable NBA center who could play some defense and run the floor, which was intriguing since he was still in his early twenties. While the Latvian big man became a fairly regular double-double threat and received a lucrative six-year, $63 million extension in 2008, Al Jefferson, J.R. Smith, and Jameer Nelson were all talented prospects then who are still playing years after Biedrins flamed out.

In July 2004, Mullin made his first big signing, luring point guard Derek Fisher from the Los Angeles Lakers with a six-year, $37 million contract. Fisher was a pro's pro with a championship pedigree, having won three championships with Shaquille O'Neal and fellow 1996 draftee Kobe Bryant. Even with that success, the Lakers did not want to give Fisher the contract he requested, which opened the door for Mullin to entice Fisher with a big deal.

That same month, he also signed Adonal Foyle to a six-year, $42 million contract extension. Foyle was a defensive specialist on his way to becoming the Warriors' all-time leader in blocks. Already 29 years old, the center was extremely limited offensively and arguably his greatest claim to fame was being drafted ahead of future Hall of

Famer Tracy McGrady. While a positive contributor on and off the court, Foyle never lived up to that contract.

Mullin would go on to say he had to overpay since the Warriors were not a desired destination, effectively a tax he had to pay until he got Golden State to a point where they could compete on the free agent market.

His best move as general manager came during that season, when he acquired Baron Davis from the New Orleans Hornets in February 2005. He got a troubled but talented franchise player for Speedy Claxton and Dale Davis, two part-time starters better served as key reserves on good teams.

Trades proved to be Mullin's most prominent strength. Less than a year after fleecing the Hornets for Davis, he also came up big by acquiring Stephen Jackson and Al Harrington from Indiana in January 2006, in a trade that also ended the disappointing tenures of Mike Dunleavy and Troy Murphy. Like Davis, the move capitalized on talented players who had become out of favor with their current teams, giving Davis more talented, experienced, and fiery players to work with.

In between those two massive deals, Mullin set up one of the most memorable seasons in franchise history with another pivotal swap, but it did not involve players. Mullin fired Montgomery and hired his former coach Don Nelson to lead the franchise. Nelson, with Davis and Jackson as his top players, made a late-season push to improbably make the 2007 playoffs. The We Believe season escalated when they pulled off one of the greatest upsets in NBA history by knocking off the top-seeded Dallas Mavericks.

Mullin's weakness was clearly drafting, as many of his picks continued the franchise's tradition of swinging and missing. He took big men Ike Diogu in 2005 and Patrick O'Bryant in 2006 and both failed miserably as the Warriors' low-post options. Mullin's greatest draft success came in the same draft as Diogu, when he took high school guard Monta Ellis 40th overall and the energetic scorer became far and away the best pick of his tenure.

In the 2007 Draft, Mullin traded beloved franchise star Jason Richardson for seventh overall pick Brandon Wright and drafted shooting guard Marco Belinelli as a potential replacement. Neither Wright nor Belinelli wound up as more than role players for the Warriors, though they both carved out serviceable careers for other teams.

The next year, Mullin chose Anthony Randolph out of LSU with the 14th pick. The enigmatic Randolph stood out as a talented big man with guard skills who looked to be something special if he were developed right, but he clashed with Nelson and immaturity stunted his growth. While his potential was undeniable, the pick hurt more as players taken after him, including Stanford big man Robin Lopez and Cal product Ryan Anderson, continued still-productive careers.

In the later years of his tenure, Mullin ended up in a power struggle with team president Robert Rowell. In 2007, he negotiated a blockbuster trade for Kevin Garnett, which included the much-maligned Jason Richardson deal, and a three-year extension for Davis, but both were nixed by owner Chris Cohan. After those disappointments and the subsequent issues with Rowell's suspension of Ellis and unilateral extension negotiations with Jackson, Mullin eventually retreated to the background and let his contract run out.

He left, however, having done at least one thing he set out to do: get the Warriors back into the playoffs.

86 The San Jose Warriors

The Oakland-Alameda County Coliseum Arena originally opened on November 9, 1966, and has been the Warriors' home for decades. It is the oldest arena in the NBA, beating Madison Square Garden by two years.

The Garden, however, is a national treasure even in its dilapidation. Oakland Arena, as it came to be known, earned a distinctly different reputation. At the same time it wore down, the 1990s saw a boon of new arenas in the NBA, including seven new venues from 1990 to 1995.

As years passed, the Warriors' home became inadequate in the new economics of the league. It was one of the smallest arenas in the NBA, with a seating capacity just over 15,000, and also lacked the bells and whistles of modern arenas. That combination of factors limited the fan experience and, importantly, the franchise's ability to make money.

With that in mind, after the 1995–96 season, the Warriors decided that their outdated venue needed an upgrade. Following brief discussions about potentially building a new arena in San Francisco or San Jose, they decided to help fund major renovations to their existing home.

Starting in 1996, Oakland Arena would undergo a $121 million renovation that gutted the whole interior of the building and added a brand-new seating bowl to the arena, which helped increase the seating capacity to 19,596 for basketball games.

Since the renovations would take a year to complete, the Warriors needed a place to play for the 1996–97 season. The South Bay had the San Jose Arena, built for the NHL expansion Sharks franchise, which made for a natural fit. San Jose Arena was only three years old at the time, so the Warriors and their fans had the chance to experience a season in a modern facility.

Even though the team spent a season playing in a ritzy new building, they were still the same ol' Warriors.

Arguably the low point of that season came off the court, as the team decided that they would not guarantee longtime season-ticket holders in Oakland their seniority or seats once the refurbishments were complete if they did not shell out the money for the year in San Jose. Owner Chris Cohan later admitted, "That created a lot of bad feelings," and that the team "lost thousands" of season-ticket holders as a consequence.

That said, the Warriors did have a significant bright spot in Latrell Sprewell, who averaged a career-high 24.2 points during the San Jose season. It was a breakout year for the rising star, even though he once showed up near halftime for a game because he got lost in the streets of San Jose trying to beat the traffic.

The season away from Oakland proved revelatory for the Warriors. Just three years earlier, they won 50 games behind the exciting combination of Sprewell and Chris Webber, but a third straight season below .500 made it official that they were back to being a cellar dweller in need of a revival. A 30–52 record inspired the franchise to make sweeping changes to prepare for their new home.

The team fired both head coach Rick Adelman, who replaced Don Nelson after he resigned in 1995, and general manager Dave Twardzik.

That summer, the Warriors also traded Chris Mullin, who had been the steady face of the franchise for years. His place on the 1992 Dream Team brought national attention to the team and the perennial All-Star was beloved by the fan base. The last member of Run TMC went to the Indiana Pacers for center Erick Dampier and forward Duane Ferrell.

After the year in San Jose, the Warriors even traded their uniforms. The Run TMC era's royal blue and gold shifted to navy blue, orange, and gold while the classic "Warriors" across the chest now had a lightning bolt from the W stretching across the top with another orange bolt down the side of the jersey. Thunder and lightning was the new theme, including a dunking mascot and all.

In another significant development, the Warriors drew well during their season in San Jose. The arena's larger capacity pushed the total attendance to 621,844, the highest in franchise history. Plus, it completed a Bay Area circuit, since the franchise started in San Francisco before spending decades in Oakland. The Warriors truly became the Bay Area's team since the East Bay, West Bay, and South Bay each could claim their place in franchise history.

87 Coaching Carousel

From 1988 to 1995, the Warriors had some stability at the head coaching position.

During those seven seasons, Don Nelson was the man in charge. He led the team to four playoff appearances during his seasons and oversaw Run TMC, one of the most entertaining trios in NBA history.

Even with recent success and excitement, the Warriors suffered a 14–31 start to the 1994–95 season after Nelson's rocky relationship with burgeoning star Chris Webber, and the subsequent trade that November robbed the franchise of its future centerpiece. Before the end of that season, Nelson was out as head coach and by the start of the next season, he was in New York and the Warriors began a two-decade journey to replace Nelson's presence.

The first crack went to Bob Lanier, who served as interim coach after Nelson's midseason departure. The Hall of Fame center finished the year 12–25, making it clear he wasn't the successor.

Rick Adelman took over in 1995. In his previous five seasons coaching the Portland Trail Blazers, Adelman led the team to three Western Conference Finals, twice making it to the NBA Finals. He was the credible, proven coach the Warriors needed. Two years later, the team fired Adelman after amassing a record of 66–98.

Latrell Sprewell looks at his former coach, P.J. Carlesimo, in the fourth quarter of a 1999 game. (AP Photo/Ben Margot)

P.J. Carlesimo was the next man up. Just like he had done in Portland, Carlesimo took over for Adelman to begin the 1997–98 season. The former Seton Hall coach led the Blazers to three straight playoff appearances, but he was not able to duplicate that success in Golden State. The Warriors failed to make the playoffs in Carlesimo's first two seasons before he was fired in December of 1999, with his lasting impact on the franchise coming from getting choked by Latrell Sprewell.

Garry St. Jean, the general manager at the time, took his crack as the head coach for the remainder of the 1998–99 season. Without the team's best player in Sprewell, St. Jean loaded up on experience. He acquired John Starks, Mookie Blaylock, and Terry Cummings, but all three were past their prime by the time the Warriors got them. St. Jean went 13–42 as the head coach before the team fired him from both jobs.

St. Jean assistant and Hall of Fame player Dave Cowens started the 2000–01 season as the head coach, but won just 25 of 105 games before being fired the morning after the team Christmas party in 2001, when news of his dismissal had already run in that day's newspaper. Brian Winters stepped in and did not do much better, finishing the 2001–02 season with a 13–46 record.

For their next hire, the Warriors went young. They brought in 37-year-old Eric Musselman to inject some freshness into the franchise. The Warriors had a stable of young talent after the 2001 Draft, selecting Jason Richardson, Gilbert Arenas, and Troy Murphy. That season, the Warriors won 38 games, the most by the franchise in nine years, and Musselman finished second to former Nelson assistant Gregg Popovich in NBA Coach of the Year voting.

Even after the franchise lost Gilbert Arenas in free agency and traded anchor Antawn Jamison, Musselman still kept the team afloat in his second year. While the Warriors missed the playoffs, their 37–45 record gave them back-to-back 30-win seasons. The only other coach to do that after Nelson left was Adelman.

At the same time, the team hired Warriors legend Chris Mullin as the new general manager. Even with Musselman's promise as a young coach, Mullin wanted to go a different direction, choosing someone with greater name recognition and more experience teaching young men the nuances of basketball.

Mike Montgomery, who had led the nearby Stanford Cardinal to 10 straight NCAA Tournaments and a 1998 Final Four appearance, was supposed to bring the discipline and fundamentals to the undermanned Warriors. They took a small step back in Montgomery's first year by winning 34 games, but a mid-season trade for All-Star point guard Baron Davis improved the talent level. The next season, the Warriors flipped the calendar with a winning record for the first time since 1994.

Despite that relative success, Montgomery's rigid style did not mesh with Davis. Also, Montgomery was hard on talented rookie guard Monta Ellis, Mullin's second-round gem. After posting a second consecutive 34–48 season, Mullin fired Montgomery.

Part of the reason for the change is that Mullin had a big idea: bringing back Nelson. Eleven years after he left the franchise in shambles, Nelson returned in hopes he could make something of the Warriors' mess. Finally, the Warriors filled the hole he left.

88 Adios, Nellie II

It was not a strange sight to see Don Nelson walking out the side door of the Warriors practice facility with a Bud Light or a cup of coffee in his right hand and Lucky, his Jack Russell terrier, shuffling behind him. He might throw his empty hand up and wave to no one without breaking his stride or looking up.

In many ways, Nelson made his exit from the Warriors and from basketball in the same fashion. Quietly. Unceremoniously. Out the side door.

The Warriors fired Nelson in September 2010, a week before the start of training camp. He was axed by his good friend, then–general manager Larry Riley, acting on behalf of incoming CEO Joe Lacob, and the team replaced their Hall of Fame coach with the assistant he had been grooming in Keith Smart.

It was clearly the end for Nelson. The rigors of the job did not seem to match his levels of patience and energy anymore, a bad fit for a franchise that was a year away from starting over. He was primarily sticking around to collect the final $6 million on his contract.

While it was an odd ending for one of the greatest coaches of all time, it was almost fitting for Nelson, who over the years had become as unconventional and tumultuous as they come. While his 29 years as a coach lent themselves to a different kind of sendoff, the difficulty that centered on him for a series of franchises made it more likely he would eventually face that sort of exit.

Nelson's second and final stint with the Warriors was a microcosm for his coaching career: electric, fun, messy, and exhausting. It had several great moments and plenty of behind-the-scenes drama.

When the Warriors hired him for a second time, in August 2006, it was a celebrated move. Nelson, the last coach to lead the Warriors to playoffs way back in 1994, brought credibility back to a franchise mired in mediocrity under Mike Montgomery, the legendary coach at Stanford who made the jump to the NBA.

After coaching the We Believe team and picking up a definitive playoff upset over a Dallas squad filled with players he coached and drafted, it looked like the Warriors were on the way up. Over the following 16 months, Golden State's old nature kicked back in as they traded away Jason Richardson and alienated Baron Davis, who left in July 2008 for the Clippers.

Despite the talent exodus, the Warriors gave Nelson a contract extension three months later. Around that time, due to losing a power struggle with team president Robert Rowell, Mullin retreated into the shadows until his contract expired. In May 2009, Mullin was officially out and the team promoted Nelson's longtime assistant coach, Larry Riley, to the position of general manager.

The grand parts of Nelson's tenure were pretty much done. What was left was the toll such a brutally honest, temperamental, master of mind games can take. Center Andris Biedrins went from a productive starting center to a shell of himself, a mentally broken reserve who never recovered from the pressure of Nelson's thumb. With all his confidence lost, Biedrins went from averaging 11.9 points per game to 5.0. He was never the same, leaving the NBA after his extension expired.

Draft pick Anthony Randolph, a raw-but-talented versatile forward the Warriors selected No. 14 overall in 2008, spent most of his two seasons with the Warriors paralyzed by frustration. His talent never blossomed, as Nelson did not have time for Randolph's emotional immaturity and rookie mistakes.

While Nelson's trouble with less-established players proved problematic in the long-term, a more pressing concern was his eroding relationship with star guard Monta Ellis. The two clashed frequently in 2009–10, as Ellis was unhappy with the franchise and did not take well to his coach's sharp tongue. Nelson was increasingly moody and had little interest in dealing with his disgruntled star.

There was one big highlight in 2010, on April 7 in Minnesota. The 116–107 victory over the host Timberwolves was the Warriors' 24th win of the season, but marked career win 1,333 for Nelson, passing Lenny Wilkens for the most wins in NBA history.

The Warriors players celebrated right in front of the bench on the opposing court. He was mobbed by players who doused him with Gatorade on the court and danced with him in the locker room. It was an odd collection that could scarcely win on the court, but that perhaps made the moment better.

Rookie guard Stephen Curry had 27 points, 14 assists, eight rebounds, and seven steals as he willed the Warriors to the landmark victory. Veteran forwards Corey Maggette and Devean George were excited again. NBA Development League call-ups Anthony Tolliver and Reggie Williams, whom Nelson gave a chance, felt privileged to be part of the occasion.

"Every coach says, 'It's a joy to coach you guys,'" Curry said about Nelson after the game. "But you could tell he meant it."

It was the last great moment of a Hall of Fame career.

89 Shootout in Denver

The Denver Nuggets were beginning a new era, having just hired Paul Westhead from Loyola Marymount with the goal of unleashing his run-and-gun style of basketball on the NBA. Denver was going to outscore the world.

The league's schedulers gave them the Warriors in the 1990–91 season opener and the result was the highest-scoring NBA game ever.

The teams combined for 320 points in regulation on November 2, 1990, which is more than seven points per minute. And here is the real shocker: only six three-pointers were made. Neither team played defense worth mentioning.

Denver's new philosophy was to get the ball up the court quickly and shoot before the defense set up. They played fast. Denver took 130 shots *and* 55 free throws in four quarters. Eight players took at least seven shots.

On the other hand, the Warriors' approach was instead to let their elite scorers go to work, prioritizing quality over quantity and they showed off their offensive prowess in the most offensive game in NBA history. Golden State looked like world-beaters offensively, as Tim Hardaway absolutely ran circles around the Nuggets while Chris Mullin and Mitch Richmond seemed to be open all game.

The final score: Warriors 162, Nuggets 158. The numbers from this game are astounding:

- The Warriors set a franchise record with 87 points in the first half—and they only led by four at the break.
- Mullin, Hardaway, and Richmond combined for 99 points and they did it in just 72 field goal attempts.
- Hardaway had 18 assists to go with his 32 points. He assisted on 48.4 percent of his teammates' baskets while he was on the floor.
- Rod Higgins did not miss a shot: 4-for-4 from the field, including one three, and 8-for-8 from the free throw line.
- Starting center Alton Lister did not attempt a shot from the field in his 13 minutes.

This game was a microcosm for the season and the legacy of the Run TMC Warriors, while that Nuggets team was closer to a gimmick. They had good players—Walter Davis, Michael Adams, Orlando Wooldridge—but could not be taken seriously. They led the league in scoring because they took the most shots, 1,400 more than second place, but also gave up a league record 130.8 points per game.

The Warriors, though, proved to not be a gimmick. They simply had a special trio of players and a coach who knew how to maximize their special skill sets. They finished the season second in scoring behind Denver, but their 116.6 points on 48.5 percent shooting was far more efficient. As the first game of the season helped to show, the Warriors were a real offensive juggernaut, not a system.

90 Larry Smith

Old-school Warriors fans remember the time when fans would wear hard hats to the game. A section of fans looked like union workers who came straight to the arena from manual labor, but you would also see kids in hard hats and women donning the construction gear.

It was all for Larry Smith, a staple of Warriors basketball in the 1980s. He was a reason for pride in a woeful era because, win or lose, fans could count on one thing each game: Smith would bring the effort.

Smith was not an All-Star. His game was not pretty. He did not score a lot of points or entertain with his skill. He worked hard. And the fans' appreciation for that was expressed by wearing hard hats. His No. 13 jersey became popular for such an understated player and fans cheered his extra effort as if they were baskets.

"It was unbelievable," Smith told Warriors.com of his reaction to seeing the hard hats for the first time. "I got really, really teary-eyed because it was so much of an honor for people to really appreciate the little things you did. There are no better fans than the Warriors fans. They were tremendous to me. They supported me throughout my whole career. If I played lousy, they still supported me. I always tell my friends about the fans there. Out of all the places I've been, Warriors fans are the best fans in the NBA."

Smith's effort shone in his rebounding, where effort can make a major difference. He went after rebounds like kids go after candy. Smith averaged 10.4 rebounds in his nine seasons with the Warriors, who drafted him 24th overall (second round) out of Alcorn State University in the 1980 Draft. He still ranks third in franchise history with 6,440 rebounds and only Nate Thurmond and Wilt Chamberlain grabbed more boards in a Warriors uniform.

The Mississippi native brought blue collar to the Blue and Gold immediately, averaging 12.1 rebounds his rookie season—which held up as the highest average (and most total rebounds in a season) in his 13-year career. He made the All-Rookie team that season.

Smith averaged his lone double-double in 1984–85 with 11.1 points and 10.9 rebounds. During 1987, his first playoff appearance, Smith led the entire playoffs with 13.7 rebounds per game. "Everybody wants to score—who doesn't want to score?" Smith said. "But at the end of the day, rebounding gives you an opportunity to win games. That's something that I really took pride in, I really worked hard at it and I became pretty good at it."

His game was about hustle and toughness. He was only 6'8", 215 pounds, but he played like a seven-foot-tall weightlifter. It really stood out with the Warriors. On a finesse team loaded with scorers, Smith became a fan favorite by doing the dirty work. He played next to Joe Barry Carroll, Bernard King, World B. Free, and Purvis Short when he entered the NBA. His grind shined against his teammates' skill and his intangibles were bold next to their stats.

The Mr. Mean nickname made perfect sense, too. Though it was his college sports information director that gave him the name because he never smiled, Smith, as a pro, did what needed to be done. If it meant an elbow, sturdy bump, hard foul, aggressive dive, going up strong, being a brick wall on a screen, or matching up with bigger and better players, he did it without apology.

Oddly enough, behind his steely stare and gritty style of play was a Southern kindness that endeared him to everyone.

"The only thing mean about Larry Smith," Houston coach Don Chaney said after Smith got 22 rebounds in a 1991 game, "is the way he plays."

91 Chase Center

It did not take long for new owners Joe Lacob and Peter Guber to show they were looking toward San Francisco. After all, they held their first press conference at the Epic Roasthouse on the Embarcadero on November 15, 2010, and also had the press conferences for Jerry West and Mark Jackson at San Francisco's St. Regis Hotel the following year.

It also made financial sense as San Francisco was the largest city in the United States without an arena of that size and that void meant that the first entity to build there would also likely benefit from numerous other events and the significant revenue that comes from them. That eventual income stream also helped explain and justify the then-record $450 million purchase price for the franchise despite their current building not being a part of the deal.

As such, it was not a surprise that when Lacob, Gruber, and the Warriors announced their plans to build a new arena for their burgeoning franchise in May 2012, the new facility would be in San Francisco. The team held an extravagant ceremony on the planned building site at Piers 30–32, including NBA commissioner David Stern, Ahmad Rashad, and San Francisco mayor Ed Lee, that served as a window into their grandiose vision for the franchise.

The announced move was hard to swallow for Oakland and the East Bay. After all, they played a massive role in consistently filling the arena and giving Oracle a truly special atmosphere long before the team became consistently competitive. For many fans used to the Warriors being centrally located in Oakland and the team being an intrinsic part of the underappreciated grassroots vibe of the city, the decision to move the Warriors across the Bay Bridge was taken as a betrayal that fed into long-held notions that the upper crust does not like Oakland.

"The reason we're not staying in Oakland is not because of the fans," Lacob explained. "Look, we have great fans. And I actually like the arena, overall. But it can't last forever. I have to think long term for the franchise.... If you're thinking longer term, you kind of need to think about the next generation. If you're going to make the kind of investment we made, you're going to make it where you have the chance to build the best brand and the best business."

The Warriors put out designs of a space-age arena that capitalized on the Bay views and hired Rick Welts—a longtime NBA mover and shaker who ran the Phoenix Suns after a long stint in the NBA offices—to be the team president and chief operating officer. Welts' experience and expertise would be integral in the pursuit and later development of the new arena.

However, the Warriors met major resistance from San Franciscans on their proposal. From environmental hurdles to concerns about obstructing the views to stringent building requirements, they had lots of hoops to jump through to even make the arena possible, the greatest of which was rebuilding the decrepit pier on which the stadium would rest. Eventually, those costs far exceeded the estimates, doubling to $120 million.

Over time, it became clear the opposition would not go away and the project faced the additional challenge of having to be on the ballot for an election due to exceeding the height requirements for new developments on the pier.

In April 2014, the Warriors gave up on the Pier 30–32 project and purchased land at another waterfront. For about $150 million, according to the *New York Times*, the Warriors bought a 12-acre plot of land from cloud computing giant Salesforce in the Mission Bay district.

While the project still had opposition to contend with, the change to Mission Bay removed the necessity of being on the ballot and a few other headaches. On January 17, 2017, the Warriors broke ground on the Chase Center and found out on the same day that the California Supreme Court would not hear appeals on two legal challenges to the project.

Now projected to be open for the 2019–20 season, the Chase Center will hold 18,064 (about 1,500 less than Oracle Arena) and incorporate many of the myriad technological advancements that have come since Oracle Arena's 1996–97 renovation. The complex will also include a new practice facility, more than 100,000 square feet of office space, and 3.2 acres of public space, including a public plaza along the waterfront.

As expected, even before the move was announced, ownership's vision for the Chase Center includes use for many non-Warriors events, including concerts and conventions. The franchise currently estimates that there will be more than 200 events per year, including the Warriors' home schedule.

One central tenet of the new stadium is that the $1 billion project is 100 percent privately financed, following the model of the San Francisco Giants and AT&T Park almost 20 years earlier. Inevitably, that will lead to higher ticket prices and could change the atmosphere from the current standard. It is entirely possible that the Warriors will lose some of the home-court advantage they have wielded at Oracle, but that will likely be chalked up to the price of change and the modern economics of sports franchise ownership.

While there are conflicting points of view and open questions about changes to the in-game atmosphere, the Chase Center will be the Warriors' first new permanent home in more than 50 years.

92 Kezar Pavillion

While it has been decades since the Warriors called San Francisco home, there is a place in The City that can be one of the best places to connect with the team's players.

Kezar Pavilion opened in 1924 and has hosted college basketball, concerts, roller derby, and many other events over its 90-plus years. Located in the southeast corner of Golden Gate Park, it has an official capacity of 4,000.

In 1979, the San Francisco Bay Area Pro-Am Summer Basketball League started as a way for the community to stay active during the summer. The league typically runs from mid-June through mid-August and does not charge admission, making it incredibly fan friendly. While the Pro-Am has a schedule and team rosters, one of its most interesting elements is that players can join those rosters at any point during the season, even for one game. Since NBA players often spend time in the Bay Area during the off-season, that flexibility opens the door for some special experiences.

While Jason Kidd, Gary Payton, and Steve Nash never played for the Warriors, all three local stars participated in the Pro-Am at Kezar Pavilion, a tradition that has continued with current players like Damian Lillard and Aaron Gordon. Kidd actually played in the Pro-Am after his senior year of high school in 1992 and said, "A lot of players in college aren't playing with the pros daily. That will help me learn what to do and help me want the ball at crunch time," which ended being a major part of his college and NBA career.

Unsurprisingly, plenty of Warriors have participated as well, including Tim Hardaway, Gilbert Arenas, Jason Richardson, Adonal Foyle, Jeremy Lin, and Kent Bazemore. While many of those players participated in a smaller capacity, Bazemore used his time there in 2013 "to try to get into basketball shape, to get up and down, and to try to get ready for Vegas." Bazemore had to prove his mettle as a point guard in the Las Vegas Summer League and he started that season as the Warriors' backup point guard.

A recent standout event happened when Stephen Curry played a game there on July 2, 2014. To the delight of the crowd, he scored 43 points, including nine three-pointers, the summer before winning his first Most Valuable Player Award.

The special combination of access and game-watching experience makes Kezar Pavilion and the San Francisco Bay Area Pro-Am something for Warriors fans and Bay Area basketball fans more broadly to put on their lists.

93 Robert Parish

While Robert Parish's legacy with the Warriors largely consists of the infamous trade that sent him to the Boston Celtics, his four years in Oakland should be a significant part of his story as well.

The seven-foot center took a genuinely unusual path to the NBA, having starred at Centenary College of Louisiana while the school was on probation. While working in the shadows at Centenary, Parish also had the chance to prove himself in the 1975 Pan American Games, where he made the team via a tryout, then was chosen as a captain and starred in their win over Cuba as the U.S. won the gold medal.

The next year, the Lakers owed the Warriors a first-round pick as compensation for signing Cazzie Russell in 1974, so Golden State received the eighth pick in the draft. They reaped the rewards early on, as Parish became a part of their rotation immediately and increased his role from 18 minutes per game to 24 his second year and 31.7 his third season.

Part of Parish's initial challenge was coach Al Attles still having so many options at center. Both Clifford Ray and George Johnson had been key pieces on the Warriors' championship team just two years earlier, and while Attles used a deep bench, that limited Parish's opportunities. During that season, Golden State traded Johnson for a first-round pick, opening up more time for the rookie center.

While the Warriors were declining as a West power, Parish's role grew as he shared center duties with Ray during his second season. In 1978–79, the 25-year-old big man supplanted the veteran in the rotation and actually led the league in defensive rebound percentage, securing 29.2 percent of available boards on that end, outpacing Jack Sikma, Moses Malone, and Kareem Abdul-Jabbar. He also finished fourth in block percentage, foreshadowing a strength in his All-Star seasons. While that team missed the playoffs with a 38–44 record, Parish actually led the NBA in Defensive Rating, as opponents only scored 94.4 points per 100 possessions when he was on the court.

Parish stayed at that level for the 1979–80 season, but the Warriors had lost so much of what made them competitive. Phil Smith was not the same after his knee injury, Rick Barry left for Houston in 1978, and the team did not have the talent to pick up their slack, especially after trading their 1979 first-round draft pick for aging Celtics point guard Jo Jo White.

After a 24–58 season, Golden State was looking at rebuilding and Parish did not fit in as a talented center who was about to make substantially more money. The team became infatuated with big man prospect Joe Barry Carroll, but the Celtics had the first overall pick. Attles traded Parish in order to move up from No. 3 to No. 1 and Boston also sent back the 13th pick.

Danny Leroux

In four seasons as a Warrior, Parish averaged 13.8 points, 9.5 rebounds, and 1.8 blocks per game, despite spending two of those years behind Ray in the rotation.

After the trade, he thrived as a member of a reliably competitive team, making nine All-Star teams and two All-NBA teams as a Celtic. Boston won three championships with Parish and Kevin McHale, the player Red Auerbach chose with the third pick of the fateful 1980 Draft.

Parish's four years with the Warriors became less than one-fifth of his NBA career, as he played a remarkable 21 seasons and a league-record 1,611 games. Chosen as one of the NBA's 50 greatest players in 1996, Parish was inducted into the Naismith Memorial Basketball Hall of Fame in 2003.

94 World B. Free

During pregame warm-ups back on February 25, 1982, Warriors coach Al Attles informed the Dallas Mavericks public address announcer that his starting guard had legally changed his first name. He requested the announcer not announce No. 21 by his former name.

But sure enough, when the Warriors starters were announced, "Lloyd B. Free" echoed through Reunion Arena.

He refused to get off the bench. Him not jogging out onto the court, as is tradition, prompted the announcer to say it again. "Lloyd B. Freeeeeee." Still the 6'2" guard from Brooklyn, in his seventh season, refused to get off the bench.

Attles went back to the announcer. But he refused to call him World. He called him Lloyd again.

Angry, Free had extra motivation. He lit up the Mavericks for 31 as the Warriors built a big lead and held on for a nail-biter.

"I went at them every time I saw them," Free said in a Q&A with Sixers.com. "By the third meeting with the Mavericks, this guy was calling it like 'Woooooorld Beeeeeee Freeeee!'"

Free has one of the most memorable names in NBA history, changing it officially December 8, 1981, during his second season with the Warriors, as a statement. Born Lloyd Bernard Free, he changed his first name to promote global peace.

Of course, Free's legacy extends beyond his unique name change. The Brooklyn native was an incredible talent and an explosive guard at a time when athleticism wasn't so rampant in the NBA. Just 6'2", he was quick, had a 44-inch vertical, and was known for doing 360-degree dunks on the playgrounds of New York.

Free combined leaping ability and shot making with his slithery quickness and was the quintessential New York point guard, a scorer who thrived in one-on-one play and got buckets with flamboyance. He spun off defenders like a ballet dancer and would pull up for jumpers and just hang in the air, his high-arching jumper negating excellent defense. He totaled 4,299 points in two breakout seasons with the San Diego Clippers, twice finishing behind George Gervin for scoring champion honors. He made the 1980 All-Star Game, starting in his only appearance. The next season, he joined the Warriors as an elite scorer.

He was a gunner, a volume shooter who usually missed more than he made. Free also lived at the free throw line and when he did score, it was beautiful, making him a natural fit for a Warriors team that needed some punch.

He graced the cover of *Sports Illustrated* in his first season as a Warrior and was dubbed "The Prince of the Mid Air." He led the Warriors in scoring (24.1 points) and was second in assists in 1980–81 as the Warriors improved by 15 wins. The next season, they improved from 39 to 45 wins as Free finished right behind Bernard King for scoring honors.

King signed with the New York Knicks for the 1982–83 season, and the Warriors' compensation was troubled-but-talented point guard Michael Ray Richardson, a three-time All-Star. That same off-season, the Warriors drafted a point guard in the first round, Oakland native Lester Connor, so the Warriors traded Free to Cleveland in December '82.

Trading Free, who dominated the ball while working his magic, freed up the offense to center around seven-footer Joe Barry Carroll and created the opportunity for Purvis Short to flourish, but Richardson, whose battle with drugs would eventually get him banned from the NBA, lasted 33 games with the Warriors before they traded him to the Nets. Plus, Connor was a defensive specialist and Ron Brewer, who was averaging 19.4 points for the Cavaliers when the Warriors acquired him for Free, did not come close to replicating Free's scoring punch.

Free, however, averaged at least 22 points per game in each of his four seasons in Cleveland and is even credited with saving the Cavaliers in Cleveland. The franchise was reportedly on the brink of being moved before Free carried them to the playoffs in 1985, giving the new owners a glimpse of what basketball could be in Cleveland.

Free was a show all his own. That is really how he got the name World, long before he officially changed it. They started calling him that in Brooklyn, though the exact reason is obscured by time. Perhaps it was because he spun like a globe on his 360 dunks, or because his midrange jumper worked all over the court, or "around the world." Maybe it was just that he was too good a player for the mere All-City or All-County or All-State descriptions most star players received.

Whatever the reason, the inner-city basketball world had been calling him World for years. He just made it official with the Warriors.

95 Fight with Blazers

Maybe he had a gun. Maybe he did not.

"I'm not 100 percent sure if he was," said one player on the court that night, "but knowing where he comes from and who his homeboys are, I'm pretty sure somebody in that car was strapped."

Either way, Chris Mills was not going to let the Portland Trail Blazers' bus pass this crazy night in Warriors history. He and his cohorts pulled their SUVs in front of the bus' path, keeping Portland trapped at the Arena in Oakland as he practically begged for them to come out and "fight like a man."

Before the Malice at the Palace—the infamous all-out 2004 brawl between a few Indiana Pacers and Detroit Pistons fans—the Warriors were involved in a scary situation in Oakland that was oh-so-close to becoming one of the NBA's worst incidents of all time.

On December 20, 2002, Portland forward Rasheed Wallace hit a fade-away jumper at the buzzer to beat the Warriors in Oakland 113–111. From the time the shot went up, Mills and Portland guard Bonzi Wells got tangled up battling for a rebound. After Wallace's shot went through, they barked at each other and shoved one another. Soon forward Troy Murphy got involved, then Warriors coach Eric Musselman joined the fray. Portland forward Ruben Patterson and Murphy got into it and the situation quickly became mayhem on the court.

Both benches emptied. Depending on who was giving the account, Jason Richardson and Murphy threw a punch and Gilbert Arenas threw a chair. Referees' attempts to hold players back proved futile.

Fans started rushing onto the court and throwing objects from the stands. Police officers ran into the crowd to unsuccessfully detain offending fans. As Portland left the floor, they were showered with popcorn and soda and food debris. One fan pegged Wallace with a wad of gum, prompting him and a teammate to try to go in the stands to get the fan.

That Portland squad was known as the "Jail Blazers" for a reason, as multiple players on the team had issues with drugs or domestic violence cases, and apparently they loved to fight. That narrative led to the story playing out as another issue for a troubled team, the poster children for the NBA's reputation as a league of thugs.

The league suspended Wells, who torched the Warriors for a game-high 28 points, two games for throwing a punch at Mills while fining Wallace $15,000 for trying to run into the stands. After reviewing the footage, neither Richardson, Murphy, nor Patterson were suspended.

Mills? He received the heftiest punishment with three games because even though the ruckus was done on the court, it was not over behind the scenes.

Mills—a Los Angeles native known in NBA circles for having serious street connections—was so upset with Wells, he tried to finish the altercation in the visiting locker room. Security had to restrain him from getting into Portland's locker room and fighting Wells. After failing to get to Wells there, Mills saw the Blazers bus pulling out of the facility as he was leaving. With a car full of people, he stopped the bus and practically begged for the Blazers to come finish the fight.

"Chris Mills engaged in some actions at the conclusion of the game," NBA senior vice president Stu Jackson said when announcing the punishment, "and well after the conclusion of the game that, quite frankly, we cannot accept and will not tolerate."

While the incident never gained the resonance or permanence of the Malice at the Palace, it foreshadowed a significant blemish of the NBA's reputation that regrettably persists to this day.

96

162–99

It still looks inconceivable.

162–99.

Heading into March 19, 1972, the Warriors were trying to secure a playoff berth with just four games left in the season and a strong 49–29 record. However, that fateful Sunday was their fourth game in four nights and pitted them against the Lakers, a team that had already set the still-standing NBA record 33-game win streak and later established the single-season wins record at 69 before winning the championship.

Still, a 63-point defeat was an embarassment for a franchise that was in a stronger place at that point, particularly since it retained that place in history for almost 20 years.

Eight Lakers scored in double figures, a number increased by the fact that Los Angeles' starters did not play in the 42–22 fourth quarter. To make matters worse, seven different Lakers had more points than the Warriors' leading scorer and current television announcer Jim Barnett's 15.

Amazingly, the Warriors only trailed by 15 points at halftime after outscoring the Lakers 32–29 in the second quarter. However, the Lakers poured it on with a 49–21 demolition in the third quarter and another 20-point margin (42–22) in the fourth to establish the ridiculous margin of victory.

That 63-point differential was the largest in NBA history to that point, topping Syracuse's 62-point win over New York in 1960, and the record stood for almost 20 years before Cleveland beat Miami by 68 in 1991. In a strange turn of events, the 1991–92 Warriors almost broke the single-game margin record themselves when they crushed the Sacramento Kings 153–91 on the same day they traded Mitch Richmond for Billy Owens.

Further adding insult to injury, the 1971–72 Lakers had a few significant connections to the Warriors. Both Wilt Chamberlain (just 10 points) and Keith Erickson (nine points) previously played for San Francisco, while Lakers head coach Bill Sharman coached the team from 1966 to 1968.

While that stunning defeat produced some shame and embarrassment, the Warriors did win two of their final three games of the season, so they ended up securing the final Western Conference playoff spot anyway.

97 Attend Warriors at Kings

Over the years, the Warriors and Kings have had a fascinating and sometimes contentious relationship.

Amazingly, the two franchises have never finished over .500 in the same season, despite sharing Northern California for 31 years, taking away the possibility of a playoff series that could build memories and ratchet up the tension.

That said, there have been memorable moments, including Klay Thompson's 37-point third quarter in 2015.

The dynamics between the two franchises have changed in recent years, both with Golden State's success and the influx of figures with Warriors connections to Sacramento. Former Warriors minority owner and vice chairman Vivek Ranadivé stepped up to buy the Kings when it looked like they were going to leave Sacramento and his presence has opened the doors to former assistant coach Michael Malone and players including Carl Landry,

Matt Barnes, Anthony Tolliver, Marco Belinelli, and Stephen Curry's younger brother Seth.

One of the rites of passage for Warriors fans has long been making the trip to Sacramento to see the closest possible Golden State road game. The atmosphere in the building shifts along with the balance of power between the two franchises but the experience has consistently been an interesting one. At its best, the contentious relationship between the longtime Kings fans and their Northern California interlopers parallels the defiance at Oracle Arena in the early 2000s when the Lakers came to town. For longtime Warriors fans, seeing that surreal reversal in person will be worth the trip.

On top of that, the experience of seeing the Warriors play in Sacramento has also changed significantly with the Kings opening their new arena, the Golden 1 Center. After 28 seasons at the Sleep Train/ARCO Arena on the outskirts of town, the Golden 1 Center's placement near Old Town and the Capitol makes it far more conducive to spending the day or evening in town before the game.

Also, as the NBA's newest arena, there are elements of the Golden 1 Center that will likely inspire the Warriors' Chase Center, which is scheduled to open in 2019. Seeing the current high-water mark in person could help fans set their expectations for the new building and then serve as a fascinating comparison when it is finished.

Considering the often shorter-than-expected travel time and the feeling of being unwelcome guests in another team's building, particularly when Warriors fans overrun the place, a trip to the Golden 1 Center for Warriors at Kings should be on every fan's list.

98 Manute Bol

While NBA players are all anomalies, Manute Bol stood out from even that unusual pack.

At 7'6¾" (measured by *The Guinness Book of World Records*, no less), with a remarkable 10'5" standing reach and 8'6" wingspan, Bol used that extreme length to become a force as a shot blocker. His 397 rejections in the 1985–86 season are still the second-most in league history and his career block rate (8.6 blocks per 100 possessions) is still the highest in NBA history. In fact, Bol is the only player with more than 30 minutes played to have more blocks than points and it was not even close: 2086 to 1599 during his 10-season career.

Born in what is now the South Sudan, Bol began playing basketball at 15 years old and played in his first NBA game just eight years later. Amazingly, Bol was actually drafted in 1983 by the San Diego Clippers, but the league ruled him ineligible since his passport listed him at 19 years old, then too young to join the NBA. That same passport also listed Bol at 5'2" because he was sitting down when they measured his height.

After two years of college basketball in the United States, the Washington Bullets drafted Bol in the second round and he played there three seasons before joining the Warriors. He became a fan favorite and a fascination due to his unusual physical characteristics and game. While blocking shots was always a hallmark of his game, Bol's long arms and slender frame made him a better fit on the perimeter than in the post offensively and coach Don Nelson encouraged him to extend his range on that end. After shooting a total of three three-pointers as a Bullet, Bol attempted 91 in his first season under Nelson and another 48 in his second. He mostly

Warriors center Manute Bol battles for a rebound against Portland Trail Blazers center Kevin Duckworth at Memorial Coliseum. (USA TODAY Sports Images)

came off the bench that first year, but ended up starting 20 games in 1989–90, the first season of Run TMC.

While Coach Nelson unlocked new parts of Bol's game during those two seasons, he and the front office traded him in the 1990 off-season for the first-round pick that eventually became Chris Gatling, meaning Bol just missed being a part of the Warriors' 1991 playoff squad with his Run TMC teammates.

After four seasons away, Bol returned to the Warriors for the 1994–95 campaign and made the opening day roster. His highlight that season came in his first game back in Oakland as a member of the Warriors, when Bol played 29 minutes and turned in an unforgettable fourth quarter when he made three three-pointers to the stunned delight of the Oakland Arena crowd. One week later, after starting a game against the Charlotte Hornets and former teammate Muggsy Bogues, Bol suffered a season-ending knee injury and that ended up being his final NBA game.

Despite playing just 160 games as a Warrior, he still has the fourth-most blocks in franchise history at 592 and it will be years before any current member of the team challenges him.

 **17–65**

While Warriors fans became accustomed to bad basketball in the years following the trade of future star Chris Webber and the ensuing resignation of Don Nelson, they had not experienced anything like this.

The Warriors won 19 games in 1999–2000, leading to major changes by general manager Garry St. Jean. He fired coach P.J. Carlesimo in December and in February, St. Jean gave up a draft pick to get promising young guard Larry Hughes, who was to team with star Antawn Jamison to give the Warriors a one-two scoring punch. In June, another three-team trade sent forwards Billy Owens and Jason Caffey to Milwaukee while netting two more guards: Bob Sura and Vinny Del Negro. Then, before training camp, the Warriors were involved in a four-team deal, shipping away Donyell Marshall and Bill Curley while receiving big men Danny Fortson and Adam Keefe. A month later, they brought back franchise legend Chris Mullin after a three-year stint in Indiana.

And after all that, the Warriors turned out to be even worse. They won just 17 games in 2000–01.

Even with that horrifying record, the season did not start out in disastrous fashion. One of their wins was an overtime thriller over the defending champion Lakers when Jamison went toe-to-toe with Kobe Bryant and each scored 51 points. Hughes added 24 points and nine assists, keeping pace with Shaquille O'Neal's 25, while Sura added 16 as the Warriors pulled the upset.

It looked as if the off-season moves had some promise. Golden State closed 2000 with two wins, including one over the playoff-bound Utah Jazz. The Warriors were 10–20, on pace for 27 wins, and they had two overtime losses and another seven defeats by eight points or less. They could have been flirting with .500.

Then the bottom began falling out. First a five-game losing streak, then a six-gamer, then another five-game skid and an eight-gamer. They got a win in Chicago—against a Bulls franchise that was even worse than the Warriors, spiraling since Michael Jordan's retirement—and followed that with 11 more losses in a row.

The Warriors were 14–28 after a home win on January 24 gave them victories in three of their last four. After that, the Warriors imploded: 3–37, which including losing the final 13 games of the season by an average of 15.5 points.

"I just thank God it's over," Antawn Jamison said after the game. He was the only player to start all 82 games that season. "The nightmare is over. We got in this situation where everything was going wrong, and we couldn't get out of it."

Head coach Dave Cowens got out of it early. His first season as coach of the Warriors concluded with him being ejected in the final minutes of the third quarter. He left to an ovation.

What happened? Injuries, as the Warriors led the NBA with 421 games lost.

Fortson, the bruising undersized forward who was supposed to bring some toughness and defense, played just six games before a foot injury ended his season. He was averaging 16.7 points and 16.3 rebounds when he went on the shelf.

Chris Mills, the shooter expected to be a weapon off the bench, was done by early December. Hughes and Sura missed more than one-third of the games. Center Erick Dampier, who looked like the long-lost center the Warriors desperately wanted two years earlier and traded Mullin to get, endured another injury-plagued season that included missing most of December, all of January, and most of February, totaling just 43 games played.

Seven players from the opening night roster were unavailable by the season finale.

Guard Mookie Blaylock, who the Warriors acquired for a first-round pick that became guard Jason Terry, checked out earlier than that. On February 4, he scheduled a tee time in San Antonio after the Warriors' 10:00 AM practice, but Cowens changed the practice to 1:00 PM. Blaylock, however, did not change his tee time. He skipped practice. As punishment, Blaylock lost his starting job for the loss at San Antonio the next night and was stripped of his title as one of the team captains.

Blaylock, when asked about the penalties he incurred, revealed the dysfunction of this historically bad season.

"Doesn't bother me none," he told reporters. "I'd do it again."

100 Thunder

A great test for any who claim to be a true Warriors fan or simply a way to divide the bandwagoners from those who suffered for this new reality of Golden State dominance: What was the name of the Warriors' last mascot?

His name was Thunder.

With a listed height that reads "stands above the clouds" and weight that reads "lighter than air," Thunder jumped off of trampolines and threw down highlight-reel dunks to the delight of fans for years.

As opposed to most mascots who are fluffy and cuddly, Thunder was a chiseled blue man character decked out in a Warriors uniform with a thunderbolt sticking out of his head. The list of celebrities Thunder dunked over is impressive and includes Jamie Foxx, Roger Craig, Kristi Yamaguchi, and Pete Sampras.

According to the Mascot Hall of Fame, Thunder attended "Sir-Slam-A-Lot High School" and "Dunk-U-Very Much University" before being drafted in the "1997 Mascot Supplemental Draft."

He had two trademark dunks. The Thundersault was a front flip off the trampoline where he brought the ball through his legs mid-flip and the Double Funk required Thunder to whip the ball between his legs from his right hand to his left and back again before capping the dunk with a one-hand tomahawk.

The mascot fit in perfectly with the logo change that took place in 1997. The team ditched the traditional "Warriors" lettering used from 1988 to 1997 in favor of a new script featuring a thunderbolt across the team name while another bolt shot down the side of the jersey.

Those uniforms lasted from 1997–98 until 2002–03 but Thunder would remain with the team for a few more years. He mysteriously disappeared in 2008 when the team returned from a trip to China and Thunder was nowhere to be found.

What happened to the Warriors mascot, who was the best highlight in many ugly losses?

His departure coincided with the Seattle SuperSonics' 2008 move to Oklahoma City. As a part of the relocation, the team became renamed and rebranded as the Oklahoma City Thunder, which may be why Thunder was nixed.

Another working theory: Chris Mullin, the Warriors legend who became general manager, did not like the gimmicky mascot. The famously crew-cutted star was on a mission to change the team's culture and a mascot did not strike the tone he wanted. Even before 2008, the Warriors had removed Thunder from his previous role by hiring a team of young men dunkers to entertain the crowd, isolating Thunder to kids' birthday parties and other team-affiliated appearances.

Was it Mullin who exiled Thunder?

New owners Joe Lacob and Peter Guber bought the team in 2010 and changed the Warriors' logo to one inspired by the famous City uniforms. At that point, any connection with Thunder and the old logo/uniform scheme was extinguished.

Shockingly, there was a sighting of the Warriors' old mascot on a 2013 trip to China. A video on Warriors TV showed Thunder, still ripped and navy blue, casually walk past the camera during a segment. Thunder left a message for Warrior fans who wondered what happened to the mascot, saying he met the love of his life in China and would live there from now on.

Acknowledgments

While the process of writing a book often feels like a solitary endeavor, it also provides an amazing demonstration of both the necessity and efficacy of a strong support system.

For me, that starts with my family, specifically my parents, sister, and grandmother. They gave me space and patience when I needed it, then motivation in the rough patches. None of this would be possible without them helping mold me into the person I am today before ensuring that I lived up to my own expectations.

My friends were also great, checking up and providing a welcome change of pace while also being understanding during some of the longer periods of radio silence toward the end of the process.

I am so lucky to have started covering the Warriors when I did. Back in 2009, the group of people in the media room was truly amazing. Sam Amick, Marcus Thompson II, Rusty Simmons, Marc Spears, Monte Poole, and Tim Kawakami were generous mentors to a brash 24-year-old then, and valued friends now. That media corps eventually expanded with some truly remarkable people, including Ethan Sherwood Strauss, Adam Lauridsen, and Nate Duncan.

When I started covering the team, Golden State had a top-flight PR staff led by Raymond Ridder and that excellence has continued to this day through the massive increase in attention due to the team's success. Raymond, Dan Martinez, Brett Winkler, and the rest of their amazing team have been a constant that also answered queries enthusiastically and quickly for this book.

Jim Barnett, Marcus Thompson II, and Tim Kawakami deserve specific thanks; their invaluable insight into the history of this team and their fan base helped breathe context and life into every page.

My basketball media circle also helped make this book a reality.

Nate Duncan, Kevin Pelton, Seth Partnow, Ben Golliver, Tim Bontemps, and Dan Feldman consistently hone my insight and served as vital sounding boards at points in this process. Similarly, Sam Vecenie, Adam Lauridsen, Seerat Sohi, and Jared Dubin were a wonderful source of support during this endeavor.

When I graduated from college, my best friend from UCLA, Rahim Kurwa, offered space at a blog he and our buddy Derrek Hibar started as a potential creative outlet. Using it as a stress release during law school made the horrors of 1L much more bearable and eventually changed my life.

Incredibly, my legal mentors, Rob Epstein and John Diamond, enthusiastically supported my sportswriting during and after my time at UC Hastings and then my decision to pursue it as a career afterward. I cannot describe how inspiring those conversations were as I grappled with complicated choices and incredible uncertainty.

Eight years ago, Chris Reina replied to an email I sent about a piece of his, opened a door for me, and immediately established himself as an ardent advocate and wonderful friend. His support played an invaluable part in everything that followed and continues to this day.

Along a similar line, all of my employers during the Warriors' 2016–17 season were supportive and understanding when I took on this project in addition to my other work. The Athletic (Adam Hansman and Alex Mather), Dunc'd On (Nate Duncan), Sporting News (Adi Joseph and Jordan Greer), Locked on Warriors (David Locke), RealGM Radio (Chris Reina and Nick Gelso), and Twitter NBA Show (Ali Jafari and Nate Duncan) all encouraged me to pursue this to its fullest despite that lessening the time I could give them and I am deeply thankful.

This book would not have been possible without amazing work from so many other writers from across the decades. It was an absolute joy to discover material in a variety of formats from all over that provided some of the depth and color to these stories. I want to single out Basketball Reference and the *Sports Illustrated* Vault as unbelievable free resources that kept on providing worthwhile information.

I wanted to end this with the people who give me inspiration. Matt Christopher and Roald Dahl helped foster my love of reading, George Orwell taught me the power and resonance of the written word, and Bill Simmons inspired me to consider sportswriting as an outlet, then a potential career.

Additionally, thank you to all of my teachers and professors throughout the years for bringing the best out of me while augmenting a lifelong love of both learning and sharing that knowledge with others.

While writing this book, reading the work of other people provided inspiration and motivation. Jonathan Abrams' *Boys Among Men*, Ken Korach's *Holy Toledo*, and Lee Jenkins' material for *Sports Illustrated* reminded me to always convey the emotional and human elements along with a strong factual foundation.

Finally, my deepest thanks to Triumph Books and their amazing team for making this ambitious project a reality. It was such a thrill to be asked to share these stories and their support proved essential to making a book worthy of its audience.

Sources

http://www.sfgate.com/warriors/article/For-Stephen-Curry-basketball-in-hands-is–6037999.php

http://ftw.usatoday.com/2015/11/
watch-steph-curry-complete-the-most-insane-ball-handling-drill

http://www.si.com/vault/1968/11/25/670152/old-days-and-changed-ways

https://www.youtube.com/watch?v=M0faQ–6RJyA

http://www.si.com/vault/1967/08/14/609424/the-education-of-mr-barry

http://www.nba.com/history/players/barry_bio.html

http://www.remembertheaba.com/oakland-oaks.html

http://www.nba.com/history/players/barry_bio.html

http://www.nba.com/history/players/barry_bio.html

http://www.nba.com/warriors/photogallery/rick_barry_1.html/

http://www.nba.com/2010/news/features/steve_aschburner/12/15/point-forward/

http://www.nba.com/2010/news/features/steve_aschburner/12/15/point-forward/

http://www.usatoday.com/story/sports/nba/2014/11/11/
sixth-man-stigma-manu-ginobili-andre-iguodala-isaiah-thomas/18883329/

http://www.si.com/nba/2015/06/29/
stephen-curry-warriors-steve-kerr-nba-championship-lebron-james

http://www.si.com/nba/2015/06/12/
warriors-steve-kerr-nick-uren-andre-iguodala-andrew-bogut-nba-finals-cavaliers

http://thecomeback.com/crossoverchronicles/2015-articles/who-were-those-guys-a-look-back-at-the–1974–1975-warriors.html

http://www.sfgate.com/sports/ostler/article/50-years-on-reluctant-Warrior-Al-Attles-is-the–3203061.php

http://thecomeback.com/crossoverchronicles/2015-articles/the–1975-western-conference-finals-where-the-magic-began.html

http://thecomeback.com/crossoverchronicles/2015-articles/the–1975-western-conference-finals-where-the-magic-began.html

http://thecomeback.com/crossoverchronicles/2015-articles/the–1975-western-conference-finals-where-the-magic-began.html

http://www.nba.com/bulls/history/sloan_750511.html

http://thecomeback.com/crossoverchronicles/2015-articles/the–1975-western-conference-finals-where-the-magic-began.html

http://www.foxsports.com/nba/story/
golden-state-warriors-washington-bullets–1975-nba-finals-champions–052815

http://thecomeback.com/crossoverchronicles/2015-articles/the–1975-nba-finals-the-warriors-turn-the-nba-upside-down.html

http://www.foxsports.com/nba/story/
golden-state-warriors-washington-bullets–1975-nba-finals-champions–052815

http://www.foxsports.com/nba/story/
golden-state-warriors-washington-bullets–1975-nba-finals-champions–052815

http://www.sfgate.com/sports/ostler/article/50-years-on-reluctant-Warrior-Al-Attles-is-the-3203061.php

http://www.si.com/vault/1975/10/27/613689/when-golden-state-glittered

https://www.nytimes.com/2015/05/27/sports/basketball/al-attles-part-of-warriors-past-is-still-a-presence.html?_r=0

http://online.anyflip.com/mguy/mwkl/mobile/index.htmlNo. p=33

http://www.sfgate.com/sports/ostler/article/50-years-on-reluctant-Warrior-Al-Attles-is-the-3203061.php

http://www.sfgate.com/sports/ostler/article/50-years-on-reluctant-Warrior-Al-Attles-is-the-3203061.php

http://www.mercurynews.com/2017/03/02/anniversary-the-night-wilt-chamberlain-scored-100-points/

http://www.sfgate.com/sports/ostler/article/50-years-on-reluctant-Warrior-Al-Attles-is-the-3203061.php

http://www.sfgate.com/sports/ostler/article/50-years-on-reluctant-Warrior-Al-Attles-is-the-3203061.php

https://www.nytimes.com/2015/05/27/sports/basketball/al-attles-part-of-warriors-past-is-still-a-presence.html?_r=0

http://online.anyflip.com/mguy/mwkl/mobile/index.htmlNo. p=33

http://www.sfgate.com/sports/ostler/article/50-years-on-reluctant-Warrior-Al-Attles-is-the-3203061.php

http://www.nytimes.com/1992/04/29/sports/basketball-sonics-edge-the-warriors-to-take-a-2-1-lead.html

http://www.espn.com/nba/story/_/id/8341678/nba-don-nelson-luckiest-guy-world

http://www.nytimes.com/1994/12/16/sports/pro-basketball-a-warrior-s-continuing-battles.html?pagewanted=all

http://articles.latimes.com/1995-02-14/sports/sp-31971_1_general-manager

http://articles.latimes.com/1996-03-09/sports/sp-44917_1_don-nelson

http://www.deseretnews.com/article/598685/Mavs-oust-Cleamons-Nelson-to-step-in.html?pg=all

https://www.nytimes.com/2016/05/01/sports/basketball/the-birth-of-hack-a-shaq.html

http://sports.yahoo.com/blogs/nba-ball-dont-lie/mark-cuban-contends-don-nelson-once-wanted-trade-204121022--nba.html

http://www.slamonline.com/nba/original-old-school-run-shoot-shoot/No.bAO8UlIe8JreuSfT.97

http://www.nba.com/2015/news/features/fran_blinebury/06/09/RunTMC-gave-franchise-and-league-glimpse-of-the-future/

http://articles.latimes.com/1991-05-04/sports/sp-822_1_golden-state

http://www.slamonline.com/nba/original-old-school-run-shoot-shoot/No.bAO8UlIe8JreuSfT.97

http://www.nba.com/2015/news/features/fran_blinebury/06/09/RunTMC-gave-franchise-and-league-glimpse-of-the-future/

http://articles.latimes.com/1991-05-11/sports/sp-1219_1_run-dmc

http://www.nytimes.com/1991/05/13/sports/basketball-lakers-near-another-conference-final.html

http://articles.latimes.com/1991-11-02/sports/sp-478_1_billy-owens

http://www.slamonline.com/nba/original-old-school-run-shoot-shoot/No.
    Yh3bAc4zvcMYJWzU.97
http://www.nba.com/2015/news/features/fran_blinebury/06/09/Run
    TMC-gave-franchise-and-league-glimpse-of-the-future/
http://www.nbcnews.com/news/asian-america/
    warriors-super-fan-paul-wong-celebrates-nba-championship-n377861
https://www.newspapers.com/image/98448105/
http://www.si.com/vault/1976/05/24/614854/
    have-the-suns-risen-in-the-west-yesNo.
http://www.si.com/vault/1976/05/24/614854/
    have-the-suns-risen-in-the-west-yesNo.
http://www.si.com/vault/1976/05/24/614854/
    have-the-suns-risen-in-the-west-yesNo.
http://www.si.com/vault/1976/05/24/614854/
    have-the-suns-risen-in-the-west-yesNo.
http://archives.chicagotribune.com/1976/05/17/page/65/article/
    suns-stun-warriors-gain-final
http://archives.chicagotribune.com/1976/05/17/page/65/article/
    suns-stun-warriors-gain-final
http://www.si.com/vault/1976/05/24/614854/
    have-the-suns-risen-in-the-west-yesNo.
http://www.mercurynews.com/2015/10/04/
    luke-walton-suddenly-warriors-interim-coach-has-basketball-pedigree/
http://www.espn.com/nba/story/_/id/17790252/
    golden-state-draymond-green-problem
http://www.si.com/nba/2016/04/14/
    golden-state-warriors—73-wins-chicago-bulls-nba-record-legacy
http://www.slamonline.com/nba/original-old-school-run-shoot-shoot/No.
    dRO1v9uDGpWGrbps.97
http://articles.latimes.com/1991—11—02/sports/sp—478_1_billy-owens
http://www.slamonline.com/nba/original-old-school-run-shoot-shoot/No.
    dRO1v9uDGpWGrbps.97
http://www.si.com/vault/1968/11/25/670152/old-days-and-changed-ways
https://news.google.com/newspapers?nid=1129&dat=19860710&id=Na9RAAAAIB
    AJ&sjid=xG4DAAAAIBAJ&pg=6796,3112165&hl=en
http://bleacherreport.com/articles/2698627-we-were-a-bunch-of-draymond-greens-
    how-we-believe-warriors-shook-up-nba
http://www.nytimes.com/1999/01/19/sports/basketball-knicks-will-most-likely-get-
    sprewell.html
http://blogs.mercurynews.com/warriors/2011/02/08/the-ghost-of-marcus-williams/
http://www.sfgate.com/sports/ostler/article/50-years-on-reluctant-Warrior-Al-Attles-
    is-the—3203061.php
http://www.slamonline.com/nba/100-grand/No. fRgTofKOKq42m1bC.97
http://www.nba.com/warriors/catching_up_meschery.html
http://www.espn.com/nba/story/_/id/8341678/nba-don-nelson-luckiest-guy-world
http://www.sfgate.com/sports/article/SPECIAL-REPORT-The-man-who-owns-the-
    Warriors—2874504.php

http://www.espn.com/nba/news/story?id=5383261

https://books.google.com/books?id=vvySt6hPeLwC&pg=PA231&lpg=PA231&dq=
cohan+warriors+119+million+-lacob&source=bl&ots=ZUrS-fQdow&sig=F3-tQr
PDMVB0qnwHDSwwOCEidW8&hl=en&sa=X&ved=0ahUKEwisvO3rrd_
SAhUE12MKHaWKANI4ChDoAQglMAMNo. v=onepage&q=cohan
percent20warriors percent20119 percent20million percent20-lacob&f=false

http://www.nba.com/media/warriors/GSW_2Staff.pdf

http://www.sfgate.com/sports/ostler/article/Captain-Spree-should-remain-a-
landlubber–2508631.php

http://nba.nbcsports.com/2015/06/16/report-jerry-west-threatened-to-resign-if-
warriors-traded-klay-thompson-for-kevin-love/

http://www.cbsnews.com/news/warriors-sign-jason-caffey/

http://www.essence.com/2009/06/19/la-lakers-star-derek-fisher-on-how-his-d

http://www.sfgate.com/sports/article/Dampier-Remains-A-Warrior-Center-team-
agree-to–2912225.php

http://www.espn.com/nba/news/story?id=1867027

http://www.espn.com/nba/news/story?id=3470016

http://www.sfgate.com/sports/article/J-Rich-Murphy–6-years-Warriors-beat-
deadline–2638865.php

http://www.sfgate.com/sports/article/Jamison-stays-for-big-bucks-Warriors-
sign–2885280.php

http://archive.jsonline.com/blogs/sports/157015455.html

http://www.sfgate.com/sports/article/Jim-Fitzgerald–1926–2012-Ex-Warriors-
owner–3609143.php

http://cdn.espn.go.com/nba/playoffs/2015/story/_/id/13096860/
andre-iguodala-golden-state-warriors-named-nba-finals-mvp

http://bleacherreport.com/articles/2698627-we-were-a-bunch-of-draymond-greens-
how-we-believe-warriors-shook-up-nba

http://www.slamonline.com/nba/original-old-school-run-shoot-shoot/No.
sXZi9AWRO1DtDR5d.97

http://www.nba.com/history/players/wilkes_bio.html

http://www.insidesocal.com/lakers/2012/12/28/
jamaal-wilkes-reflects-on-his-career-and-looks-ahead-to-jersey-retirement/

https://www.nytimes.com/2015/05/27/sports/basketball/al-attles-part-of-warriors-
past-is-still-a-presence.html?_r=0

http://sports.yahoo.com/blogs/nba-ball-dont-lie/dunk-history--chris-webber--charles-
barkley-and-a-poster-preserved–214137431.html

http://www.nytimes.com/1995/07/02/sports/pro-basketball-one-blot-on-nelson-s-
impressive-resume.html

http://www.nytimes.com/1994/05/05/sports/pro-basketball-suns-sweep-warriors-as-
barkley-goes-swish.html

http://www.nytimes.com/2001/02/22/sports/guy-rodgers-an-nba-all-star-dies-at–65.
html

http://nba.nbcsports.com/2015/06/06/
strength-in-numbers-is-not-just-marketing-slogan-its-philosophy-for-warriors/

https://www.cbssports.com/nba/news/
speights-says-his-clippers-have-a-lot-to-learn-from-the-warriors/

http://www.nytimes.com/2001/02/22/sports/guy-rodgers-an-nba-all-star-dies-at–65.
html

http://www.si.com/vault/1968/11/25/670152/old-days-and-changed-ways

http://bkref.com/tiny/YToVK

http://www.nytimes.com/2001/02/22/sports/guy-rodgers-an-nba-all-star-dies-at–65.
html

http://www.ibabuzz.com/warriors/2008/11/06/mullins-right-hand-
man-fired/?doing_wp_cron=1490334267.09745693206787109375
00

http://blogs.mercurynews.com/kawakami/2009/10/14/
robert-rowells–25-fire-able-offenses-as-warriors-colossus/

http://www.mercurynews.com/2008/11/17/
warriors-sign-jackson-to-contract-extension/

http://www.mercurynews.
com/2009/11/11/a-stephen-jackson-trade-is-inevitable-warriors-coach-says/

http://www.nytimes.com/1995/07/02/sports/pro-basketball-one-blot-on-nelson-s-
impressive-resume.html

http://www.nytimes.com/1995/07/02/sports/pro-basketball-one-blot-on-nelson-s-
impressive-resume.html

http://www.nytimes.com/1994/12/16/sports/pro-basketball-a-warrior-s-continuing-
battles.html?pagewanted=all

http://www.nytimes.com/1994/11/18/sports/pro-basketball-sign-him-trade-him-
webber-becomes-bullet.html

http://www.espn.com/nba/news/story?id=3219421

http://www.ibabuzz.com/warriors/2016/02/03/ex-warriors-assistant-brian-scalabrine-
describes-dysfunctional-events-leading-up-to-mark-jackson-firing-him/

http://www.nba.com/2014/news/features/david_aldridge/05/12/
david-aldridge-morning-tip-mark-jackson-firing-wizards-qa-with-derek-fisher/

http://www.newsday.com/sports/
nba-report-jamison-kobe-get–51-in-overtime-shootout–1.272820

http://web.kitsapsun.com/
archive/2000/12–04/0040_the_nba__sonics_win_despite_51_by.html

http://www.cbsnews.com/news/jamison-kobe-each-pour-in–51/

http://www.si.com/vault/2000/12/18/294116/nifty–50s-erupting-for–51-points-in-
back-to-back-games-the-warriors-antawn-jamison-shot-his-way-into-the-spotlight-
and-stole-some-thunder-from-his-old-college-classmate-vince-carter

http://www.sfgate.com/sports/article/Amazing-Antawn-Jamison-s–51-point-nights-
might–3238283.php

http://www.si.com/vault/2000/12/18/294116/nifty–50s-erupting-for–51-points-in-
back-to-back-games-the-warriors-antawn-jamison-shot-his-way-into-the-spotlight-
and-stole-some-thunder-from-his-old-college-classmate-vince-carter

http://www.nba.com/video/2016/12/06/20161206-week-history-bryant-jamison-duel

http://www.newsday.com/sports/
nba-report-jamison-kobe-get–51-in-overtime-shootout–1.272820

http://www.sfgate.com/sports/jenkins/article/Warriors-announcer-Jim-Barnett-not-
retiring-after–5565909.php

http://www.ibabuzz.com/warriors/2014/07/31/
warriors-broadcaster-jim-barnett-energized-age–70-dont-want-retire-ok/

http://www.nytimes.com/2002/01/22/sports/alex-hannum–78-won-titles-as-coach-in-two-pro-leagues.html

http://www.si.com/vault/1968/11/25/670152/old-days-and-changed-ways

https://prohoopshistory.net/2013/07/18/paul-arizin-philadelphia-warriors/

http://articles.latimes.com/2014/jan/26/local/la-me-tom-gola–20140127

http://www.nytimes.com/1989/11/05/magazine/a-soviet-hoopster-in-the-promised-land.html?pagewanted=all

http://www.nba.com/warriors/news/jenkins-sarunas-marciulionis

http://www.nba.com/warriors/catching_up_marciulionis.html

http://www.nba.com/warriors/news/jenkins-sarunas-marciulionis

http://www.espn.com/espn/feature/story/_/id/18376747/
how-kevin-durant-landed-bay

https://theundefeated.com/features/
strength-in-numbers-convinced-kevin-durant-to-join-warriors/

Warriors Owner Opens Up;Few Fans Know Much About The Man Who Has Shunned Reporters And The Spotlight Since Buying The Franchise In 1994, December 5, 2001 (Contra Costa Times)

http://www.sfgate.com/sports/article/SPECIAL-REPORT-The-man-who-owns-the-Warriors–2874504.php

http://sanfrancisco.cbslocal.com/2017/01/17/
state-supreme-court-denies-petition-to-halt-warriors-new-arena/

http://www.chasecenter.com/vision

http://www.chasecenter.com/vision

http://www.sanfranciscoproam.com/

http://www.sanfranciscoproam.com/quotes.html

http://sanfrancisco.cbslocal.com/2014/07/03/stephen-curry-scores–4three-points-in-san-francisco-summer-league-game-basketball-golden-state-warriors/

http://www.sfchronicle.com/warriors/article/Bazemore-tries-to-earn-bigger-role-with-Warriors–4638758.php

http://sanfrancisco.cbslocal.com/2014/07/03/stephen-curry-scores–4three-points-in-san-francisco-summer-league-game-basketball-golden-state-warriors/

For players with more than 25 minutes played: http://bkref.com/tiny/Uimnp

http://www.si.com/vault/2010/06/28/105954613/
a-gift-from-on-high